Space Clearing

VOLUME 1

BY THE SAME AUTHORS

Karen Kingston
Clear Your Clutter with Feng Shui

Karen Kingston & Richard Kingston
How to Clear Your Clutter
Space Clearing, Volume 2: How space clearing works

This book has been written with safety in mind. The utmost care has been taken to provide the information that is needed to do space clearing safely. However, the reader must understand that a range of energies can be found in buildings and space clearing may involve some risks. Some of the techniques also involve the use of lit candles, so the reader needs to be aware that these must be positioned with care and caution, and never left to burn unattended.

All guidelines need to be followed carefully and warnings heeded, and neither the authors nor the publisher can accept any responsibility for any injuries or damage, however they may arise. The authors and publisher also make no guarantees concerning the level of success the reader may experience by following the methods in this book, as the results will differ for each individual.

CONSCIOUS LIVING SERIES

Space Clearing

VOLUME 1:

The art of clearing and revitalizing energies in buildings

Karen Kingston & Richard Kingston

Clear Space Living

SPACE CLEARING, VOLUME 1: The art of clearing and revitalizing energies in buildings

Copyright © Clear Space Living Ltd 2024

First published in Great Britain in 2024 by Clear Space Living

A CIP catalogue record for this book is available from the British Library.

Paperback ISBN: 978-1-8382504-1-6
Ebook ISBN: 978-1-8382504-7-8

Clear Space Living
www.clearspaceliving.com

Contents

Introduction

The term "space clearing" is fairly new, although the concept is not. Most traditional cultures around the world have purification practices that can be performed by ordinary people in their own homes on a regular basis, with an expert being called in to handle more complex situations such as a traumatic event or a death.

House purification practices used to be so much a part of life that they were seen as being essential to good health and wellbeing. They were used to clear out old or unwanted energies in homes that can have detrimental effects on the lives of the occupants. Handed down from generation to generation, the methods rested on spiritual forces and beliefs that were specific to each traditional culture and addressed the particular types of energy issues that were endemic to it.

But times have changed.

With the widespread influence of television, the internet, and other modern inventions, most cultures have become westernized to a large extent. Their purification practices have lapsed, and this has brought about a huge loss in their quality of life.

The types of energies in people's homes and other buildings are also now very different to those generated by the slow-moving, rural ways of life of bygone years. The purification techniques that have been used for centuries no longer work so well in the cultures they were originally developed for and hardly have any effect in modern homes.

Burning smudge sticks, for example, worked fine as a purification technique for some Native American tribes long ago within the context of their lifestyle. However, it was not designed for the densities or types of energies we are immersed in today, which are very different.

Something new is needed for our twenty-first-century lifestyles.

The space clearing system that Karen has pioneered since 1978, and we have developed together since 2005, has been created for our times and can be used by people of all cultural backgrounds, religions, and spiritual beliefs. Since the publication of her first book about space clearing in 1996, Karen has received a continuous stream of feedback from people all over the world attesting to its effectiveness.

Providing you follow the steps, observe the cautions, and don't take shortcuts or add inventions, the space clearing system you are about to learn will work for you as it has for the millions of people who have already benefited from it. It has been used in the homes of Christians, Hindus, Buddhists, Sikhs, Muslims, Jews, people who have other religious or spiritual beliefs, and those who have no spiritual inclinations at all. It has proved to work equally well in them all.

Who we are

We are widely recognized as the world's foremost authorities on space clearing and leading experts in clutter clearing. At the time of writing, we have 65 years of experience in these fields between us (Karen for 46 years and Richard for 19 years).

To give you some background, Karen was born in England and Richard was born in Australia. We met and fell in love in 2004, started working together in 2005, and have dedicated our lives to developing deeper levels of space clearing, clutter clearing, and other aspects of conscious living. Karen lived in Bali for 20 years from 1990 to 2010 and was joined there by Richard for the last five years. We now live in England, which has become our permanent home.

Karen's first two books, written before she met Richard, immediately became international bestsellers. *Creating Sacred Space with Feng Shui* was published in 1996 and sold over a million copies in 15 languages. *Clear Your Clutter with Feng Shui* was published in 1998 and has so far sold over two million copies in 26 languages.

Clear Your Clutter with Feng Shui has been regularly updated and is now in its fifth edition. It has established itself as a classic in its field.

However, when we attempted to update *Creating Sacred Space with Feng Shui,* we quickly realized it wouldn't work. Our space clearing knowledge and skills have developed so much since it was published that a complete rewrite is needed. It is therefore no longer in print and has been replaced by two volumes:

- *Space Clearing, Volume 1* (this book) covers everything you need to know to be able to do space clearing in your own home and the homes of close friends and relatives.
- *Space Clearing, Volume 2* contains the story of how we pioneered and developed space clearing, deeper understandings of how it works, the many ways it can be used, and a debunking of the most common misconceptions about energy clearing.

Who this book is for

This book is for people who want to live a more conscious and awakened way of life. If you've never done space clearing before, you're going to discover an extraordinary new life skill. And if you *have* done it before, you'll gain a whole new level of insight into what it is and how to do it.

Space clearing has made a profound difference to our lives. We hope it will make a similarly profound difference to yours too.

How to use this book

This book is in eight parts. You will get the most from it if you read it cover to cover before doing your first space clearing. Each chapter contains information that will help you to get the best possible results. You can then use it as a reference book that you return to from time to time to refresh your knowledge and improve your skills. To facilitate this, we have briefly repeated some of the information at times or pointed out when it is necessary to read other sections for completeness.

The first three parts of the book contain vital information that everyone needs to know before doing space clearing:

- **Part One**: What is space clearing?
- **Part Two**: How to get the best space clearing results
- **Part Three**: Space clearing equipment and materials

The middle section of the book is about how to do space clearing:

- **Part Four:** When and where to do space clearing
- **Part Five**: How to prepare to do a space clearing ceremony
- **Part Six**: How to do space clearing

The final two parts of the book are reference sections:

- **Part Seven**: Resources
- **Part Eight**: Glossaries

Please be aware that this book is written in British English, which sometimes has different punctuation, spelling, and terminology to other styles of English.

The terminology used in this book

A major challenge in writing a book about space clearing is that there is a lack of vocabulary in the English language to describe the unseen worlds and how things work energetically. There is also the problem that the words that do exist are often vague or have different meanings to different people, depending on which spiritual school they have studied with or what they have read. This can lead to many misunderstandings, which we sincerely want to avoid. What's needed is a common vocabulary that can be clearly understood by everyone.

Why naming things is important

Naming things brings a much higher level of awareness to experiences. To give an example, on a stroll through the countryside you may see dozens of plants you don't know the names of. You can admire their variety and beauty. However, if you want to go deeper, there comes a point when you either name them yourself or discover what other people are calling them. Otherwise, everything you see will just wash over you in a blissful haze.

When we lived in Bali, we learned the Balinese names of all the common flowers there. It completely changed our relationship with our own garden and what we saw as we travelled around the island. Plants were no longer a blur of flowers and leaves. They became individual species that brought the landscape vividly to life.

After moving to the UK in 2010, we embarked on a similar project by learning the names of trees. Again, this transformed our world from a jumble of branches, leaves, and blossoms to an awareness of the rich array of the different types of trees. We started noticing trees everywhere we went and appreciating them in ways we had never done before.

An even more intriguing aspect of naming things emerges when venturing into non-physical realms, such as the states that are experienced during meditation and the energy changes that happen during a space clearing ceremony.

Imagine Karen's delight, therefore, to meet Samuel Sagan in 2000 and learn that he and his students in the Clairvision School of meditation had been engaged in a systematic mapping of consciousness since 1990, which had resulted in the compilation of a unique reference work called *A Language to Map Consciousness* (ALTMC for short, pronounced "alt-em-SEE"), designed to create a unifying language of spiritual terms that could be used by everyone.

We were present for some of the mapping sessions involved in its creation (Karen from 2000 and Richard from 2003). We were both very impressed by the methods that were used and the care that was taken to create terms that would be meaningful to people from as many spiritual streams as possible.

A Language to Map Consciousness (ALTMC)

ALTMC has provided us with the means to describe aspects of space clearing we previously had no words for, which has led to the development of whole new vistas of space clearing knowledge and skills.

With the permission of Samuel Sagan and the Clairvision School, we have incorporated some of the ALTMC terminology into this book. It is our hope that this will spread awareness of its existence and the adoption of its use, to create a common language for everyone who works with non-physical energies in any way. We use this terminology ourselves, both professionally and in our daily lives. It helps to make the energy worlds as clear and accessible as the physical worlds, which greatly facilitates living a more conscious way of life that bridges the two.

It's not necessary to read ALTMC or refer to any other Clairvision material to learn to do space clearing. However, most people who have an affinity with our work find that they also resonate with Clairvision teachings, so we have included resources, where relevant, for those who may wish to explore further.

ALTMC can be accessed online for free at clairvision.org. For ease of reference, in Part Eight of this book you can find an abridged version called the ALTMC Glossary.

Space clearing terminology

In this book, we want to pass to readers a much deeper level of knowledge than in Karen's first book about space clearing (*Creating Sacred Space with Feng Shui*), so we're going to need to use more precise terminology.

All specialists develop their own terms to describe the intricacies of what they do, and space clearing is no exception. Most people attending a meeting of professional space clearers would understand very little of what we say.

In addition to using terminology from ALTMC, there are words that we have coined ourselves to describe aspects such as the types of energies in spaces, the issues they cause, the techniques we use to clear them, the results we achieve, and so on. We have included some of these terms in the Space Clearing Glossary in Part Eight of this book.

How to use the glossaries

Single asterisk

When you come across a term that has a single asterisk after it (like this*), flip to the ALTMC Glossary in Chapter 41 to get clarification.

Double asterisk

For a term with a double asterisk after it (like this**), refer to the Space Clearing Glossary in Chapter 42.

To avoid peppering the text with multiple asterisks, each term has usually been asterisked only the first times we use it in the book.

PART ONE

What is
space clearing?

1

Early beginnings

by Karen Kingston

One fine summer evening in 1978, I was driving over to visit a couple of friends who had just moved into a new apartment when an idea occurred to me that would completely change the course of my life.

I arrived on their doorstep and asked them if I could try an experiment. Instead of letting them show me around their new home, I asked them to allow me to explore it blindfolded. For a couple of years, I had been developing my abilities to sense energies with my hands. I had practised a lot in my own home and public buildings but had never tried it in anyone else's home before and never blindfolded.

They were as interested as I was to try this, so I waited outside while they found a thick, black silk scarf and tied it tightly around my eyes. I couldn't see a thing.

Hand sensing

My friends guided me into the apartment and closed the front door. I took off my sandals, removed the ring I was wearing, and rolled up my sleeves. They guided me to a sink where I could wash and dry my hands, then led me back to the entrance hall.

Starting at the front door, I followed the inner perimeter of the space and used my hands to sense the energies of the walls, furniture, and other objects from 5–10 centimetres (cm) (2–4 inches) away. My friends steered me, when necessary, so that I didn't bump into things or trip up.

The first thing I discovered was that I could easily tell the difference between the furniture that belonged to them and the pieces that belonged to their landlord. My friends' items were vibrantly imprinted with their energies and felt well loved, whereas the landlord's things felt lifeless and dull.

"See if you can tell us what pictures we have on the wall," my friends challenged me.

This wasn't something I'd ever tried before, but sure enough, I found I could easily tell the difference between clear stretches of wall and places where pictures were hanging. I could sometimes discern colours and the types of images depicted too. One that felt hot and prickly turned out to be an image of a battle scene. Another that felt cool and calming was a beach panorama with rippling ocean waves.

My friends also had some framed photos of famous people and mutual friends. By hand sensing** them, I discovered I was able to name who some of them were. I hadn't seen any of these pictures before. They had all been acquired for this new place, which was their first real home together.

Whatever it was we had planned to do that evening had long since been abandoned by this point. "Let's see what else you can do," my friends enthused. They were totally fascinated now.

They collected a variety of decorative items from around their home, put them on a table in front of me, and asked me to tell them which ones were theirs. It felt very clear to me that only one of the pieces belonged to them, but they said that wasn't correct. I tried again and got exactly the same reading, yet they still insisted I was wrong. I found this very puzzling until I asked them more about the history of the items and discovered they were mostly antiques that had been purchased from markets. The reason I couldn't feel my friends' energies in them was because they were so heavily imprinted by the previous owners.

This gave me the idea to do another circuit of the apartment, hand sensing at a deeper level, to see what I could discover about the previous occupants. This time, I perceived a predominant frequency of someone who was mentally inflexible. I also felt fleeting aches in my bones, especially the joints of my fingers.

My exploration continued for the rest of the evening, hand sensing all kinds of things. Some of the items were so small that I had to sense them with my fingertips rather than my whole hand. Some, such as a treasured teddy bear, were so lovely that I lingered over them for a long time. The entire experience was like a fabulous sensory extravaganza. I kept my blindfold on the whole time I was there and only took it off as I was leaving.

A week later my friends excitedly called to say they had asked their landlord about the previous tenant. They learned he had lived there for 20 years and was a very obstinate old man who suffered with severe arthritis, especially in his hands.

Developing space clearing

The experience of that evening motivated me to improve my hand-sensing skills even more, which naturally led me to wanting to develop ways to clear the unsavoury energies I was finding in buildings, especially in my own home. That's how space clearing began.

If you'd like to know more, you can find the full story of how Richard and I developed space clearing in *Space Clearing, Volume 2.*

2

Why all buildings need space clearing

Have you ever wondered why it is that so many people prefer new things to second-hand?

Apart from the fact that new things are in pristine condition physically, a large part of the joy of new ownership is that an item arrives in your life as an energetically blank canvas, ready for you to use and imprint with your own energies to make it yours. It feels very different to acquiring something that someone else has used before you.

This applies to buildings as well as objects. When you move into a new home, you will want to take ownership of the space. Physically, this often involves decorating and furnishing it to your own taste, and perhaps making some structural changes too.

But what about the energies of the space? You need to take ownership of these too.

A property that has had other occupants before you will contain residues of their energies, and the longer it has been occupied, the more imprinted it will be. Even a brand-new home can be imbued with the frustrations and setbacks experienced by the builders who created it.

Buying or renting a home is one of the largest personal expenditures most people ever have, so you want to get it right. Yet it's a game of chance what types of energetic frequencies will be embedded in the walls and how they will affect you. Knowing how to change this is an essential skill for any homemaker.

How energy imprints can affect you

The imprints left by previous occupants of a home build up in layers and are collectively known as predecessor energy. This happens in all properties and, short of knocking down and rebuilding, only one thing can completely remove them – space clearing.

If your home is a fairly new one and the people who lived there before you were healthy and happy, the imprinting will probably only be light and will not affect you too much. Space clearing will easily clear these residues and help to make your new space quickly feel like home.

It's a very different story if you move into a place where the previous occupants got sick, divorced, went bankrupt, suffered a tragedy of some kind, or experienced other misfortunes while living there. Those astral imprints** will still be embedded in the walls, floors, ceilings, fixtures, fittings, and any furniture they have left in the place, and they will tend to cause history to repeat itself. Similarly, if the people who lived there before you were lazy, argumentative, or had other deeply entrenched behaviours, you may find yourself picking up those habits yourself.

People in this situation often lament, "Life started going wrong when we moved here". Unless they know about energy imprints, they tend to look for external causes and rarely realize that the property itself may be the source of their problems.

After you move in, you and anyone you share your home with will create more imprints, day after day, layer upon layer. Most people wouldn't want to live in a home that isn't kept physically clean, but unless you space clear regularly, you'll be living in the energetic equivalent of a garbage bin without even knowing it. This can cause a range of problems that can make it very difficult for you to move forward in life with ease.

Why space clearing is an essential life skill

The loss of purification practices in modern times has caused a corresponding loss of sacredness in our way of life. It's a strong contributing factor to why so many people feel spiritually disconnected and unable to find any deeper meaning in their lives.

While we are incarnated here on earth, physical cleaning is needed to maintain the physical levels of existence. But it's not enough. To be able to access higher levels of consciousness and navigate through life with integrity, we need higher levels of purification too. Clearing and revitalizing the energies of your home is one of the most important of these practices. No matter how much personal development work you do, it will have minimal effect if you continually live surrounded by your own or other people's historical imprints.

We personally use space clearing extensively in our lives, in every home we live in, and every place we stay in. This includes each of the homes we have owned or rented on three continents (in Bali, Australia, and the United Kingdom), as well as all the hotel rooms, self-catering apartments, and houses we have rented in the many countries we have travelled in.

To give an example of short-term usage, we once spent a couple of months in Sydney, Australia, where we rented a series of four self-catering apartments to experience living for a few weeks in different parts of the city. Each had substantial predecessor energy of one kind or another when we arrived. Some were so awful that we initially felt we didn't want to stay there at all. Space clearing improved them immediately. Even we were surprised at the radical difference it made in one of the places we stayed, which had seen a huge amount of use and initially felt beyond redemption.

These were not cheap rentals, by the way. We paid a good rate for them, and they were well furnished and fitted out. The problem is that rented properties can have imprints of hundreds or even thousands of previous occupants. The apartments we stayed in were in popular locations and were as energetically saturated as they get.

The beautiful thing about space clearing is that it can be used to clean up the energies of anywhere you live so that you can truly have a fresh start and make it your own. There's no need to live with anyone else's energies in your home ever again or with the historical imprints of your own challenges and struggles that will inevitably build up over time.

Space clearing can change your life

Space clearing has made a world of difference to the quality of experiences we have had in each place we have lived. It has supported our spiritual development, fortified our health, deepened our relationship, enabled our business to grow and prosper, and helped us to work through all life's ups and downs with greater clarity and ease.

We get similar reports from the clients we have space cleared for and the people we have taught the skills to.

Space clearing is not something to put on your to-do list and perhaps get around to doing someday. It's a vital twenty-first-century life skill that everyone can benefit from learning, as the next two chapters explain.

3

What space clearing is and is not

All buildings, no matter how well designed, and all people, no matter what their beliefs, can benefit from space clearing.

The five levels of home maintenance

To create a home environment that nurtures and supports you, it's common sense to keep it in a good state of repair, clean, organized, tidy, and clutter-free. We hope that if you're reading this book, this is something you already do or at least aspire to do.

Space clearing goes much further. It is the highest level of home maintenance for people who are energetically aware and value their quality of life, as this diagram shows.

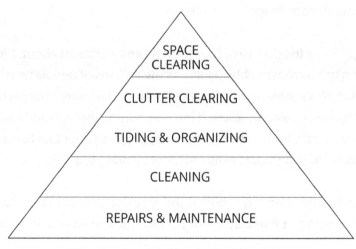

The five levels of home maintenance

Space clearing works best if the lower levels of home maintenance have already been taken care of. It is also easier to do space clearing if it is done regularly, in the same way that physical cleaning is easier to do when grime is not allowed to build up.

You can live your entire life without doing space clearing. But once you've learned how to do it and experienced the difference it makes, you'll never want to be without it again. We hope that, after reading this book, you will join the many people who choose to make it part of their regular building maintenance programme to keep their spaces energetically as well as physically clean and clear.

Space clearing is not the same as clutter clearing

Space clearing is sometimes confused with clutter clearing because both result in a type of clearer space. The difference is that clutter clearing mainly results in physically clear space. Space clearing works at a higher level to create space that is energetically clear.

Another difference is that clutter clearing needs no equipment, except for a few boxes or bags. The level of knowledge and skills needed to do it are also at a much more basic level. Space clearing needs specialized equipment, knowledge, and skills.

Finally, there's the degree of change that can be brought about. Clutter clearing brings remarkable results, as the millions of people who have read Karen's clutter clearing book or taken online courses or personal sessions with us already know. It involves sorting through and clearing physical objects from a space, and it may progress after that to mental, emotional, and spiritual levels of clutter clearing too.

Physical clutter clearing is one of the essential preparatory steps for space clearing. It can also be done without any intention of doing space clearing or even any knowledge that space clearing exists. The changes that space clearing can bring about are at a much higher and more profound level.

The purposes of space clearing

Space clearing can be used for a range of different purposes:

- Clearing and revitalizing energies in buildings
- Taking energetic ownership of a space
- Raising the level of consciousness in a space
- Facilitating spiritual connection
- Spiritually presencing a space

The best known of these is clearing and revitalizing energies in buildings, and it's the one we will be focusing on in this book. You will learn how to confidently do this first in your own home and then in the homes of close friends and relatives, if they invite you to do so and you wish to help them. We'll also be touching on some aspects of taking energetic ownership of a space.

The other purposes listed here are more advanced and only possible after you have become proficient at clearing and revitalizing energies, so we'll be exploring them more in *Space Clearing, Volume 2*.

What we mean by space clearing

Karen first started developing her space clearing skills in 1978 and coined the name space clearing ten years later. As a result of the success of her first book, it has been adopted by others as a generic term for all kinds of energy clearing techniques, some of which are very odd indeed and bear no resemblance to anything you will read about here.

We therefore want to make it very clear that any references we make to space clearing are about the method Karen originally developed and how it has evolved since we met and started working together. We cannot vouch for the efficacy of any other energy clearing techniques.

We also want to clarify at this point that none of the space clearing techniques in this book have any resemblance to traditional Balinese purification practices, except for the mudra that is used to activate flower offerings**, and even that is done very differently in space clearing to the way it is generally practised in Bali. As we explain in *Space Clearing, Volume 2*, Karen started developing space clearing 12 years before she visited Bali. The only reason we use Balinese equipment for space clearing is because it is by far the highest quality available anywhere in the world for space clearing purposes.

Space clearing is not just a series of techniques

The space clearing ceremony you are about to learn involves doing several circuits of the inner perimeter of a property, using a series of techniques that include clapping and bell ringing. In some versions of the ceremony, a space clearing altar is also created with flower offerings and exquisitely beautiful Balinese altar cloths and colourizers**.

This has led some people to mistakenly assume that a space clearing ceremony can include a variety of techniques, loosely strung together in any order. In our experience, if that achieves anything at all, the results will be insubstantial and short-lived.

Space clearing consists of a precise series of steps that need to be performed in a specific order. This applies to all forms of space clearing that are practised in traditional cultures around the world, as well as to the space clearing methods we use. Each step of the ceremony creates a foundation for the next step, so if you change any of the steps, change the order, or substitute energy clearing techniques you have learned elsewhere, the space clearing won't work as well as it could, won't work at all, or can have unwanted effects.

We are not claiming that our form of space clearing is the only one that works, although we do firmly believe it is the most applicable to modern life. What we are saying is that for *any* space clearing system to work, its archetypal integrity must be upheld. Mixing one or more systems together will only create a hybrid that lacks whatever integrity the individual systems originally had, and randomly changing the order will dilute and weaken its effectiveness, as we will explain in detail as this book unfolds.

You don't have to believe in space clearing for it to work

From time to time, someone contacts us who shares their home with a partner who is sceptical about space clearing. They often ask whether it is necessary to believe in space clearing for it to work.

Our answer is that no belief in space clearing is needed at all. It either works or it doesn't. And that is not determined by how much you hope, believe, or intend that it will bring about changes. The determining factors are how skilfully the space clearing is done, and the quality of the equipment and materials used to do it. The results then speak for themselves.

This is why we say that space clearing is essentially a higher level of home maintenance. You don't have to believe in physical house cleaning, tidying, organizing, or decluttering for those techniques to work. You can see the difference, and sensitive people can also feel it.

Space clearing does not create visible results, but the changes it brings about can certainly be felt energetically. Many people tell us that visitors have walked into their home after they have space cleared and have stopped in their tracks, astonished at how different it feels. They ask if it has been redecorated or physically changed in some way, as they try to find a logical reason to explain it.

We do understand scepticism about space clearing and feel it's very healthy to have it, especially since there are now so many bizarre energy clearing methods that have sprung up since Karen's first book was published. We'll be examining some of these in *Space Clearing, Volume 2*, so you'll know what to look out for.

4

Energies in buildings

We spend more time inside buildings now than at any time in human history. It's therefore more important than ever to understand how the energies of the places you occupy affect you and what you can do to improve them.

We live in an ocean of energy

We think of ourselves as solid, physical beings living in a solid, physical world. In fact, we are energetic beings living in an ever-changing ocean of energy. The breath you just took as you read that last sentence has been scientifically calculated to contain about 4.3×10^9 molecules of the air that was breathed by Leonardo da Vinci during the 45 years he was alive. It also contained about five molecules of the last dying gasp of everyone who has ever lived. Every breath you ever take does.

If you talk to physicists, there is arguably no physical world at all since everything is made of atoms, and all atoms consist almost entirely of empty space. The only reason we perceive objects to be physical is because the electrons that revolve around atoms repel each other and keep them apart.

If you are sitting in a chair reading this, you may think you are physically sitting on the chair. The truth is that you are hovering one angstrom (10^{-10} or one ten-billionth of a metre) above the chair, held there by the electrons of your body and the electrons of the chair repelling each other.

There is also much more to a human being than just a physical body. We each have an etheric body* too, made of life force energy, an astral body* made of thoughts and emotions, and a Higher Self, which is our spiritual essence.

Similarly, there is more to a building than just bricks and mortar. Each room within a building will contain energies of some kind that will affect you, whether you are aware of them or not. These unseen elements are what may have caused you to say, after walking into a house, "Wow! This place feels great!" Or perhaps, "This place feels awful. I could never live here."

The starting point of this book, before we talk about how to do space clearing, needs to be an exploration of these energies. They are not as distinct as physical objects, which means there can be some intermingling, but the main characteristics of each type are sufficiently different that they can be categorized. This will give you more awareness of the energies that may be in your home, and a better understanding of what space clearing can do and why it's so vital.

What kind of space does space clearing clear?

There are some words in the English language that have such a wide range of meanings they almost defy definition. "Energy" is one of these. "Space" is another. Changing the energy of spaces is what space clearing is all about, so it's crucial that we define what each of these terms means.

In the *Oxford English Dictionary*, two of the main definitions of space are:

- The dimensions of height, depth, and width within which all things exist and move
- A continuous area or expanse which is free, available, or unoccupied

These describe the physical features of a space very well, but they take no account of its energetic qualities, which lie beyond the expertise of lexicologists.

The space we are referring to in the context of space clearing consists of various types of energies and the levels of consciousness they are permeated with. These can be discerned through certain subtle body* structures* that anyone can develop, although few people do.

If you're interested to learn more about this, we've included some information about subtle body building* in Part Two of *Space Clearing, Volume 2*. For now, all you need to know is that what we're about to explain is not based on theories. It's the result of decades of first-hand exploration and cognizing of the unseen worlds of energy, which have become as tangible to us as the physical worlds. Our perceptions also correlate exactly with independent mapping done over many years by Samuel Sagan and the students of the Clairvision School.

Types of energies in buildings

The two main types of energies that can be found in buildings are:

- Etheric*
- Astral*

Etheric energies

All humans, animals, and plants have an etheric body. It permeates the physical body and extends beyond it. The Chinese call it *chi*. The Japanese call it *ki*. In India, it is known as *prana*. In English-speaking countries, it is often called life force energy. Etheric energies make things grow and give living things vitality.

One of the easiest ways to feel your own etheric body is to monitor your energy levels during the day. When you wake up full of energy in the morning, your etheric vitality is at its best. As the day progresses and you become tired, that's the feeling of your etheric energy getting depleted. A primary function of sleep is to recharge it.

Buildings do not have an etheric body in the same way that humans, animals, and plants do, but each room in a building will have what is known as an ambient etheric**. This results from the combined qualities of a range of factors such as the nature of the land energies below the building, the materials used to construct the property, how well energies flow around the space, the type of ventilation, what the room is used for, how much clutter it contains, and so on.

There is a world of difference between living in a home that has clear, vibrant, etheric energies and living in one that does not. It can affect whether you thrive or just survive, whether you fulfil your potential or just get by. We all flourish and grow in etherically nurturing spaces, which is one of the main reasons why space clearing is so beneficial. It addresses the three unwholesome types of etheric energies that can be found in buildings:

- Etheric debris**
- Stagnant energies**
- Perverse energies*

Etheric debris

Etheric debris is elemental* in nature. It is formed by the energetic excretions that are a natural function of all living organisms. There is often a physical component to it, such as dust, grime, sweat, mould, or grease, and sometimes an odour too. Living rooms, bedrooms, bathrooms, and kitchens tend to accumulate more etheric debris than other areas of a home because they are the most frequently used.

Allowing etheric debris to build up in your home will impact your etheric body. It has a clogging effect that will prevent you from being able to function at your best.

Etheric debris tends to sink to floor level and also collects on flat surfaces, in the same way that dust does. And like dust, the remedy for etheric debris isn't space clearing. It's good, old-fashioned, roll-up-your-sleeves household cleaning, which is why cleaning your home from top to bottom is an important preparatory step for space clearing.

Regular sweeping, mopping, or vacuuming the floors of your home, and cleaning all surfaces as part of your regular housekeeping, will remove most types of physical and etheric debris. Vacuuming, in particular, instantly makes any room feel fresher, providing you use the type of equipment that has an efficient dust particle filter, which you empty regularly. Even if you don't have the time or energy to do space clearing, making sure the floors of your home are kept clean will help to support your etheric wellbeing.

If damage has occurred to the structure of a building as a result of dampness or other issues, then physical repairs will be needed as well as cleaning in order to remove both the physical and etheric debris.

Stagnant energies

In the same way that water stagnates if it is not moving, so buildings can stagnate if there is a poor flow of energy around the space. Entire properties can fill with stagnant energies or just individual rooms or parts of those rooms.

Stagnant energies often mingle with etheric debris. In fact, a good way to appreciate the quantity of stagnant energies there may be in your home is to imagine how much dust would have built up if it had never been physically cleaned since the day it was built. Most people would not want to live or work in such a space. But that is exactly what it may be like energetically if it has never been space cleared.

Architectural design, furniture positioning, and poor ventilation can all contribute to the quantity of stagnant energies that accumulate. Physical changes can be made to improve energy flows, which is why it's useful to learn enough about feng shui to be able to do this. However, this won't clear any stagnant energies that have already built up or those that will build up in the future. Space clearing is needed for that.

Stagnant energies have a dull, heavy feel to them. They tend to gather in rarely used or neglected areas of a building, such as basements, attics, junk rooms, and guest rooms. They also collect in corners and in the gaps between things – anywhere spiders like to create their webs. The lack of activity in these areas will cause energies to pool and come to a stop (hence the clever strategy of the spider to build its web and wait there for prey). Children are generally more etherically aware than adults, which is why they may feel uneasy about dark corners and spaces under beds, where stagnant energies tend to collect.

Many cultures traditionally preferred buildings without corners. Native American tribes lived in wigwams or tipis. Some South African tribes lived in domed buildings or circular tents. Inhabitants of some central Asian countries lived in circular yurts. The Celts and other ancient communities in North European countries lived in roundhouses.

Architects and historians tell us that the benefit of circular structures is that fewer materials are needed than for square buildings, they are more resistant to the ravages of the elements such as strong winds, earthquakes, and heavy snowfall, and they are easier to keep warm or cool. There are energetic benefits too, because circular structures have no corners where stagnant energies can gather. The more etherically-based humans of ancient times would have been more aware of this than most people are today.

In most homes, stagnant energies extend about 5 cm (2 inches) from the walls. In some properties we have visited, where generations of people have lived and died, the layers may extend up to 30 cm (12 inches) from the walls. Ancestral homes that are centuries old are usually the most imprinted of all. The build-up can be a metre (3 feet) thick in such places, where doing hand sensing** (a technique you'll be learning about later in the book) can feel like the energetic equivalent of pulling your hand through thick syrup.

One of the biggest causes of stagnant energies in a home is clutter. If you have ever decluttered an area of your home and then wondered why you feel grubby after, even if the items you were handling were stored inside boxes and were physically clean, it will be because they were coated in stagnant energies. That's why it's always a good idea to take a shower after clutter clearing, or at least wash your face, hands, and forearms, to wash off any etheric debris and stagnant energies that have stuck to you.

You can find detailed information about how to clear your clutter in Karen's book *Clear Your Clutter with Feng Shui*. Removing clutter from your home will remove the stagnant energies that are embedded in the items, but not the stagnant energies that will have accumulated around them. Space clearing is needed for that.

Stagnant energies are a problem because you are energetically connected to your home and all your belongings. When stagnant energies are allowed to build up, they cause a corresponding stagnation in some aspects of your life that will make you feel stuck.

This can take many forms. You may feel stuck in a job you don't like or a relationship that doesn't nurture you, or be unable to find a job or a loving relationship at all. Your finances may be stuck, your creativity, or your progress in some other aspect of your life. You may find it hard to shake old habits, lose weight, become fitter, and so on. Generally, you'll feel like you're in a rut, going around in circles, with no new opportunities coming your way. It can get to the stage where you feel like you've hit a wall, unable to move forward at all in life.

Space clearing can revitalize the stagnant energies in your home to get your life moving again. The changes it can bring about, especially when combined with clutter clearing, are substantial.

Perverse energies

Most people reading this book will not have perverse energies in their home. They are a type of etheric energy that can be found in some buildings, so we are including information about them for completeness.

The main places we have encountered perverse energies is in buildings that are very neglected or permeated with damp, and in the homes of people who have hoarding behaviour, where some of the rooms can no longer be used for their intended purpose.

It's fairly easy to discern when a place is brimming with perverse energies because it will feel awful. It can also smell damp or fetid or may make you feel unclean as soon as you enter. The physical odour can linger energetically in your nostrils, sometimes for days after you have been exposed to it.

Perverse energies tend to float in the air and stick to you. This is known as the pancake* effect, because it can feel like the energetic equivalent of having a sticky pancake thrown at you. In some buildings, there are so many perverse energies floating around that you quickly become coated in them.

The problem with perverse energies is that they can creep into your etheric body and nest in it, causing a range of health issues. They are not negative, wrong, or evil. They just don't belong inside a human body, just as fungi are an essential part of a forest ecosystem but some types can cause health problems if they enter the human organism.

No matter how resilient you are or how well developed your perception is, there is no way to avoid getting pancaked if you walk into a place where these types of energies are prevalent. If you immerse yourself in water, you will get wet. If you spend time in a place that is swarming with perverse energies, you will get caked in them.

There is no foolproof way to protect yourself against them, although someone with good discernment and an awakened etheric (explained in more detail in *Space Clearing, Volume 2*) can deflect some of them. After you walk out of a property that has perverse energies floating around, you will feel like you are coated in lumps of energetic crud. If you don't know how to quickly clear them, they can enter your system and cause problems.

In some cases, there may be no permanent solution for perverse energies. For example, if a property has been built in a location that is not fit for human habitation, such as a swamp or an area that often gets flooded, any changes that space clearing brings about are likely to be only temporary before the perverse energies come back.

In other cases, where the cause of perverse energies is a side-effect of human activities within a building or a result of neglect, rather than being caused by environmental factors, there are advanced space clearing techniques that can be used to reclaim the space. We have not included those methods in this book because they can only safely be used by those who have received practitioner-level training.

Astral energies

The two main types of astral energies that can be found in buildings are:

- Astral imprints**
- Entities*

Astral imprints

If you've ever had the experience of walking into a room just after there has been an argument, you know that you can literally feel it hanging in the air. People sometimes say, "You could have cut the air with a knife", meaning the astral frequency of the argument was so raw and dense that it was tangible in the room, even after the people who were engaged in the quarrel had left.

Everything that happens in a room creates astral ripples in the space, similar to the effect of a stone being dropped in a pond. The astral imprints of this are then recorded in the walls, floor, ceiling, furniture, and objects in the space, and will remain there, layer upon layer, unless they are cleared. Repetitive actions and behaviours get deeply imprinted. Events accompanied by strong emotions or trauma are the most strongly imprinted of all.

In the same way that we leave elements of our personal microbial cloud and a trail of physical dust in our wake (a substantial proportion of household dust comes from skin), so we also leave astral imprints everywhere we go and on everything we touch. A large part of what makes a house feel like a home is imprinting it with our own energy in this way, but it can also keep us stuck in the past, if the imprints are allowed to build up.

Clearing astral imprints is more difficult than revitalizing stagnant energies, so if your home is heavily imprinted, we recommend doing one of the longer versions of the space clearing ceremony described in this book (Essential Space Clearing** or a Full Space Clearing** ceremony) rather than the shorter version (Basic Space Clearing**). Depending on your skill and level of experience, it may also be necessary to repeat the ceremony several times over a period of weeks or months.

Some people get concerned that space clearing will clear out happy imprints as well as unwanted or unhappy ones, but it doesn't work like this. It clears out the lower levels that unhappy memories are attached to and leaves the higher levels intact. In fact, it enhances the higher levels because the lower levels are not weighing them down.

Entities

Entities are energetic parasites that are primarily astral and may also have etheric components. Known in Chinese as *kuei*, in Sanskrit as *bhuta*, and often referred to as ghosts or attachments, some are elemental beings that come from nature. Most come from the shattering process of the astral body that happens to all humans after they die. They are crystallized, non-physical fragments* of a deceased person's astral consciousness and etheric life force energy.

Like physical parasites, energetic parasites need a host in order to survive, so they will usually seek out a live human or animal to attach themselves to. This can cause physical, mental, or emotional problems in the host, which normal health treatments will be unable to resolve.

Entities can also sometimes be found in buildings. They tend to gravitate to crossing points of earth lines or regions of dense elemental energies that they can tap into as an energetic food source. It's not easy to detect when there is an entity in a building. They do not want to be seen and are very good at hiding. The biggest clue is often an inexplicable feeling of being watched.

Entity clearing is far beyond the scope of this book. There is a very advanced level of space clearing that can be used for this purpose, and we have considerable experience of doing this. At the time of writing, we have not yet trained any of our practitioners in this skill. The method we advise them to use when there is an entity in a home is to space clear first and then use the Clairvision entity clearing method, if they have been trained how to do that.

If you search the internet, you'll find people who offer entity clearing services, sometimes using terms such as exorcism, ghost busting, or spirit-attachment removal. These are usually well-meaning folk although, in our experience, their methods are rarely effective. They attract vulnerable people who are desperate for help, and they may use absurd techniques such as entity clearing from a distance or visiting a property in person to talk to an entity and tell it to go. Some claim to work with angels who they believe will come when called to do their bidding.

If you have ever had physical parasites inside your body, such as intestinal worms, you'll know it can be difficult to get rid of them. Energetic parasites are just as tenacious. Once they have nested into a person, animal, or building and are feeding off it as their host, they don't want to leave. Therefore, the notion that telling an entity to go will have any effect at all is, at best, wishful thinking and, at worst, hopelessly unrealistic. There are angelic beings that can assist with entity clearing, but they are extraordinarily high-level presences* and are not at our human beck and call. The level of inner stillness required to commune at will with such presences is beyond the capability of most humans.

We are going into so much detail here because the problem with attempting to clear an entity unsuccessfully is that it is worse than not attempting it at all. It can cause the entity to bury deeper into the host, which will make it much more difficult to clear if attempted again. This is therefore not a situation where you want to "have a go" at clearing an entity yourself or invite someone with dubious credentials to do so. It needs to be done by capable experts.

The Clairvision School has an international network of the most proficient entity clearers we know of. If you suspect you have an entity in your home and are not able to find a Clairvision-trained entity clearer who is also a certified space clearing practitioner, our best advice is to get the entity clearing done first, then decide whether to do the space clearing yourself or hire a certified space clearing practitioner to do it.

If you are interested to learn more about entities, the best book we have ever found on this topic is *Entities: Parasites of the Body of Energy* by Samuel Sagan (published in the United States as *Entity Possession: Freeing the Energy Body of Negative Influences*). However, be assured that you do not need to know anything about entities to be able to do the level of space clearing described in this book.

PART TWO

How to get the best space clearing results

5

What you need to know

The information in this book is not intended for professional use, so no previous experience of working with energy is needed to learn the three levels of space clearing ceremonies described in these pages. However, there are some fundamental aspects you will need to understand first, which will have a significant effect on the depth of results you are able to obtain.

We therefore encourage you to read this part of the book in full. The topics covered range from the practical to the profound:

- How to determine the main entrance to your home
- The importance of MC-ship
- Why it works best to keep your sleeves rolled up
- Hydration
- Breathing and throat friction
- Involution

Some of the information in these chapters may not make much sense at first because you don't yet have a context for it, but its relevance will become clearer as the book progresses.

6

How to determine
the main entrance to your home

Most space clearing techniques take the form of a circuit that starts at the main entrance, follows the entire inner perimeter of your home, and ends back at the main entrance. The reason for this is that the main entrance to a home is the main portal through which people, and the energies that accompany them, enter the space.

If your home has only one front door that is always used as the main entrance and everyone who lives in your home wants to be included in the ceremony, it's very simple. Each circuit of the ceremony needs to begin and end at the front door.

If your home has other doors that are sometimes used to enter and leave, or you share it with people who do not want the areas they occupy to be included in the ceremony, you'll need to read this chapter to discover which door to use as your main entrance for space clearing purposes.

If your home has two front doors

If your home happens to have two front doors (perhaps because it consists of two properties that were at one stage joined together), your main entrance will be the one that is used the most frequently.

If your back door
is used more often than your front door

In some countries, such as Ireland, the back door may be the entrance that is used the most. It is seen as being much friendlier than using the formal front door, so much so that in some Irish homes the front door is completely nailed shut. In such homes, treat the back door as the main entrance for space clearing purposes.

If a side door is used more often than your front door

In this situation, your side door will be the main entrance at which all circuits of the ceremony begin and end.

If your home has an attached garage

An attached garage is one that is connected to your home by a door. If you regularly park your car in a garage of this type and then enter your home through that door instead of the front door, then for the purposes of space clearing, the door connecting your garage to your home will be the main entrance.

This is common in many modern homes, especially in the United States, because it's so convenient. Unfortunately, in many cases, it can have unintended effects. It usually means you enter through a generally unexciting or cluttered area instead of a more tastefully designed foyer that your front door opens into. Habitually entering through such a route is the equivalent of using a servant's or tradesperson's entrance. Your foyer may be a delightfully welcoming space for visitors, but if you rarely experience this effect yourself, you'll miss out on the feeling of energetically owning the space that entering through the front door would give you. This can lead to issues such as low self-esteem, always putting other people's needs before your own, or feeling out of control in your life.

Another problem caused by having an attached garage is that each time you enter the home after parking your car, you will swamp your home with toxic chemicals from car fumes. You will also unwittingly carry with you a mishmash of energies that the vehicle has collected on its travels, which can cause chaotic effects inside your home.

Most Eastern cultures understand very well that there needs to be a clear separation between outdoor and indoor energies, which is why they observe the strict practice of removing their shoes before entering a building. They know how disruptive it can be to trample outdoor energies through a home, and this is not even taking into account the chemical cocktail of pesticides that we pick up on the soles of our shoes, even in urban areas. Other cultures tend to have very little awareness of this, and modern garage designs now take this one step further by mingling the energies of cars as well.

If you or any people you share your home with commonly enter your home through a door connected to a garage, then this is the one you will need to use to begin and end each circuit of the space clearing ceremony, however unappealing it may be.

Alternatively, you can make the decision to start using your front door from now on instead of the garage door, in which case you can use your front door as the main entrance for the space clearing ceremony. This means that in future you will need to park your car in your garage, exit through your garage door, close it behind you, then enter your home through the front door. If there is shopping to be brought in from your car, you will then need to re-enter the garage through the door connecting it to your home to retrieve it. This simple change of behaviour can result in beneficial changes on many different levels. Even if you cheat occasionally and enter through the internal garage door when it's pouring with rain, you're still likely to notice a marked improvement.

When there is equal usage of two or more doors

In a home where there are two or more doors that are used equally often to enter the property, choose the one that a stranger coming to visit you would presume to be your front door.

If you have a shared front door

In a property such as an apartment block, the main entrance to use for space clearing purposes is not the front door that is shared by all the owners or tenants of the building. You will need to start all the circuits of the ceremony from the main entrance to the part of the property that you have exclusive use of, which will usually be your apartment door.

If you share your home with others

If you share your home with others who do not want the areas they occupy to be space cleared (see Chapter 22), then for space clearing purposes the main entrance will be the door that opens to the area you have exclusive use of, even if that's only one room.

7

The importance of MC-ship

MC** is short for Master of Ceremonies. MC-ship** is the state of being an MC.

In everyday life, an MC is the person who has overall responsibility for an event and ensures that everything happens in the right order, such as the chairperson of a meeting, the host of an event, or the conductor of an orchestra.

In the context of space clearing, the MC is the person who conducts the space clearing ceremony and has overall responsibility for orchestrating its practical and energetic aspects.

Why every space clearing ceremony needs an MC

A space clearing ceremony needs to have an MC for the same reason that it doesn't work to have two people trying to drive a car at the same time. Someone needs to take overall responsibility for making decisions about what happens.

It's also necessary because the superastral* architecture of a space clearing ceremony works top-down, not bottom-up. A bottom-up approach would be to do the techniques mechanically, one after another, with all kinds of mundane chitter-chatter going on inside your head as you do so. The result would be ineffectual or mediocre at best. A top-down approach involves holding the overview of the focus for the ceremony throughout, giving each step your full attention, and maintaining conscious awareness of the changes being brought about. The best way to achieve this is when MC-ship is held by just one person.

It doesn't work to share MC-ship of a space clearing ceremony because some things will inevitably get missed. One person will assume the other person is taking care of a particular aspect when, in fact, they are not. This applies to any project involving two or more people. It usually works best for one person to take MC-ship and the other person or people to assist. It's especially important in space clearing because the person who has MC-ship also holds the overview and the energy of the space and works from there.

How to choose the best person to MC a space clearing ceremony

The best person to MC a space clearing ceremony is someone who has well-developed superastral structure*, etheric know-how, the ability to stay involuted*, and a comprehensive knowledge of the steps of the ceremony.

To do space clearing in your own home, all that's needed is that the MC must have read and understood this entire book first, have practised the main techniques in it, and be able to do the ceremony on behalf of all the occupants of a home, without weaving their own agenda into it.

If you live alone

If you live alone and decide to space clear your own home, you are automatically the MC.

If you share your home with other people

Other occupants of the home can help the MC with the preparations for the ceremony, such as picking the flower heads and carrying flower offerings to where they are needed, but it's not a good idea to delegate the buying of flowers or the making of the flower offerings. Those aspects need to be taken care of personally by the MC.

All activities in the home will need to come to a standstill during the ceremony so that everyone is fully focused on it while it is in progress. Ideally, everyone present will follow the MC around to experience the changes that happen during each circuit. If someone decides not to do that, or is not physically able to do so, they will need to sit in silence, preferably somewhere near the altar, and not engage in any other activities while the ceremony is in progress (including reading a book, using any kind of digital device, or eating). If they have no real interest in the ceremony, arrange to do it at a time when they will be out.

If you share your home with a partner

If you share your home with a partner and you are equal heads of the household, you will need to decide which of you will be the MC.

The best person to be MC is usually the one who first thinks of doing the space clearing, providing they are fit, healthy, and knowledgeable enough to do so. If you have both read the book and both have good space clearing skills, you can alternate MC-ship with each ceremony you do, which will have the bonus of helping you to take equal energetic ownership of the space.

Being MC does not mean you have to do everything yourself, though. There are some aspects of the ceremony you can delegate to your partner. Please bookmark this section and return to read it after you've read the rest of the book, by which time it will make much more sense.

Focus

You can both be involved in making the decision about the best focus for the ceremony. The MC's responsibility is to hold the overall focus of the ceremony throughout.

Preparations

The MC is responsible for making sure all the preparations are taken care of. The partner can help as directed by the MC.

Hand sensing

The MC must lead the way with hand sensing the inner perimeter of the space. The partner can follow around behind the MC, doing hand sensing too, if they wish to.

Altar design

The partner can help to pick the flower heads according to the instructions given by the MC. The MC will be the one to create the flower offerings and the altar design, then place the flower offerings on the altar.

Activating the first flower offering

The MC makes the space clearing water** and activates the first flower offering** on the altar.

Other flower offerings

It is the MC's responsibility to make sure all the flower offerings are placed in locations where the candles will burn safely. The partner can help to carry the flower offerings to the various parts of the home and carry the coasters and matches.

It usually works best for the MC to activate all the other flower offerings. An exception to this could be a flower offering in a room that the partner has sole use of, where the MC may choose to invite them to activate it themselves, holding the space for them while they do so.

The circuits of the ceremony

Each circuit must be completed before starting the next one. Trying to save time by one person doing one circuit while the other person is doing the next circuit won't work because the foundations for the next circuit will not yet be in place.

In any case, you will get the best results if the partner accompanies the MC on every circuit and the MC accompanies the partner during any circuits that are delegated to them. This will allow the MC to continuously hold the space.

Clapping

Clapping** is usually done by the MC, although it is possible to delegate the entire circuit to the partner (for example, if the partner is much better at clapping than the MC). In a very large building, it's also possible for the MC to start the clapping circuit and hand over at some point to the partner, if they start to feel tired or their hands become sore. When this is done, it feels like the energetic equivalent of passing a baton in a relay race.

Belling

The belling** circuit is one the MC must do. It cannot be delegated.

Harmony ball infusion and frequencing

The MC must be the one to lead the harmony ball** infusion process and the frequencing circuit described in detail in Chapter 33, Step 20. The partner can either share the same personal harmony ball or use a personal harmony ball of their own. It will work best if the partner follows around after the MC during the frequencing circuit, using their own harmony ball or a neutral harmony ball.

8

Why it works best
to keep your sleeves rolled up

You will get the best results if you do the entire space clearing ceremony with your sleeves rolled up above your elbows, or wearing a top that has short sleeves or no sleeves at all.

There are a number of reasons why this is important:

- To improve your sensitivity
- To prevent stagnant energies from becoming entangled in your clothing
- To engage MC-ship
- To enhance your etheric awareness

To improve your sensitivity

Hands and forearms are parts of the body that are very sensitive to energies. Rolling up your sleeves will expose these areas and help you to do space clearing at a deeper level.

Note that there is a huge difference between rolling your sleeves up a little and fully rolling them up above the elbow, which is what is needed here. If you are interested to learn more about this, there is a section about it in *Space Clearing, Volume 2*.

To prevent stagnant energies from becoming entangled in your clothing

Stagnant energies are sticky in nature, which is why they have the effect of making you feel stuck. During the clapping circuit of the ceremony, it is therefore important to keep your sleeves rolled up so that these energies do not get entangled in your clothing. At the end of the circuit, you can then rinse your hands and forearms under running water to easily wash off any energies you have collected.

To engage MC-ship

The physical act of rolling up your sleeves puts you in action mode, which will help you to engage MC-ship of the ceremony more dynamically.

To enhance your etheric awareness

People who naturally live with their sleeves rolled up generally have more etheric awareness, more etheric interaction with their environment, and more etheric know-how than those who do not.

If you're the kind of person who doesn't usually keep your sleeves rolled up as you go about your daily life, we invite you to try doing this more and to be especially vigilant about doing it when space clearing. Awakening your etheric and cultivating etheric know-how will open entire new worlds of spiritual experiences to you that you will have been completely unaware of before. If you'd like to know more, we've included an entire chapter about etheric awareness in *Space Clearing, Volume 2*.

9

Hydration

Be sure to drink plenty of water before, during, and after a space clearing. Many space clearing techniques have an etheric component. Water is the element that is most closely associated with the etheric body, so keeping yourself hydrated will help to keep your etheric fresh and vital, which in turn will help you to do space clearing more effectively.

It's fine to drink water from an open glass while preparing to do a space clearing, but during the ceremony, be sure to cover your drinking glass with a plate or switch to drinking out of a sealed container. Otherwise, the water will be likely to absorb some of the stagnant energies you are clearing.

About water

A reason why most people tend not to drink enough water is that we do not get excited by drinking the flat, lifeless water we get in our homes or even spring water that has been stored in a bottle. We instinctively know that it lacks etheric vitality. There is a world of difference between these fluids and water obtained directly from a clear, fresh mountain stream.

Drinking flavoured, sweetened, or carbonated water isn't the answer. Nor is consuming quantities of tea, soft drinks, or other liquids instead. Nothing has the marvellous purifying effect that water has.

For bottled or filtered water that lacks vitality, there is an ancient Hindu method of boosting prana you can use to re-energize it. Pour it quickly through the air from one glass to another several times to add more life to it.

An even better solution, if you can afford it, is to invest in a volcanic mineral water filtration system for your home that will revitalize the water and remove bacteria, viruses, chlorine, chloramines, cysts, fluoride, heavy metals, rust, sediment, asbestos, fluoride, herbicides, and pesticides. They are a wonderful investment in your own health and the health of everyone you share your home with. The water tastes and feels delicious to drink.

10

Breathing and throat friction

How you breathe, and how much awareness of your breath you have, can make a huge difference to the space clearing results you get.

Awareness of the breath

One of the major purposes of space clearing is to clear and revitalize energies in spaces. It's therefore essential to keep the energies in your own body moving while doing a ceremony, which can be helped a lot by maintaining conscious awareness of your breath.

As the space clearing ceremony progresses, the energies become clearer and more refined. Some people start to hold their breath when this happens, which will make it more difficult to clear the space. Keep breathing fluidly and remind anybody present who starts holding their breath to breathe fluidly too.

Breathe through your nose, not your mouth

Humans are designed to breathe through their nose. Mouth breathing is only supposed to be used in extreme fight or flight situations of stress, to get you out of danger. Breathing through your mouth at other times will keep you anchored in lower levels of consciousness, which is counterproductive when conducting a space clearing ceremony. Nose breathing has numerous health benefits and can also be actively cultivated to facilitate access to higher, more refined levels of consciousness.

Learn the throat friction technique

Throat friction* is an advanced technique that can be used during the space clearing ceremony to greatly enhance the results. It's a simple technique, yet one of the most profound you will ever learn, with far-reaching applications. It's an essential part of third eye* meditation and can be used to cultivate the extraordinary subtle body structures of the larynx.

When Karen first started developing space clearing, she used to call this "power breathing". It's identical to the Clairvision technique known as throat friction, so this is the name we now use for it.

In *Awakening the Third Eye* Samuel Sagan explains, "The friction is generated during both inhalation and exhalation. It creates a 'wind' type of sound... The correct friction comes from the larynx and the lower pharynx, meaning the lower part at the back of the throat."

He further clarifies, "The throat friction is an energetic rather than physical technique. It quiets the mind and instantaneously induces a more focused and internalized state of consciousness, with enhanced receptivity to all manner of subtle perceptions."

To help you to learn throat friction, you can find an in-depth description and audio examples in *Meditation, Portal to Inner Worlds*, which is currently available as a free download at clairvision.org. A deeper level of knowledge about the technique is in *Knowledge Track Portal One* (available to purchase on the same website).

Throat friction can be used throughout the space clearing ceremony and is especially effective during these parts:

- Hand sensing
- Making space clearing water
- Activating flower offerings
- Clapping
- Belling
- The harmony ball infusion process

11

Involution

Being able to hold a higher level of involution* during a space clearing ceremony will help a great deal to improve the effectiveness of the techniques. This is why we have devoted an entire chapter to this important topic, together with the related topics of exvolution* and de-exvolution*. All three terms have been coined by the Clairvision School to describe states of consciousness that there were previously no precise words for in the English language.

Exvolution

The starting point for understanding involution is its opposite state, which is exvolution. That's because most humans live in a state of exvolution, so it is the state you will be most familiar with.

Exvolution is defined in ALTMC as follows:

> A turning outwards of consciousness, towards grosser levels of existence. The opposite movement of involution. Excessive exvolution is one of the central characteristics of the present human condition. Dwelling in a human body, consciousness is constantly drawn outwards through the senses, towards the material world. Consciousness loses touch with its inwards essence, its non-manifested roots. This engrossment in the senses is an exvolution, an extroversion by which consciousness forgets its own nature of infinity and

becomes assimilated to physical limitations. Human beings forget they are immortal Spirits, they believe themselves bipeds bound by the constraints of a three-dimensional universe. Consequently, to know itself consciousness must follow a path of involution.

Most people think that an exvoluted way of life is normal, yet it is far from how we are created to be. Human consciousness comes from Highness, and it is possible for us to remain connected to high spiritual realms while incarnated in a human body. However, our 21st-century lifestyle makes that incredibly difficult. Life is generally lived at the level of ordinary mental consciousness*, locked in the mental and emotional cage that is formed by a person's own astral body and samskaras*. From birth to death, there is often no knowledge that anything more exists.

In our online course The Seven Levels of Consciousness**, we call this band of existence Level 6. There is a level below it that some people unfortunately fall into (Level 7), and there are five levels above it (Levels 5, 4, 3, 2, and 1) that are accessible to us all, although very few people ever experience the higher levels. It is these levels, starting with Level 5, where involution begins, together with its synonym de-exvolution, which is the undoing of exvolution back toward more uncorrupted, original states of consciousness.

De-exvolution

De-exvolution means the same as involution. It is defined in ALTMC as follows:

> A de-exvolution is an involution. Calling it de-exvolution emphasizes the fact that in its original state, human consciousness was far more involuted than it is now. So in de-exvoluting, there is a return towards more primordial and less fallen states.

Involution

Involution is defined in ALTMC as follows:

A turning inside of consciousness. Consciousness letting go of the senses and internalizing itself, turning towards its source and cognizing itself. The opposite of involution is exvolution. Just as a glove can be turned inside out, so consciousness is turned outside in through involution. However, it would be more accurate to say that consciousness is turned inside out through exvolution, and that involution brings it back to its original state. Hence the key direction: consciousness knows itself through involution.

There is a world of difference between conducting the ceremony at Level 6, with all kinds of thoughts going on inside your head, and conducting it in a more involuted way at Level 5, which is how space clearing is supposed to be done.

Beyond that, there is a phenomenal difference between these levels and the level at which our professional space clearers are trained to do space clearing, which is Level 4. And it doesn't end there. At its highest level, space clearing is conducted with the profound levels of stillness and spiritual presencing that are the hallmark of Level 3. That's the level at which we do the ceremony ourselves.

How to involute

It can take years to build the subtle body structures to be able to access the higher levels of involution we have described. The best way to do this is by developing the type of meditation practice that is based on silencing your thoughts.

If you already have such a meditation practice and are familiar with involution, the best way to prepare yourself to do space clearing is to meditate just before the ceremony. You don't need to learn how to meditate in order to space clear your own home, though. All you need to do to begin is to take the first baby steps of shifting your awareness from the level of everyday thoughts and emotions to a more de-exvoluted level for the short time when you are conducting the ceremony.

To learn how to do this, stand or sit with your head and spine perfectly vertical. Calm and centre yourself by taking a few conscious breaths, with your awareness on your in-breath and out-breath.

Then do the following:

- Slowly tilt your head to the right and then back up to the vertical position
- Slowly tilt your head to the left and then back up to the vertical position
- Slowly tilt your head forward and then back up to the vertical position
- Slowly tilt your head backward and then back up to the vertical position

With each movement, what you are looking for is the energetic click that happens as you come back into verticality*. This will help you to locate your vertex (the centre top point of your head), from which the line of energy known as the central thread* emanates vertically upward.

Next, gently shift your awareness to being above your head. Do this by moving your awareness vertically upward along your central thread, involuting, and transposing your consciousness from being inside the mental chatter of your head to being above your head, where it is possible to silence your thoughts. In other words, stop thinking with your mind* and transpose your awareness to above your head, to gain access to higher parts of yourself through your column above*. This is where stillness, through the absence of thoughts and emotions, can be found.

Shifting your awareness to above your head may feel vague at first. Don't try to do it perfectly or expect too much of yourself. Don't try too hard, and especially don't think about it, because as soon as you do, you'll be back in your mind. What's needed here is a fluid receptivity to a new way of being and resting your consciousness. Remember, involution is a more natural state for a human than being exvoluted. Higher parts of you already know how to do this and long for you to return to it.

It's ideal if you can remain as involuted as possible throughout the entire space clearing ceremony. This will probably only be possible if you are very familiar with the techniques and are also an experienced meditator. Otherwise, it's likely your level of involution will not be very deep, and it won't be long before your thoughts start up again. It's still worth aspiring to do, though, because of the huge difference it will make to the space clearing results you can achieve. Keeping your head as vertical as possible throughout the ceremony will help you to stay more involuted.

The parts of the ceremony where involution is most important are:
• Hand sensing
• Making space clearing water
• Activating flower offerings
• Clapping
• Belling
• The harmony ball infusion process

These will all be covered in detail later in the book.

PART THREE

Space clearing
equipment and materials

12

Levels of space clearing

To determine which space clearing kit you need, you will first need to decide which level of space clearing you wish to do.

In the 46 years we have pioneered the development of space clearing, four distinct levels have emerged. In order of effectiveness from low to high, they are:

- Basic Space Clearing
- Essential Space Clearing
- Full Space Clearing
- Practitioner Space Clearing

Basic Space Clearing

When Karen first started doing space clearing in 1978, it was just a set of techniques. She would do a circuit of hand sensing, a circuit of clapping in corners, a final circuit of ringing her bell, and that was it. With hindsight, she says that at best you could call it "space helping". It was very superficial compared with how the ceremony has evolved since then.

Basic Space Clearing is a vast improvement on this early version of the ceremony, with an added harmony ball circuit and the option to leave out the hand-sensing circuit. It's the best one to start with, to get a feel for what space clearing can do.

If you then decide to progress to Essential Space Clearing or Full Space Clearing, you can continue to use Basic Space Clearing as a quick refresher in between space clearings or to quickly raise the energy of a particular room when needed, such as when staying in a hotel for a night. It's the equivalent of washing your face and hands instead of taking a full bath or shower.

Having said this, while writing this book Richard taught a teenage friend of ours how to do Basic Space Clearing in a room he had moved into that had previously been occupied by his sister. He said he felt some energy shifts while doing the ceremony, but it wasn't until he went out shopping and came back that he felt the full effects. The words he used to describe the changes were "surprising" and "shockingly different". He said the room felt lighter, the walls felt cleaner, and there was a depth of stillness in the space that hadn't been there before. He also felt a marked change in his relationship with the room.

So even if you only do Basic Space Clearing, it can transform your space and help you to take more energetic ownership of it. Over the years, we've heard from thousands of people who have only ever done Basic Space Clearing, and it has been enough to bring about significant changes to their home and their life.

Essential Space Clearing

Essential Space Clearing is the method we encourage most people to use to space clear their own home. You'll need to buy some flowers to make a flower offering, and it takes a bit longer to do than Basic Space Clearing, but it's well worth the extra cost and effort because the results are much deeper and last much longer.

We recommend doing Essential Space Clearing the first time you space clear your home and then once a year after that. It can also be done whenever you move into a new home, feel stuck, go through a major life change, or need help with any of the many other uses explained in detail in *Space Clearing, Volume 2*.

Full Space Clearing

Full Space Clearing is the top level of space clearing described in this book. It's an exquisitely beautiful ceremony that is substantially more effective than Essential Space Clearing, has much longer-lasting results, and will help you to forge a much more conscious relationship with your home.

It requires a Full Space Clearing kit and flower offerings for all the main rooms of your home, so it takes longer to do and costs more. It may not even be possible for you to immediately purchase the Full Space Clearing kit that is needed because there are a limited number of craftspeople in Bali who have the calibre of skills needed to create all the items included in it, so there can sometimes be a waiting list to order some items.

This level of the ceremony is the ultimate one to aim for. Most people find it works best to gradually work up to it rather than begin with it. The depth of changes it can bring about are remarkable.

Like Essential Space Clearing, a Full Space Clearing can be done the first time you move into a new home and then once a year after that, or whenever you feel the need.

Practitioner Space Clearing

This is the level at which our professionally certified space clearing practitioners conduct ceremonies in people's homes and businesses. It can bring about profound levels of transformation, in both the space and its occupants.

To learn practitioner space clearing requires the cultivation of specific subtle body structures and many years of personal development work. The ceremony is performed with an enhanced level of etheric, astral, and superastral awareness, perception, and skill. This know-how cannot be learned by reading a book. It is taught through a process of transmission from teacher to student, which is why the key elements of our professional training are always taught in person, never virtually.

Practitioner Space Clearing kits contain additional equipment that is considerably more expensive and only available to those who train professionally, so we have not included information about it here.

13

Space clearing kits

It can take a few weeks to gather the equipment and materials you'll need to do your first space clearing ceremony, so be sure to allow enough time for this.

A space clearing kit consists of three types of items:

- **Space clearing equipment** – Specialized items you will need to purchase
- **Household items** – Things you are likely to have in your own home or can purchase locally
- **Materials** – Consumable items you can purchase locally

The space clearing kit you need will depend on which level of the space clearing ceremony you decide to do and the size of the property or properties you intend to use it in. The three different types are:

- A Basic Space Clearing kit
- An Essential Space Clearing kit
- A Full Space Clearing kit

A Basic Space Clearing kit

Space clearing equipment

- A Balinese space clearing bell and stand
- A Balinese harmony ball and stand

Household items

- None

Materials

- Brass cleaner and a soft cloth to clean your bell and harmony ball
- Unscented hand cream (if you need to moisten your hands before the clapping circuit)

An Essential Space Clearing kit

Space clearing equipment

- A Balinese space clearing bell and stand
- A Balinese harmony ball and stand
- A space clearing water pot and saucer
- A white tablecloth
- A Balinese altar cloth (optional)

Household items

- A small plate or saucer for the flower offering, made of porcelain, *not* bone china, glass, or plastic
- A coaster to put under the flower offering plate or saucer to protect the surface below from scorching when the candle burns down

Materials

- An unscented tealight candle in a heat-resistant holder
- Flower heads (see Chapter 18 for details)
- A mini carnation flower head (white or pastel coloured)
- An unopened bottle of still spring water
- A box of long matches
- Brass cleaner and a soft cloth to clean your bell and harmony ball
- Unscented hand cream (if you need to moisten your hands before the clapping circuit)

A Full Space Clearing kit

Space clearing equipment

- A Balinese space clearing bell and stand
- A Balinese harmony ball and stand
- A Balinese altar cloth
- Balinese colourizers
- A comb
- A space clearing water pot and saucer
- A white tablecloth
- A set of three harmony balls and plate (optional)

Household items

- Small plates or saucers (one for each flower offering), made of porcelain, *not* bone china, glass, or plastic
- Coasters (one for each flower offering) to protect the surface below from scorching when the candles burn down
- A tray to carry flower offerings on (only needed if you have a large home)

Materials

- Unscented tealight candles in heat-resistant holders (one for each flower offering)
- Flower heads (see Chapter 18 for details)
- A mini carnation flower head (white or pastel coloured)
- An unopened bottle of still spring water
- A box of long matches
- Brass cleaner and a soft cloth to clean your bell and harmony ball
- Unscented hand cream (if you need to moisten your hands before the clapping circuit)

Where to purchase space clearing equipment

It took Karen many years to put together her first space clearing kit. Now it's much easier for anyone to do this because most of the items can be purchased from our online shop at www.clearspaceliving.com, which has the highest-quality space clearing equipment available anywhere in the world.

Karen travelled all over the island of Bali to find the most skilled bellmakers, woodcarvers, and weavers, whose skills have been handed down from generation to generation. There are only a handful of craftspeople of this calibre. We certainly wouldn't be teaching space clearing today if she hadn't discovered this extraordinary resource for space clearing equipment.

The best approach to take when creating your own space clearing kit is to think of it as a long-term investment in your life rather than a short-term, quick-fix expense. After you've learned how to do space clearing and have experienced the extraordinary difference it can make, it's something you'll want to do again and again.

The following chapters contain information about the space clearing equipment, household items, and materials you will need to do a space clearing ceremony. You will only need to read the sections that are relevant to the level of the ceremony you have decided to do.

14

Balinese space clearing bells

☑ *Basic Space Clearing*
☑ *Essential Space Clearing*
☑ *Full Space Clearing*

Balinese bells are in a class of their own and the best in the world to use for space clearing. Karen has tested hundreds of bells from other parts of the world and has never found any that even come close to the astonishingly beautiful, resonant tones they have or the excellent space clearing results they can achieve.

Why Balinese bells are so special

A Balinese bell consists of a hand-carved wooden handle, a high-quality hand-cast bronze dome, and a bronze clapper inside the dome that produces the sound when the bell is rung.

These bells are so extraordinary because of the way they are handcrafted, the combination of metals they are made of, and the level of consciousness they are attuned to. Each bell has its own unique sound, and it feels very special to own one.

What's also unique about Balinese bells is that they highlight stuck energies and can be used to clear them. When doing space clearing, you can literally hear the sound of the bell momentarily fade as you walk past a stagnant area in a room and then hear it return to full volume one pace further on. No other bells we've ever found do that.

In our space clearing workshops, we usually demonstrate this effect on four or five volunteers from the audience. They come to the front of the room and sit on chairs in a row, facing the audience. Then one of us does a technique called personal belling**, which involves ringing a Balinese bell close to the front of each person's body, from the root charge* area to above the head, gearing the sound into their central channel* (the energy channel that runs up the centre of the body). Even people who have no experience of working with energy can immediately hear how the sound of the bell changes as it passes over areas where there is stuck energy.

By the time we have done this with the second or third person, there are gasps of amazement from the audience as they realize how different each person sounds. If someone is in good shape, the bell ring is clear and resonant all the way up. If they have energy blockages, the sound will momentarily fade in that area of their body. Karen has experienced a few occasions when the sound has died completely for a second or so, then resumed. This usually indicated a medical condition of some kind that needed to be addressed. (Please note that this skill takes many years to develop, and we are certainly not suggesting it as an alternative to consulting a medical professional.)

For space clearing purposes, the most important quality of Balinese bells is that when the sound is consciously directed into the walls and furniture in a room, it can simultaneously revitalize stagnant energies and shatter embedded historical imprints. These effects are not automatic, of course. Skill is involved, and there is a tremendous difference between the level of clearing an experienced, certified space clearing practitioner can achieve and that of a complete beginner.

Even so, the energy changes that can be brought about by a novice using a Balinese space clearing bell are far more substantial than can be achieved using any other type of bell.

The difference between large and small Balinese space clearing bells

Space clearing bells are currently available in large and small sizes. They both have the same purity of tone. The main difference is the size of dome, which is what determines the volume of sound. They also have slightly differently shaped handles and different sizes of carved wooden bell stands that are designed to go with them.

Large and small Balinese space clearing bells and stands

The large Balinese space clearing bell

A large space clearing bell is needed for a home that has many rooms or rooms up to 200 square metres (approx. 2,000 square feet). It can also be used in smaller homes or smaller rooms. In other words, it's multipurpose.

The small Balinese space clearing bell

A small space clearing bell can be used in smaller homes (1 or 2 bedrooms) or homes that have rooms up to 50 square metres (approx. 500 square feet). The sound starts to get lost in rooms that are larger than that, so it's not as effective.

Note: If you have a room that has a lot of clutter or a lot of soft furnishings that absorb sound (carpet, curtains, sofas, cushions, etc), then a large bell will usually be needed, even if the room is small.

Can other types of bells be used for space clearing?

When Karen first started teaching space clearing workshops, she encouraged people to do what she had done and use the best bell they could find. Later, when she published her first book *Creating Sacred Space with Feng Shui*, she hedged around the topic, not wanting to give the impression that she had any ulterior motive to sell space clearing products. She truly regrets this lack of clarity now, having heard from many people who have tried various options. She wishes she had stated plainly from the start that if you want to do effective space clearing, don't even think about using anything other than a high-quality Balinese bell.

Tibetan bells, tingsha cymbals, and similar items, are not of a high enough quality to be used for space clearing, and improvising with a ceramic bell, a wind chime, tuning fork, or other sound-producing objects will have little or no effect at all. The results you'll get will hardly be likely to inspire you to do space clearing again. It's much better to wait and save up to buy the right equipment for the job.

We do appreciate that Balinese bells are expensive. That's because of the purity of the metals used to create them, the skill involved in making them, and the time it takes to produce them. Handcrafted items are always more expensive than mass-produced ones, and there are only a handful of Balinese craftspeople who are skilled enough to make them. They are the one piece of equipment you absolutely must have to do space clearing. Even if you need to scrimp on other parts of your space clearing kit, at least invest in a Balinese bell.

And what if you really can't afford a Balinese bell, or are not able to purchase one immediately because they are temporarily sold out? We're sorry, but it won't be possible to do any of the three levels of space clearing ceremonies described in this book. The best we can suggest is doing the clapping technique described in Step 17 of the ceremony, which can be done without any equipment and will at least help to break up lumps of stagnant energies in your home. This will usually make a noticeable difference.

Is it OK to use a singing bowl instead of a Balinese bell?

Definitely not. Singing bowls are not designed to do space clearing. If you are interested to know why, you can find information about this in the energy clearing misconceptions section of *Space Clearing, Volume 2*.

Balinese space clearing practitioner bells

Each space clearing practitioner we train receives a Balinese temple bell that has been paired with a harmonizing small space clearing bell. This is essential for the range of skills that are required at practitioner level. It takes most trainees at least a year to learn how to ring the two bells correctly, and that's only the basic level. There are more advanced techniques that we teach after that. Belling skills can be developed to an extraordinarily high degree.

To the outside observer, it may not look as if much is happening when watching us, or one of our professionally trained practitioners, during the belling circuit of a space clearing ceremony. To someone with well-honed perception, though, it can be an astonishing feast of vision*. A Balinese bell can be used to orchestrate multiple changes simultaneously. When Karen first developed space clearing, she never imagined there could be so much to bell ringing. New levels of skills have continued to be developed with each passing year. This voyage of discovery has been one of the greatest joys of her life.

The process of pairing up practitioner bells is a long and artful one. In Bali, they call this finding the *jodo* for a temple bell (*jodo* is a Balinese word used to mean a person's perfect romantic mate, and it applies very aptly to pairing up bells too). Richard is the only person Karen has ever succeeded in teaching how to do this. Our bellmaker doesn't have the ear for it, even though we have tried for years to teach him. Sometimes we have to go through as many as 400 small space clearing bells to find perfect matches for 12 temple bells. It can take many days to do this, so it's not a service we offer to anyone other than trainee practitioners.

If you have a genuine calling to train professionally, you can find more information about this in Chapter 39.

If you want a bell for personal use, then the space clearing bells we sell through our online shop are all tested individually by us and are of the highest quality. We're happy to report that, in the 30+ years we have been selling our large and small space clearing bells to people all over the world, we can count the number of bells that have been returned to us for a refund on the fingers of one hand. Most people are so thrilled by the quality and sound of the bell they receive that it immediately becomes one of their most treasured possessions.

A number of people we've heard from have travelled to Bali, hoping to find a temple bell to buy. Unfortunately, riding on the success of Karen's first book, a few unscrupulous entrepreneurs have set themselves up in business there selling poor-quality temple bell look-alikes that are of no use at all for space clearing. Like other tourist paraphernalia, they are churned out using substandard materials. No Balinese priest or priestess would ever buy or use one of these.

From time to time, someone has turned up at one of our workshops proudly clasping a temple bell they have purchased in this way. When they hear the difference between the tone of their bell and the superb sound of a genuine space clearing bell, they realize they have been duped. We feel sincerely sorry for anyone this has happened to. It is totally beyond our control. Although Bali has a unique spiritual culture, it is also an island of self-employed entrepreneurs, some of whom will jump at any opportunity to make a quick profit from visitors.

How to care for a Balinese space clearing bell

Treat your bell respectfully

Equipment that is used for purification needs to be treated respectfully and used only for its intended purpose. For this reason, be sure to wash your hands before touching your bell, place it in an elevated position on a bell stand instead of directly on a table, and never use it casually.

How to welcome a Balinese space clearing bell into your life

When you first receive your bell, we recommend that you create your own ceremony to welcome it into your life. This is best done alone and in a quiet place where you will not be interrupted. It does not need to be elaborate – just something that is meaningful to you, using some flower heads and a candle. If possible, don't open the box or ring the bell until you are ready to do this small ceremony.

How to store a Balinese space clearing bell

Each Balinese bell comes in its own box that it can be kept in when not in use. The best place to store it is in an elevated position, such as the top shelf of a cupboard or closet. The rest of your kit can be stored in the same location if you have enough space there, or elsewhere and at a lower level, if that is more practical.

Be discerning about who touches your bell

Items that are used for sacred purposes are much more effective when used only by one person, whose energies they become attuned to.

This is well understood in highly developed spiritual cultures, where there is always a clear differentiation between secular items and those that are used for spiritual purposes. Spiritual items are handled consciously, with reverence, and are always kept separate from everyday objects. Usually, they are not left on open display when not in use. If they are, then they are put in a special place where everyone knows they are not to be touched.

We therefore recommend that you are selective about who touches your bell and why. Certainly, do not leave it in a place where any curious visitor to your home can pick it up and ring it, or where children can play with it. The only person we ever allow to handle our own bells is each other. Because we are married, our energies are already intermingled on every level, so this works fine. Even so, we never do this casually. We always treat each other's bell with just as much respect as our own.

71

How to clean a Balinese space clearing bell

The dome of a Balinese bell is made of high-quality bronze. This material and the remarkable crafting skills of Balinese bellmakers give these bells their excellent sound and space clearing capabilities. They do tarnish a little when exposed to air, though. This won't affect the function of the bell, but it's another reason why it is best to keep it stored in its box rather than left on display, to reduce tarnishing.

As part of preparing to do a space clearing ceremony, apply a good-quality metal cleaner to the outer surface of the dome of your bell, using a clean, soft cotton cloth. Then gently buff the metal to a shine using another clean, soft cotton cloth. If needed, the wooden handle can be cleaned with a damp cloth.

How to safeguard a Balinese space clearing bell

Once in a while – thankfully, extremely rarely – we receive a mournful email from someone who has dropped their Balinese bell and it has lost its ring. They write to ask how to get it repaired.

Unfortunately, if a Balinese bell is dropped or banged against a hard surface, this can cause a hairline fracture in the bronze casting, and it will never ring again. The only way to repair it is to ship it back to Bali to have it reforged, which takes such a long time and costs so much more than buying a new bell that no one ever does it.

We think of metal as being strong and durable, so it's something of a surprise to discover that handcrafted bells need such careful handling. The type that are made of cheap metal alloys and mass-produced in factories are usually hardier. However, the unremarkable quality of sound they produce means they are of no use at all for space clearing. Handcrafted Balinese bells are made from a unique type of bronze that puts them in a completely different league. So, even though they are more fragile, they are well worth the extra care that is required.

15

Balinese harmony balls

☑ *Basic Space Clearing*
☑ *Essential Space Clearing*
☑ *Full Space Clearing*

Harmony balls are used in the final part of a space clearing ceremony to infuse the space with new higher frequencies.

Made of shiny brass-plated metal, they are handcrafted in Bali and measure approximately 4.5 cm (1.75 inches) in diameter. When you hold a Balinese harmony ball in your hand and shake it to hear the beautiful sound it makes, it is worlds apart from the cheaper Chinese stress balls that may look similar in a photo. It has a very different effect energetically too.

How to use harmony balls

Harmony balls can be used in two ways:

• As a personal harmony ball
• As a neutral harmony ball

Personal harmony balls

A personal harmony ball is one that you infuse with the frequencies of your own higher aspirations*. It comes complete with a hand-carved wooden stand to put it on.

A Balinese harmony ball and stand

You can reuse a personal harmony ball whenever you repeat the space clearing ceremony in the same place or in a new home that you move to.

Neutral harmony balls

Neutral harmony balls can be used to add extra volume and energetic oomph during the harmony ball circuit. They are especially useful in a home that has large rooms or a lot of clutter, where the sound of a solitary harmony ball can get lost in the space.

They are sold in sets of three, together with a hand-carved wooden plate to put them on so that they don't roll around and accidentally fall on the floor, which may cause them to dent. If this happens, you will still be able to use them. They just won't look so beautiful anymore.

Balinese harmony balls on a hand-carved wooden plate

Neutral harmony balls are identical to personal harmony balls. It's the way they are used that is different. They are not used in the infusion process in Step 20 of the space clearing ceremony, so they never get infused with anyone's personal frequencies. This means they can be used again and again in your own home or as part of any ceremony you do for a friend or relative who has asked for your help.

How to store harmony balls

Harmony balls are made of plated brass, which tarnishes when exposed to air. It is therefore best to store each harmony ball in the box it comes in to minimize this. To avoid getting personal harmony balls and neutral harmony balls mixed up, store each type in a different place or label them clearly so that you know which is which.

How to clean and care for harmony balls

You can clean a harmony ball using any good-quality brass cleaner and a soft cloth. Gently polishing your harmony ball(s) to a beautiful shine is part of the preparation for each space ceremony you do.

How many harmony balls
do you need to space clear your own home?

The number of harmony balls you need will depend on a number of factors.

If you do a space clearing ceremony alone

You will only need one personal harmony ball. You can also use one or two extra neutral harmony balls during the harmony ball circuit if you wish to, or need to because the rooms of your home are large or contain a lot of clutter.

If one other member of your household is present

You can either share a personal harmony ball between you or use one each. Sharing works best if you are emotionally close to each other and your values and goals in life are very similar. Otherwise, it is best to use one harmony ball each. You can also both use one or two extra neutral harmony balls during the harmony ball circuit, if you wish to.

If more members of your household are present

Everyone present can share one harmony ball during the infusion process by creating what is known as a harmony ball sandwich (see Chapter 33, Step 20). Alternatively, each person can have their own harmony ball if they prefer not to mix their frequencies in a communal one. Anyone who wishes to participate in the frequencing circuit will need to have a personal or neutral harmony ball to use.

If you share your home with other people who do not wish to participate in the ceremony

A space clearing ceremony always needs to be done for the benefit of everyone in the household, not just the person doing the ceremony. So if you share your home with other people who do not wish to participate in the ceremony, you will only need one harmony ball, but be sure to infuse it with the frequencies of all occupants of the home, using the technique described in Chapter 33, Step 20.

Doing repeat space clearings in your own home

You do not need a new harmony ball for repeat space clearings in your own home. You can use the same personal harmony ball again and again, infusing it with new frequencies each time and building on the higher aspirations you have for your life. High-level frequencies do not need clearing in the same way that low-level frequencies do, so it can be very beneficial to keep using the same harmony ball.

An exception to this would be if you previously shared your harmony ball with a partner you have separated from on bad terms. In this situation, using the old harmony ball could reconnect you to mental and emotional associations with the past, so we recommend using a brand-new harmony ball that will only be infused with your own frequencies. Most waste centres accept harmony balls for metal recycling.

If you have more than one property

If you have two properties, such as two homes or a home and a business property, it's fine to use the same harmony ball in both places if you want to. The choice will depend on whether you want to mix the frequencies of the two spaces or would prefer to keep them separate.

Space clearing someone else's home

If you space clear for a relative or friend, a new personal harmony ball will be needed so that they can fully infuse it with their own frequencies. Leave it with them so they can do their own repeat ceremonies when necessary. Don't use your personal harmony ball for this purpose because it will have your frequencies in it.

If more than one person lives in the home, it's fine for each person to have their own personal harmony ball, if they wish to.

You'll also need neutral harmony balls to use during the frequencing circuit. The recommended number is three. Hold one harmony ball in one hand and the other two in your other hand, to create the most dynamic effect.

16

Other items in a space clearing kit

Other items in a space clearing kit are:

- A white tablecloth
- A Balinese altar cloth
- Balinese colourizers
- A comb
- A space clearing water pot and saucer

A white tablecloth

☑ *Basic Space Clearing*

☑ *Essential Space Clearing*

☑ *Full Space Clearing*

A white tablecloth can quickly transform the look and feel of a table you use for everyday purposes into a clean, uncluttered space that can be used for ceremonial purposes. If you don't have a suitable table, you can use another flat surface in your home, such as a countertop or a chest of drawers.

The tablecloth only needs to be large enough for you to be able to set up the items of equipment you will be using. If you are doing a Basic Space Clearing or an Essential Space Clearing ceremony, only a small tablecloth will be needed. For a Full Space Clearing, you will need one that completely covers the table so that you can create a Full Space Clearing altar.

Ideally, use a tablecloth that is only ever used for space clearing ceremonies and has never been used for any other purpose before. If that's not possible, then at least use one that is freshly laundered.

Between space clearings, keep your white tablecloth with your space clearing kit rather than throwing it into a drawer with household items.

Why white is the best colour

White is the best colour of tablecloth to use because space clearing is a purification ceremony and white is the colour most closely associated with purification.

If you live in a culture where white is traditionally associated with funerals, don't be concerned about this. It is precisely because of white's purifying nature and reflective qualities that it is the best colour to wear to a funeral. It minimizes the risk of picking up any astral fragments, otherwise known as entities, from the disintegrating astral body of a deceased person.

Most mourners in China, and Asian countries such as India, have always traditionally worn white to limit the risk of catching an astral fragment. This used to be the case for Balinese Hindu funerals too until outside influences created a fashion trend for wearing black instead of white, which some people now do.

We realize this is contrary to well-established traditions elsewhere, where black is considered the most respectful colour to wear to a funeral. If you attend a funeral, our best advice is not to wear black and to avoid drinking alcohol or eating meat, both of which can make you more susceptible to picking up an entity from the deceased person.

A Balinese altar cloth

☐ *Basic Space Clearing*

☑ *Essential Space Clearing (optional)*

☑ *Full Space Clearing*

An altar is used in space clearing to create a symbolic representation of the focus for the ceremony and an anchorage for the frequencies of change it is designed to bring about. This increases the effectiveness of the ceremony enormously.

A beautiful cotton-silk, gold-threaded Balinese altar cloth is essential for Full Space Clearing ceremonies. It is placed on top of the white tablecloth, in the centre of the table. You can also use one for Essential Space Clearing instead of, or in addition to, a white tablecloth. An altar cloth is not needed if you are doing a Basic Space Clearing ceremony.

It took Karen many years to put together a team of the most skilled weavers in Bali to produce the altar cloths and colourizers that are available through our online shop. There's a huge amount of skill involved and a lot of patience because the cloths are all handwoven. It's very intricate, exacting work. A large altar cloth takes a weaver 20 days or more to make, and a small altar cloth takes at least 12 days.

The weavers all work in their own homes with their families around them. They are lovely people who've been with us for years and understand the care that needs to go into creating items that will be used for sacred ceremonies.

If you visit Bali and decide to look for these items in markets around the island, you'll discover it's impossible to find any of the high-quality items we stock in our online shop, and you certainly won't be able to find the full range of colours. They are highly specialized items that are made exclusively for space clearing use.

Balinese altar cloths are available in a range of sizes and colours. Choose the size that is large enough for the equipment and materials you will be using and the colour that most closely supports the main focus of the ceremony you will be doing. You can find detailed information about colours in the following pages.

Balinese colourizers

☐ *Basic Space Clearing*
☐ *Essential Space Clearing*
☑ *Full Space Clearing*

Balinese colourizers** are beautiful altar decorations in the form of strips of cloth, about 11 cm (4.3 inches) wide, made of the same exquisitely handwoven gold-threaded material that altar cloths are made of. They are used to create an altar for a Full Space Clearing ceremony.

At the time of writing, they are available in two sizes (large and small) and nine colours (white, red, pink, orange, yellow, green, blue, turquoise, and purple). Choose the size of colourizer that fits best with the size of altar cloth you have, and choose the colour or colours that will best support the focus of the ceremony you will be doing.

The following guidelines can be used to choose which altar cloth and colourizer colours you need:

- **White**: Clarity, simplicity, and purity
- **Red**: Motivation, action, and accomplishment
- **Pink**: Passion and love of life
- **Orange**: Creativity and confidence
- **Yellow**: Hope, joy, and happiness
- **Green**: Harmony, healing, and vibrancy
- **Blue**: Truth, integrity, and purpose
- **Turquoise**: Ancient resonance and inner calm
- **Purple**: Prosperity and empowerment

White

For the frequencies of clarity, simplicity, and purity

White is the combination of all colours in the visible spectrum. Made of cotton silk interwoven with gold metallic thread and small bursts of colour, the weave of the white altar cloths reflects this unique quality.

The main purpose of any space clearing ceremony is purification, so it's easy to see why using a white altar cloth is such a popular choice. Many religions use white as a symbol of spiritual purity. It's also widely associated in many cultures with the quality of cleanliness.

White altar cloths

In the context of space clearing, white is an excellent altar cloth colour choice for situations where clarity is needed to make decisions and move forward in life, where simplicity is needed to unravel a situation that has become too complicated, or when you are space clearing to prepare a room for special use, such as creating a meditation or healing space. It's also the best colour to use if you are new to space clearing and are not sure which colour to use. You can't go wrong with white.

White colourizers

White colourizers are made of the same material as white altar cloths but without the small bursts of colour. There's no need to use a white colourizer if you're using a white altar cloth. That would be an unnecessary duplication. However, it's fine to use a large or small white colourizer with an altar cloth of a different colour if an important aspect of the ceremony is to do with purity, clarity, or simplicity. For example, if your focus is prosperity and you need to gain more clarity about how to improve your financial situation, an excellent choice would be a purple altar cloth to bring in the frequencies of prosperity and empowerment, with a white colourizer in the central vertical position to highlight the frequency of clarity.

Red

For the frequencies of motivation, action, and accomplishment

A red altar cloth, or a red colourizer in the central vertical position of the altar, is a good choice if you need more motivation, action, or accomplishment in your life, and especially if one of the main reasons you are doing the space clearing is to help you get started or keep going with clutter clearing.

The red frequency is also helpful for overcoming all kinds of procrastination and inertia, such as starting or finishing a project, achieving a goal, developing willpower, becoming more dynamic or decisive, and improving stamina or physical fitness.

Pink

For the frequencies of passion and love of life

Use a pink colourizer on a space clearing altar when the focus of the ceremony is about finding your passion in life, reigniting your love of life, or reigniting the passion in a relationship. It's especially helpful after a period of putting your own needs on the back burner to fulfil other commitments or responsibilities.

Orange
For the frequencies of creativity and confidence

Orange is a warm, outgoing colour that combines the stamina of red with the cheerful optimism of yellow. It can be used on a space clearing altar when there is a need to spark creative talents and bring out more of a person's potential.

It can also be used when self-confidence needs a boost, either because it has taken a few knocks or was not strong in the first place. Its stimulating effect makes it a good choice for when someone has become withdrawn or isolated and would like to be less so.

Yellow
For the frequencies of hope, joy, and happiness

Yellow is a restorative colour, associated with sunlight. It revitalizes the spirit and is often used in a space clearing ceremony because most people can use some extra hope, joy, and happiness in their life.

It is also used in situations where life has become joyless, perhaps through being burdened with commitments or other circumstances that seem to be beyond your control, or when hope is in short supply, due to a loss of some kind or an unexpected turn of events.

When health is part of the focus for a ceremony, use yellow and green colourizers together, placed symmetrically on opposite sides of the vertical axis of the altar. If health is the most important focus, a double central vertical axis using yellow and green colourizers side by side works even better (see the Dual Focus altar design in Chapter 33, Step 14).

Green

For the frequencies of harmony, healing, and vibrancy

Green is the colour of nature. It is the principle of life and regeneration. Just looking at green is healing to the eyes. It's a good colour to use when fresh vitality is needed or when creating harmony in a home is one of the main focuses of a ceremony.

Use green and yellow colourizers together, placed symmetrically on opposite sides of the vertical axis of the altar, when health is part of the focus for a ceremony. If health is the most important focus, use a double central vertical axis with green and yellow colourizers side by side.

Blue

For the frequencies of truth, integrity, and purpose

Blue is one of the most frequently used colourizers because an essential aspect of space clearing is to facilitate a return to truth, integrity, and purpose in your life, and a clarification of what that means for you.

A blue colourizer works particularly well in the horizontal base position of an altar to create a solid foundation to rest your life on. If truth, integrity, or purpose are currently missing from your life, then it is better to place the colourizer in the even more important central vertical axis position, symbolizing the need for these qualities to become the core reference for every future decision you make.

Blue also has the effect of slowing things down, relaxing, and regulating. It's an excellent colour to use if life has become too hectic, to help restore important values and prioritize your life accordingly.

Turquoise
For the frequencies of ancient resonance and inner calm

Turquoise is used in a space clearing ceremony when there is a need to access deeper parts of yourself or to restore inner calm. It has a fluidifying effect that facilitates change. It assists with reconnection to spiritual purpose and deeper levels of meaning in your life. Use this colour when there is rigidity of beliefs or behaviour, stuckness, or too much attention being paid to the superficial day-to-day aspects of life.

Purple
For the frequencies of prosperity and empowerment

Purple altar cloths
Use a purple altar cloth when prosperity or financial issues are the focus of a space clearing ceremony. It's also a good colour to use when you need to boost self-esteem or emphasize personal empowerment, particularly if you're facing a situation where you need to take control of your life and make some important decisions.

Purple colourizers
If the creation of wealth or the boosting of self-esteem is a consideration but not the main focus for a ceremony, add purple to the altar in the form of a colourizer rather than an altar cloth. It can also be very helpful to include this colour if you're the kind of person who has trouble saying no or tend to put other people's needs before your own, sometimes to your own detriment.

A comb

☐ *Basic Space Clearing*

☐ *Essential Space Clearing*

☑ *Full Space Clearing*

A comb is needed to straighten the fringes of colourizers after you have placed them on the altar. It can be made of any material you like the feel of. It is best to use one that has never been used for any other purpose before, then keep it in your kit, to use each time you do a space clearing ceremony.

A space clearing water pot and saucer

☐ *Basic Space Clearing*

☐ *Essential Space Clearing*

☑ *Full Space Clearing*

The best type of space clearing water pot to use is an open-top circular container, 7–8 cm (3 inches) in both diameter and height, made of ceramic, porcelain, or glass. Don't use plastic, wood, or rustic-style pottery because some of the properties of these materials will be transferred to the water. A metal container is also not a good choice, unless it is made of pure silver or solid brass.

A saucer is needed underneath the water pot so that you have somewhere to place the mini carnation flower head you will be using with it. The saucer will also safeguard your altar cloth and colourizers from accidentally getting stained by water splashes.

The best type of saucer to use is one that fits the base of the space clearing water pot exactly, so that the pot will not move around or fall over when you are carrying it. To save you having to hunt around for these items, they are available to purchase as a set from our online shop at a very reasonable price.

You will need to use your space clearing pot and saucer to make a fresh batch of space clearing water each time you do an Essential Space Clearing or a Full Space Clearing ceremony. We therefore recommend storing them with your space clearing kit so they won't get used for other purposes.

If you prefer to use a pot and saucer of your own, it is best to use items that have never been used for any other purpose before. If that's not possible, then be sure to wash them thoroughly in warm, soapy water, then dry them with a paper towel or tissues so that they are sparkling clean.

17

Household items

These are items you are likely to have in your own home or can easily acquire locally.

- Flower offering plate(s) or saucer(s)
- Coaster(s)
- A tray (only needed if you have a large home)

Flower offering plate(s) or saucer(s)

☐ *Basic Space Clearing*

☑ *Essential Space Clearing*

☑ *Full Space Clearing*

Basic Space Clearing: No plate or saucer is needed because no flower offering is required.

Essential Space Clearing: You will need one small plate or saucer for the flower offering on the space clearing altar.

Full Space Clearing: You will need one small plate or saucer for the flower offering on the space clearing altar, one for each room or major area of your home that is included in the ceremony (see Chapter 26 for information about which rooms to include and exclude), and one for each matrix flower offering** (see Chapter 33, Step 13).

The best type of plates or saucers to use

Use flat plates or saucers, not bowls. The ideal size is about 15 cm (6 inches) in diameter. The best colour to use is white, and the best type of material is porcelain.

Don't use any saucers or plates that have a hairline crack or the type that are made of bone china or glass. The heat of a candle when it burns down can cause any of these to crack, creating a fire hazard. Also, do not use plastic plates because they may not be heatproof, and the material is also not conducive to landing spiritual connections*.

If you do Essential or Full Space Clearing regularly, we recommend keeping a plate/saucer or a set of plates/saucers with your space clearing kit and using them only for that purpose.

Coaster(s)

☐ *Basic Space Clearing*
☑ *Essential Space Clearing*
☑ *Full Space Clearing*

No coasters are needed for Basic Space Clearing. For Essential Space Clearing, you will need just one coaster to put beneath the offering on the altar. For Full Space Clearing, you will need one coaster for each offering.

Place the coaster beneath each flower offering to safeguard against scorching the surface below when the candle burns down. You can use the same coasters you normally use in your home to place drinks on. Just give them a good clean first.

A tray

☐ *Basic Space Clearing*

☐ *Essential Space Clearing*

☑ *Full Space Clearing (optional)*

If you have a large home, you may find it helpful when doing a Full Space Clearing to use a tray to carry the offerings from the altar to each room of the building.

18

Space clearing materials

- Flower heads
- A mini carnation (white or pastel coloured)
- Unscented tealight candles in heat-resistant holders (one for each offering)
- Long matches
- An unopened bottle of still spring water
- Brass cleaner and two soft polishing cloths
- Unscented hand cream (if needed to moisten your hands for the clapping circuit)

Flower heads

☐ *Basic Space Clearing*

☑ *Essential Space Clearing*

☑ *Full Space Clearing*

Basic Space Clearing: No flower offerings are required.

Essential Space Clearing: You will only need enough flower heads to create one flower offering on the altar.

Full Space Clearing: The number of flower offerings will be determined by the size of your home and which rooms are included in the ceremony.

Types of flower offerings

There are two types of flower offerings that can be used in a space clearing ceremony:

- Classic flower offerings – for each offering, you will need 5–6 flower heads of approximately the same size, preferably in a range of shapes and colours
- Rose-petal flower offerings – for each offering, you will need a combination of medium-sized rose petals and three or four flower heads, approximately the same size

You can find detailed information in Chapter 33, Step 13 about how to calculate the number of flower offerings you will need and how to create the two different types of flower offerings.

If you buy the flowers the day before the ceremony, it's fine to put them in a vase and enjoy them for 24 hours. This will also give any closed flowers time to open. Don't buy them a week before and then expect to be able to use them as offerings when they are starting to fade, though. Flowers used for offerings need to be fresh and etherically vibrant (full of life).

Flower colours and shapes

Choose the freshest flowers you can find rather than skimping and buying the ones that happen to be on sale.

The best colours to use are pink, orange, yellow, white, or violet. Don't use dark reds, dark purples, artificially dyed flowers, or the kind that have been sprinkled with glitter or other synthetic materials.

Also, don't use large-headed flowers such as large roses, lilies, daffodils, carnations, gerberas, tulips, and so on.

The best types of flower heads are:

- Mini or spray carnations (*Dianthus caryophyllus*)
- Chrysanthemums (*Chrysanthemum morifolium*)
- French marigolds (*Tagetes patula*)
- Alstroemerias/Peruvian lilies (*Alstroemeria aurea*)
- Orchids
- Freesias
- Roses (miniature roses and medium-sized roses that have not fully opened)

Some of these flowers are known by different names in different parts of the world, so we have created a webpage at www.clearspaceliving. com/flowers where you can see images of each one. It's fine to use other small flowers too.

Sources of flowers

Commercially grown flowers

These are usually the best type of flowers to use for a space clearing ceremony because they are robust and are available in many colours and types. If you buy them from a supermarket, try to choose ones that are not stored anywhere near fruit, especially bananas, apples, and tomatoes, which naturally emit high levels of ethylene that causes flowers to age quickly and lose their etheric vitality.

Flowers from your garden

Flowers grown in your own garden hold the frequencies of the land your house is built on, so using them brings a special quality to the ceremony. If you have a small home and a lot of flowers in your garden, this may work. If you have a small garden and a large house, you may find that your garden will look too nude after picking all the flowers you'll need for the ceremony.

If you do decide to do this, pick the flowers the day before and stand them in water to help the petals to become more turgid and not start drooping during the ceremony.

Wildflowers

Wildflowers are beautiful. However, they are not a good choice to use for space clearing because they are usually rather frail and will start to wilt as soon as they are put on the offering saucers or plates. To test this, pick a few wildflower heads a day or two before you plan to do the ceremony to see how long they retain their vitality and shape after being picked. If you find they don't last very long, you will need to use shop-bought or garden flowers instead.

A mini carnation

☐ *Basic Space Clearing*

☑ *Essential Space Clearing*

☑ *Full Space Clearing*

You will need a mini carnation (also known as a spray carnation) to use with space clearing water when activating the offering(s). The best colour to use is white. If you are not able to find white, then pale yellow or pink is the next best choice.

If mini carnations are not available in your part of the world, another option is a small marigold or any other small bushy-headed flower that will absorb and hold water between its petals when it is dipped into it.

Unscented tealight candles in holders

☐ *Basic Space Clearing*

☑ *Essential Space Clearing*

☑ *Full Space Clearing*

An unscented tealight candle in a holder is placed at the centre of each flower offering. For Essential Space Clearing, you will only need one tealight candle. For a Full Space Clearing, you will need a candle for each flower offering.

Types of candles

Paraffin candles are the cheapest and most easily available because they are made from the sludge that remains after crude oil is refined into petrol. Several studies have found that they commonly emit toxins such as benzene and toluene, so many people are now switching to healthier alternatives such as beeswax, soy, palm wax, coconut, or rapeseed oil.

To date, no scientific study has concluded that any type of candle is hazardous to human health, providing the area they are burned in is well ventilated. Be aware, though, that all candles emit volatile organic compounds (VOCs) and particulate matter in the form of soot when burned. Some are known to be worse than others.

For space clearing, all types of tealight candles will work equally well, so the choice is yours. Please bear in mind the following.

Only use brand-new candles

When burning candles to create ambience in your home, it doesn't matter how many times you relight them. For spiritual uses, including space clearing, the purpose of lighting a candle is to connect to a spiritual force of some kind, so always use a brand-new candle.

Only use plain white candles

Using candles that have been coloured with dyes or pigments does not improve the results of a space clearing ceremony in any way and may cause a variety of chemicals to be emitted that will pollute the air in your home.

Only use unscented candles

Synthetic fragrances emit phthalates when burned, which are known endocrine disrupters. It's therefore unwise to burn these in your home for any reason. Candles scented with 100% pure essential oils are generally safe, although they can cause allergic reactions in some people. Both types of fragrance will severely limit the results you can achieve during a space clearing ceremony because the aromas they emit will anchor you at the level of the physical senses. We therefore do not recommend using fragranced candles of any kind.

Only use candles with wicks made from 100% cotton, hemp, or wood

Some mass-produced candles have a wick with a lead core, which is used as a stiffening agent. Lead is highly toxic when burned.

Trim the candle wick before lighting

To minimize emissions of particulate matter, trim the candle wick to 0.6 cm (1/4 inch) before lighting. If you decide to use long-burning candles, check every four hours to see if more trimming is necessary.

Consider using glass tealight holders

If you are environmentally conscious, purchase a set of glass tealight holders and buy refill tealights instead of the ones that come in aluminium or plastic holders, which are difficult or impossible to recycle.

Don't even think about using plastic LED candles

The purpose of the candle flame at the centre of a flower offering is to anchor spiritual forces during the ceremony. This simply will not happen with an artificial LED candle, so don't even consider it.

Long matches

☐ *Basic Space Clearing*
☑ *Essential Space Clearing*
☑ *Full Space Clearing*

The best matches to use are the extra-long type that measure at least 10 cm (4 inches). Never use a gas lighter. To activate space clearing flower offerings, you need the type of fire that is created by striking a match head and burning a thin stick of wood. The quality of flame this creates is energetically far superior to that produced by a petrocarbon-fuelled lighter.

An unopened bottle of still spring water

☐ *Basic Space Clearing*
☑ *Essential Space Clearing*
☑ *Full Space Clearing*

Use water from a previously unopened bottle of still spring water. Check the label to make sure it is genuine spring water and not purified water from another source that has been processed and bottled.

If you happen to have access to water from an unpolluted mountain stream, waterfall, or well, you can use that instead, providing you collect it in a brand-new bottle that has not been used for any other purpose or wash the bottle out thoroughly before using it. Lake water is not recommended because its nature is more retentive than cleansing. River water is usually too polluted.

Don't use sparkling bottled water because that is made by injecting carbon dioxide under pressure, which changes the chemical composition of the water.

Don't use water that has had anything else added to it, such as flavourings, colourings, or sweeteners.

Don't use distilled water or water created by reverse osmosis because these processes purge the etheric vitality of the water, which makes it of no use at all for space clearing.

Don't use water from your home supply unless you have a high-quality filtration system installed. In some parts of the world, the water in people's homes comes from recycled sewerage. Even if it's not, it will have been recycled in some way and will contain many undesirable impurities together with their etheric and astral counterparts.

Brass cleaner and two soft polishing cloths

☑ *Basic Space Clearing*

☑ *Essential Space Clearing*

☑ *Full Space Clearing*

To clean your bell and harmony ball(s), you can use any good-quality metal polish such as Brasso (the wadding type is best), or an odour-free alternative such as Wiener Kalk (made of kaolinite and ground quartz, and available in German-speaking countries and some other parts of the world). Apply it with a clean, soft cotton cloth, then gently buff it to a shine using another clean, soft cotton cloth.

Unscented hand cream (if needed)

☑ *Basic Space Clearing (optional)*

☑ *Essential Space Clearing (optional)*

☑ *Full Space Clearing (optional)*

You will only need to moisturize the palms of your hands before the clapping circuit if you have very dry skin or a very large home.

Use the type of hand cream that is unscented. Many scents, especially artificial ones, will affect the level of consciousness you are able to access during the ceremony because they will anchor you in your physical senses. This, in turn, will affect the results you are able to achieve.

Also avoid greasy hand cream because it can make it difficult for you to hold your bell firmly during the belling circuit, which comes straight after clapping.

PART FOUR

When and where
to do space clearing

19

Space clearing dos and don'ts

This part of the book contains detailed information about when and where to do space clearing, and equally importantly, when and where NOT to do it, and why.

Some of the guidelines have emerged from our own experience of what works and what doesn't work, to save you having to figure this out for yourself.

Others have been included in response to the thousands of questions asked by readers since Karen's first book was published. She never imagined, for example, that anyone would crack open a six-pack of beer before doing a space clearing, but because this wasn't specifically stated in her first book as a no-no, someone tried it and then was surprised when the space clearing had no effect at all.

In this book, we have therefore taken the approach of spelling out all the dos and don'ts we know of so that you will be as clear as possible about them and understand the reasons for them.

20

When to do space clearing

Space clearing your home at least once a year, following the instructions in this book, will keep the energy of your space vibrant and clear.

There are also many other uses of space clearing – so many, in fact, that it was at this point in our writing that we realized all the information we have about this would not fit into one book.

The main uses are covered in this chapter, and you can find detailed descriptions of many of the other uses in *Space Clearing, Volume 2,* together with a recommended altar design for each one.

The three most important times to do space clearing

The three most important times to do space clearing are:
- When you move into a new home
- When you feel stuck
- When you're going through a major life change

When you move into a new home

The most obvious time to do space clearing is when you move into a new home, to clear out the energies of any previous occupants and infuse the space with your own frequencies. Until you do this, there will always be residual energies from the past affecting everything you do.

If you move into a property that no one has ever lived in before, you might think this wouldn't apply. In our experience, space clearing is still very helpful. Even a brand-new home can be problematic because of the energies imprinted by the builders, especially if the building process did not go smoothly. Space clearing clears out those imprints and harmonizes the space so that it immediately starts to feel like home.

Space clearing can also be very helpful at the various stages of moving home and settling in. It can help you to get clarity about whether to stay or move, then help you to sell your old home and find a new home. There is a beautiful practice you can do as a farewell to your old home, to complete your relationship with it. And if your home needs improvements, there's a version of the ceremony you can do before starting, to help the process go smoothly, and again after the renovations are complete, to reset the energies and make the space feel like a home again.

You can find detailed information about all these aspects in Part Four of *Space Clearing, Volume 2*.

When you feel stuck

Another important use of space clearing is whenever you feel stuck. You are energetically connected to the place where you live, so whenever you feel stuck in some aspect of your life, there will be a corresponding stagnation and stuckness in the energies of your home. Space clearing is one of the most effective ways to clear those energies, to help get your life moving again.

Wherever there are stagnant energies, there will usually be an accumulation of physical clutter too, so a deep and thorough clutter clearing before space clearing is the most effective combination for this situation.

When you're going through a major life change

Space clearing your home creates a supportive environment to help you move through a major transition with greater clarity and ease.

Other personal uses of space clearing

The following topics are all covered in Part Four of *Space Clearing, Volume 2.*

To facilitate clutter clearing

It's ideal to declutter your home before you space clear it. If you need some help to get started, there's a way to do space clearing first to clear the stagnant energies out of the space, which makes clutter clearing much easier.

To clear energies in objects

There are specific ways that space clearing methods can be adapted to clear the energies of items you own. This can be especially useful for any second-hand things you acquire that may have a dubious history.

Guest rooms

Space clearing a guest room is a wonderful way to make guests feel more welcome.

When doing home improvements

There are specific ways space clearing can be used to minimize the disruption of home improvements and help the process to go smoothly. It can also be used to change the energies of a room or building that is being repurposed.

Relationships

Space clearing can be used to help you to find a new relationship, revitalize an existing relationship, take a relationship to a deeper level, and get clarity about whether to continue a relationship or end it. It's also an essential skill to have when moving into a new home with a partner, to clear out the old energies and set the best possible space for the relationship to thrive there.

If you start a new relationship you are serious about, it's ideal to move to a place that neither person has lived in before. If this is not possible, and especially if one partner previously lived in the home and shared it with another partner, space clearing can make a huge difference. It can also help enormously after a break-up or divorce.

Health

There are specific ways that space clearing can be used to assist the healing process of someone who is sick and clear the space after an illness. The sick person can't be present during the space clearing, but they will benefit from the freshly cleared space.

Special times of the year

Space clearing can be used to create an enhanced space to celebrate special events such as a new year, springtime, a birthday or solar return, or any anniversary that is important to you.

Major life events

One of the most important uses of space clearing is to prepare a space for major life events, such as a marriage, a pregnancy, a birth, or a death.

After a disruptive experience

Space clearing can be very helpful after a disruptive experience of some kind, such as an argument, a burglary, an accident in the home, or a traumatic local or world event.

When travelling

Space clearing can be used when travelling to clear the energies of any hotel room you stay in or a guest room in someone else's home (providing they give their permission for you to do so).

To support personal development

Space clearing can be used to clarify a new direction in life, help overcome procrastination, deal with recurring problems or behaviours, promote prosperity, and open new possibilities.

Spiritual purposes

Regular space clearing is vital if you are engaged on a spiritual path, to keep the energies in your home at a high level. It can also be used to bring more meaning and purpose into your life, to create and maintain a meditation space, and to reset the space of your home after a life-changing workshop, meditation retreat, or similar event.

Business uses of space clearing

Doing space clearing for business purposes is very different to using it personally in your own home.

We have included detailed explanations in Part Five of *Space Clearing, Volume 2* about how to space clear business premises if you run your own business, as well as how space clearing can help to launch a new phase of your business, improve team spirit and productivity, prepare for an important business meeting, and boost profits. There is also a section about space clearing if you work as an employee in someone else's business.

Specialized uses of space clearing

Specialized uses of space clearing include how to use it to complement feng shui, to space clear a meeting room, to space clear a treatment or therapy room, and to prepare for and clean up after an entity clearing. These are all covered in Part Six of *Space Clearing, Volume 2*.

21

When NOT to do space clearing

Please read the list below, just before you do a space clearing ceremony, to check if any of the situations apply to you. If any of them do, you'll need to read the more detailed information in this chapter about them. If not, you can skip to the next chapter.

Do NOT do space clearing in any of the following situations:

- If you are unwell
- If you are mentally or emotionally unstable
- If you are tired or energetically depleted
- If you are pregnant or breastfeeding
- If you are menstruating
- If you have any gynaecological health problems
- If you are energetically depleted after ejaculation
- If you have any open wounds, sores, or weeping eczema
- If you have taken any psychoactive drugs:
    - Marijuana/cannabis – in the preceding 1–4 weeks (depending on your level of usage)
    - Alcohol – in the preceding 72 hours
    - Opioids such as opium, codeine, morphine, oxycodone, methadone, heroin, and fentanyl – in the preceding 72 hours
    - Stimulants such as cocaine, methamphetamine, and amphetamines (including ADHD medications) – in the preceding 72 hours
    - Hallucinogens such as LSD, MDMA, psilocybin, ayahuasca, mescaline, THC, ketamine, and PCP – in the preceding 72 hours

- Antipsychotics such as haloperidol and chlorpromazine – in the preceding 72 hours
- Designer drugs such as synthetic marijuana, MXE, and mephedrone – in the preceding 72 hours
- Sedatives, including sleeping pills and tranquilizers – in the preceding 48 hours
- Refined sugar – since waking that day
- Caffeine – immediately before or during a ceremony
- Nicotine – during the ceremony, in the area being space cleared

Here's more information about each of these aspects.

Do not do space clearing if you are unwell

You need to be reasonably physically fit and healthy to do space clearing. Don't imagine for a minute that doing the ceremony when you are ill will make you feel better. It won't. It will almost certainly make you feel worse because the weakened state of your etheric body will make you more vulnerable to picking up unwanted energies. Doing space clearing when you are unwell will also have little or no effect because you will not have the vitality to do the ceremony at the level at which it needs to be done.

So what can you do? If you have a passing illness, wait until you are back in good health before doing space clearing. If you have a chronic illness, you will need to find someone who is in good health to do the ceremony for you. As well as reading this book, they will also need to read the more detailed information we have included in the chapter about space clearing for health in Part Four of *Space Clearing, Volume 2*.

Do not do space clearing
if you are mentally or emotionally unstable

Do not do space clearing if your life is in a general period of turmoil or on a day when you are experiencing chaotic thoughts or emotions such as feeling upset, unhappy, confused, agitated, stressed, and so on. You will put those frequencies into your home and the effects could be worse than doing no space clearing at all. Wait for a time when you feel calm and centred.

If anyone in your home is mentally or emotionally unstable a lot of the time, it will work best to do the ceremony when they are not present.

Do not do space clearing if you are tired or energetically depleted

If the day of the ceremony arrives and you don't feel at your best, postpone it until another time. You need to have good vitality and a certain amount of oomph to do space clearing effectively.

Anyone can have a day when they feel energetically depleted. Karen remembers an occasion in Bali when she made an appointment with a priest to do a consecration ritual* for her new car, which is a common practice in that culture. She arrived at the agreed time only to be told by the priest that he couldn't do anything that day because he was "empty". Another member of his family, who was also a priest, stepped in to do the ritual instead.

In less spiritually discerning cultures, a more common behaviour would be for the priest to go ahead and do the ritual instead of letting someone down. The difference in Bali is that ordinary folk are much more energetically perceptive, which means they would spot the deficiency immediately. Priests therefore have to be honest if they are having an "off" day. It happens to everyone from time to time.

Most people find it best to do space clearing in the early part of the day, when their energy is at its freshest. If it's only possible for you to do it later in the day, have a short nap first, if you need one.

If you have a very large home, or a home on several floors that you will find too tiring to space clear in one day, it won't work to do hand sensing one day, set up your altar the next day, do clapping the day after that, and so on. Nor will it work, beyond Step 10 of the ceremony, to do a few steps, then take a break or have a little nap before continuing. The reason for this, and what you can do instead, is explained in detail in Chapter 35.

Do not do space clearing
if you are pregnant or breastfeeding

If you are pregnant

Preparing for a birth and cleansing a space after a birth are important uses of space clearing. However, this is not something to attempt to do yourself if you are pregnant. You will need to find someone else to do the ceremony. The reason for this is that an unborn fetus is very etherically open and vulnerable. Space clearing can expose it to energies that it is not equipped to handle.

If anyone else present is pregnant

If anyone present during a space clearing ceremony is pregnant, you must make sure they leave the building during the clapping and belling circuits (Steps 17 and 18). This is for the comfort and safety of both the mother and baby.

If you are breastfeeding

Don't do space clearing if you are breastfeeding. If you are in good health, your body's excretory systems will easily handle any traces of stagnant energies that pass into your system during a ceremony. If you are breastfeeding, these residues are likely to be passed straight to your baby through your milk.

We first became aware of this when a woman we had trained as a professional space clearing practitioner reported that each time she did a space clearing, her baby would refuse breast milk for a day or two after. Other mothers have reported similar experiences, so we now advise against it.

Do not do space clearing when you are menstruating

Menstruation is a time of internal cleansing, when the lining of the womb is shed. You will not be in peak condition to do space clearing while this is happening and may find it tiring or exhausting to do so.

Another factor is that space clearing while menstruating can put you at greater risk of picking up unwanted energies. This gives an insight into why many religions do not allow anyone who is menstruating into temples. Some people get indignant about this practice, although perhaps they wouldn't if they really understood the underlying reasons. In Bali, it is not just those menstruating who are not allowed into temples – it's anyone who is bleeding in any way. That's because blood can attract low-level astral beings that can pollute the purity of the temple space and put the person at risk too.

If you share your home with others who want to be present during the ceremony and happen to be menstruating on the day you choose to do it, be sure to ask them to step out of the building during the clapping and belling circuits. It will be fine for them to be present during the rest of the ceremony.

Do not do space clearing
if you have any gynaecological health issues

In the Professional Space Clearing Practitioner Training we offer, we have found it impossible to train anyone who has had a hysterectomy.

They lack certain subtle body structures that are essential to do space clearing at that level of proficiency.

We also strongly advise any professional space clearer who has gynaecological issues to cease working until they have regained full health, because space clearing can make these types of conditions worse.

If you have had a hysterectomy and want to space clear your own home, it is usually fine to do so, providing you have fully recovered from the surgery. We strongly advise against doing space clearing in your own home if you have any ongoing gynaecological health issues, though.

We also recommend stopping immediately if you experience any pain or discomfort in the pelvic area while doing space clearing (this is a rare occurrence but can be a sign that you have a health issue you may not yet be aware of).

Do not do space clearing if you are energetically depleted after ejaculation

Any ejaculation of semen is always accompanied by a loss of life force energy, so we recommend waiting until you feel vital again before doing space clearing.

Do not do space clearing if you have any open wounds, sores, or weeping eczema

Whenever you have an open wound, sore, or weeping eczema on your skin, there will be a corresponding breach in your energy that can make you susceptible to picking up unwanted energies. You will need to wait until the condition has healed before doing space clearing.

Do not do space clearing
if you have taken any psychoactive drugs

One of the main purposes of space clearing is to raise the level of consciousness in a space. All psychoactive drugs (recreational, prescribed, or those included in food, such as refined sugar) cause changes in consciousness, perception, mood, and behaviour, to some degree. These types of chemical substances will connect you to astral spaces that will hinder or skew the results you are able to achieve during a space clearing ceremony. Do not do space clearing if you have taken any of these substances in the time periods stated.

Marijuana/cannabis

Do not do space clearing if you have taken any marijuana/cannabis in the preceding 1–4 weeks (depending on your level of usage).

Marijuana is a psychoactive drug that is in a category of its own since it can act as a stimulant, a depressant, and a hallucinogen. Most governments do not consider it to be as addictive or harmful as Class A drugs. Scientists know that it takes a long time to process the effects of marijuana out of a person's body, and health professionals with highly developed awareness know that the energetic effects of marijuana can linger and affect a person for many years.

To remove the physical traces of the drug from your system, stop using marijuana for at least a week if you are a very occasional user, for at least two weeks if you are a daily user, and for at least four weeks if you are in the habit of using it multiple times a day.

Anyone wishing to train as a professional space clearing practitioner will usually need to have been marijuana-free for at least two years to allow time for the energetic effects of the drug to dissipate sufficiently to be able to learn the skills without putting themselves at risk of picking up unwanted energies. In some cases, even two years is not enough. We know people who gave up using the drug over a decade ago and still feel the cloudy energetic effects of it from time to time. It creates sieve-like energetic holes that can cause negative effects for years.

Alcohol

Do not do space clearing if you have consumed any alcohol in the preceding 72 hours.

It takes most people 72 hours to process every trace of alcohol out of their blood, saliva, sweat, and urine after consuming it. Moderate alcohol use is not as energetically harmful as marijuana, but it's impossible to achieve a good space clearing result while under its influence. The reason is that alcohol automatically connects you to low-level astral spaces. In other words, it has a spiritually disconnecting effect. That's why consuming alcohol of any kind is counterproductive to doing spiritual work beyond beginner's level.

The professional space clearing practitioners we train don't drink alcohol at all. It's not that they give it up. It's that after completing our training, they find that alcohol loses any appeal. They understand there is no point in developing their subtle body structures to be able to read and clear energies in buildings, then take alcohol to numb themselves and pull their energy down. They also understand that this can put them seriously at risk when doing consultations in places where there are perverse energies or entities. Having alcohol in your bloodstream while space clearing is like an open invitation to these types of energies, and once they're in your system, they're very difficult to remove.

In case you're wondering, alcohol includes wine and beer. Someone once asked about this during a space clearing workshop Karen taught in Denmark, thinking that she was surely only referring to spirits. In some countries, drinking wine and beer is so common and socially acceptable that they are thought of as being a kind of flavoured water. However, perverse energies can be attracted to alcohol, so when space clearing, don't consume anything with any alcoholic content, including wine and beer.

Opioids, stimulants, hallucinogens, antipsychotics, and designer drugs

Do not do space clearing if you have taken any of these types of drugs in the preceding 72 hours.

These types of drugs are energetically destabilizing and can cause breaches in your energy that may make you vulnerable to picking up unwanted energies. We are definitely not suggesting that you discontinue taking any prescription medications for a few days in order to do space clearing. We are saying you will need to wait until you no longer need to take these medications, or find someone else to do the ceremony for you.

Sedatives, including sleeping pills and tranquilizers

Do not do space clearing if you have taken any sedatives in the preceding 48 hours.

Space clearing is about clearing and revitalizing energies in your home, so you need to feel energized and vibrant yourself to be able to achieve this. Sedatives such as sleeping pills are designed to do the exact opposite. They shut down your awareness and can have a dulling effect that continues for a long time. It's therefore best to schedule space clearing for a time when you will not have taken any sedatives for at least a couple of days.

Sugar

Do not do space clearing if you have consumed any refined sugar that day.

You may not think of sugar as a drug until you try giving it up for a while. You'll soon discover how addictive it is. The reason so many people love sugar is because, like many other psychoactive substances, it creates an artificial high. However, it is always followed by a crash, which is what makes you want to go back for more.

This roller coaster effect needs to be avoided when doing space clearing, partly because it will destabilize you and partly because it will limit your ability to feel energies. If you are in the habit of consuming sugar every day and cannot manage without it, we recommend doing space clearing first thing in the morning and waiting until after the ceremony to have your first sugar hit of the day.

Caffeine

Do not consume any caffeine immediately before or during a space clearing ceremony.

High levels of caffeine are found in coffee, energy drinks, and sodas, and to a much lesser extent in green tea, black tea, dark chocolate, decaffeinated coffee, and kombucha. Consuming caffeine will not interfere with the space clearing ceremony as much as any of the other substances listed here. We still advise avoiding it, though, because it is a type of psychoactive drug, so it will interfere with your ability to sense energies and feel what is happening during the ceremony.

Nicotine

Do not smoke inside the property during a space clearing ceremony.

The smoke from cigarettes, cigars, pipes, and vaping devices creates an energetic greyness in a space that is counterproductive to space clearing. Don't allow anyone who is present during the ceremony to smoke or vape while it is in progress. If you are a smoker yourself, find a suitable point to pause the ceremony and go outside to smoke, if you need to (anytime before Step 15). You will get a better result that way rather than trying to continue the ceremony while distracted by nicotine cravings.

Why are anti-anxiety and antidepressant medications not included in the list?

It's not OK to space clear someone else's home if you are taking anti-anxiety or antidepressant medications (the reasons for this are explained in Chapter 36).

However, it's fine to space clear your own home. The tranquilizing effects of the medications will dull your senses and impact the depth of results you are able to obtain, but we have not found they have any other adverse effects on the ceremony.

22

Where to do space clearing

The decision to do space clearing must be made by the person who is the head of the household or by one of the joint heads of the household. The reason for this is that they have responsibility for everything that happens in a property, both physically and energetically.

This chapter gives guidelines for determining who is the head of the household in the main types of living situations you may encounter. You only need to read the section that's relevant to you:

- If you live alone
- If you share your home with a partner
- If you live in your partner's home
- If you have children
- If you live in your parents' home
- If you live in someone else's home
- If two families share a home
- If you house-sit
- If you rent a room in a house-share or apartment-share
- If you are a landlord
- If you rent part of your home to a tenant
- If you have staff who live in your home
- If you stay in a friend's home as a guest
- If you stay in a hotel or rent a vacation property
- If a close friend or relative asks you to space clear their home

If you live alone

If you live alone in a home that you own or rent, you can space clear it yourself or invite someone else to do so, if you wish to. You are the head of your own household, so you don't need permission from anyone to change the energy of your space.

If you share your home with a partner

If you jointly own your home, or rent it and are named on the tenancy agreement with your partner, it's always best to do space clearing with the full knowledge and cooperation of the other person. We certainly recommend this. However, we know from our experience of working with clients for so many years that it is sometimes the case that one partner is enthusiastic about space clearing and the other has little or no interest in it. It can also happen that a partner may be derisive about its benefits or openly opposed to doing it.

If you have a partner who has no interest in space clearing but doesn't mind at all if you go ahead without involving them, just agree on a day when they will be out for a long enough period for you to do it by yourself. Because it is your partner's home as much as it is yours, be sure to do the ceremony as much for their benefit as for your own, with no manipulative agenda.

To give an example, suppose your main reason for wanting to do space clearing is to help your stuck partner to get their life moving so that your own life will become easier. That won't work at all. What you will need to do is go higher and make the focus of the ceremony about creating a space that supports you both in fulfilling your potentials and becoming all that you can be. Then the focus of the space clearing will have integrity because you will both benefit from it equally.

If you have a partner who finds the whole idea of space clearing ridiculous or objects to you spending money to buy space clearing equipment or materials, this is more complicated to resolve. What is really being highlighted is the difference in understanding and values you both have, so it is best to at least try to have a discussion about it. For example, you may be able to agree that you go ahead and do space clearing but exclude certain rooms that your partner has exclusive use of. Or that you personally cover the cost of the entire ceremony so that your partner doesn't have to contribute anything.

If no agreement can be reached, then you have a more radical decision to make. Do you go ahead and do it anyway, or do you respect their wishes and not do it at all?

What neither of you may have realized is that you are both making energetic changes in your home all the time. This is because everything that happens in the space becomes astrally imprinted in the walls, floors, ceilings, and all the objects in the space. Stagnant energies will also be accumulating daily, in a similar way to how layers of dust build up if you don't do physical cleaning for a while. Whether you do space clearing or not, the energies of your home will be changing each day.

Another consideration is that whenever you do physical cleaning, it improves the energy of a space. So, if your partner willingly agrees to the home you share being kept physically clean, they have already agreed in principle to maintaining the space at a certain level of energetic cleanliness too, even if they haven't said so in words. The two are inextricably connected, which is why cleaning your home is one of the important preparatory steps for space clearing.

If you decide to go ahead and do space clearing without your partner's consent, choose a day when they will be out for a long enough period for you to do it. What tends to happen is that the partner will either not notice any changes when they return or, if they do, they will put it down to you having done a deeper level of physical cleaning than you normally do.

In the professional work we do, we never agree to space clear the home of a client if one partner is unaware that we have been invited to do so or strongly objects to having it done. We are non-negotiable on this point because that would be an invasion of the partner's privacy. However, it's a very different matter if you are space clearing your own home. As a joint head of the household, you have as much right to space clear as you have to sweep the floor or empty the trash.

Do be aware, though, that because space clearing clears and revitalizes old energies and replaces them with new, more vibrant frequencies, this may have an impact on your relationship. We've heard from a number of people for whom space clearing resulted in them ending a relationship because it highlighted incompatibilities so clearly, primarily that their partner didn't want to change and move forward as they did. We've also heard of happy occasions when relationships have been dramatically revived after space clearing. Karen remembers one middle-aged couple, in particular, who told her that the space clearing she did for them saved their marriage. After the ceremony, they felt so much love for each other that they put on some music, danced together in their living room, and had intimate sex for the first time in years.

If you live in your partner's home

If you live in a home that your partner owns or rents, they do not need your permission to space clear, but you will definitely need theirs. This is one of many reasons why it's always best, in a new relationship that both partners are serious about, if you can move to a home that neither of you have lived in before and that you both have equal rights to occupy.

If you have children

As a parent, you are responsible for all aspects of your children's care. If you decide to space clear your home, you will naturally want to include their rooms in the ceremony so that they receive the full benefit of it too.

People have different styles of parenting, so we want to be very clear about this. As the head of the household, or one of the joint heads of the household, you are entitled to space clear your children's rooms without their permission, and in their early years we recommend that you do. It would be pointless to ask a 4-year-old child if they want their room to be included. They do not have the intellectual capacity to understand what's involved or make an informed decision about it. You are their guardian and mentor at that age, so you need to make decisions of this type for them.

As children grow up and become more self-determining, it's good to consult them. As a general guideline, when a child reaches the age where they ask you to knock before entering their room, or it becomes obvious to you that it is right to do so, this is a sign that they are starting to have more personal ownership of their space. We recommend that you ask children who are sufficiently mature if they want their room to be included in the space clearing and respect their wishes if they do not.

If you start space clearing regularly when children are at a young enough age, this question never arises. Regular space clearing becomes as normal a practice in your home as physical household cleaning.

If you live in your parents' home

If you live with your parents or any other caregiver, then you live under their auspices and must abide by their house rules. As heads of the household, they have overall responsibility for the space and the final say about what happens in it.

This changes a bit if you pay rent. In that situation, it's fine for you to space clear the areas you have sole occupancy of. Just don't add any other areas of the home that are communal.

If you live rent-free in your parents' home, the right thing to do is to ask permission to space clear the room or rooms that you solely occupy.

An exception to this would be a situation where there has been a role reversal because your parents or caregivers are mentally or physically incapacitated, so you have effectively become the head of the household, caring for them. In these circumstances, you can make the decision to space clear, but be sure to first read all the information about space clearing for health in Part Four of *Space Clearing, Volume 2*.

Occasionally we receive a space clearing request from someone who lives at home with their parents, either because they have not yet left home or because circumstances have resulted in them moving back in. The reason for the request is usually that they are having a difficult time living there and are hoping we can fix the situation for them. Our response is always that we can only do the space clearing if the request comes from the parents. The son or daughter who first contacted us can be present during the ceremony, but we will primarily work with one or both of the parents because they are the heads of the household.

If you live in someone else's home

If you rent space in someone else's home, you have legal rights to use of the rooms you have sole occupancy of. This entitles you to space clear those areas unless that is expressly prohibited in your tenancy agreement, which is highly unlikely.

If you live rent-free, you will need to ask the permission of the owner if you want to space clear your own room. An exception would be if you have a bartering agreement by which you pay for the use of the space in some other way, such as by taking care of the owner's garden, pets, or something else.

In any case, you will need the permission of the owner if you want to space clear any rooms that you share with them.

If two families share a home

When two families share a home, the head of the household is the person who owns the property or the person whose name is on the tenancy agreement. If one family wants to do space clearing and the other family does not, then it can only be done in the areas that that family has sole occupation of, not in any areas that are communal.

If you house-sit

The main attraction of house-sitting is that you get free or reduced-price accommodation for a while. The downside is that you usually have to live with all the owner's belongings. If you value quality of life, space clearing is essential. It will remove any stagnant energies that surround the owner's possessions and, depending on your space clearing skills, it can remove the historical imprints in the walls, furniture, and objects in the place too.

It's fine to do this without the owner's permission unless they have explicitly prohibited space clearing in the terms of your house-sitting arrangement, which would be very unusual. Toward the end of a house-sitting period, it's a good idea to space clear again to clear out your own energies and hand back a fresh, energetically clear property to the owner. Most really appreciate this and comment on how good the place feels.

If you rent a room in a house-share or apartment-share

In a rented home, the head of the household is the person named on the lease. If it's a joint tenancy, each person named on the lease will be a joint head of the household and no person will have more right to say what happens in the space than anyone else. That means you can only space clear the areas of the home you have exclusive use of. If you want to space clear any other rooms that are used communally, you will need the permission of everyone you share the house or apartment with before doing so.

If you are a landlord

If you own a property that you rent to a tenant or tenants, you have the overall say about what happens in the communal areas of the building. You can decide to space clear these areas yourself or hire a professional space clearing practitioner to do it for you. However, it would be out of integrity for you or anyone else to space clear any rooms that a tenant has sole use of, unless they willingly give their permission.

If you rent part of your home to a tenant

If you have a tenant who pays you rent for exclusive use of part of your home, you can space clear the parts of your home that you share with them. Just don't include any rooms that they have sole use of unless they specifically invite you to do so.

If you have staff who live in your home

Don't include in any space clearing any rooms that your staff have sole use of. It's their private space, to use as they wish.

If you stay in a friend's home as a guest

This really depends on your relationship with your friend. For example, if we stay with someone, we make it very clear that we will want to space clear our room. They pretty much expect it of us anyway. If they didn't agree, we would find somewhere else to stay (this is pure conjecture, as it's never happened).

If you stay at a friend's house, you will need to ask them if you can space clear the room you will be staying in. If they agree, you can go ahead. If you don't ask them, or they don't agree, then it's not OK to go ahead and do it.

You may be interested to know that the professional space clearing practitioners we train will never agree to sleep in the home of a client they are doing a space clearing for. When they have to travel a considerable distance to do a clearing, some clients will offer this, either from a wish to be hospitable or because it saves the expense of paying for hotel accommodation.

However, sleeping in a client's home the night before a space clearing seriously compromises the results a space clearer can obtain. They would become subject to the energies of the space and lose the objectivity needed to be able to do a good job. Sleeping there the night after the ceremony would also interfere on many levels with the integration process that happens. The space clearer would become entangled in the energies of the space in a way that is not supposed to happen because it is not their home.

We have included this information here in case you are ever asked by a friend or relative to space clear their entire home while staying there. For all the reasons mentioned, we don't recommend it.

If you stay in a hotel or rent a vacation property

Unless it is expressly prohibited in the terms of your agreement, it's fine to space clear a hotel room or vacation property. Please respect the space of other hotel guests or neighbours, though. Our personal policy is that if we arrive in a place after 8 pm, then we consider it too late to make loud noises by clapping and ringing bells. If we are staying for a few days, we wait until a decent hour the next morning to do this.

If a close friend or relative asks you to space clear their home

If you space clear the home of a close friend or relative, the request must be made without any persuasion by you and must come from the person who is the head of the household, or from all the heads of the household if there is more than one. It would be totally out of integrity to space clear because one partner asked you to do so without the other person's agreement or awareness that you are doing so. You can find more information about how to space clear someone else's home in Chapter 36.

23

Where NOT to do space clearing

Space clearing is a wonderful skill to have. The information in this book will teach you to safely and effectively space clear your own home. After you've obtained good results doing that, you can also space clear the homes of close friends and relatives, if they ask you, and other places such as vacation rentals, hotel rooms, and so on.

This chapter is about the situations and places where it may be inadvisable to do space clearing, or where it is NOT OK to do it at all. Please read these checklists and if any of these situations are relevant to you, be sure to read the more detailed information provided about them.

If you are planning to space clear someone else's home, you will also need to read Chapter 36.

It may be inadvisable to do space clearing in your own home in any of these situations

- If someone in your home has mental health issues
- If a person or pet in your home is unwell
- If your home is so cluttered that it's impossible to walk around the inner perimeter of the space

Do NOT do space clearing in any of these places

- Public buildings (unless you are renting the space)
- Hospitals, hospices, and other places where sickness or death are common
- Churches or temples that have been consecrated to a particular religion or spiritual stream
- A place where there has been a suicide, murder, violent crime, or other traumatic event
- A place where someone you knew has recently died, and you are still grieving their loss
- A business you do not own
- The guest room of a friend you are visiting (unless they give their permission)
- Outdoor areas

If someone in your home has mental health issues

If someone in your home has mental health issues, the effects of a space clearing can sometimes be of tremendous help to them. It can also have the opposite effect and cause them considerable distress. The reason for these widely differing results is that space clearing changes the energies of spaces, which can provide a wonderful fresh start. However, if someone experiencing mental health issues has become used to resting their consciousness on those energies as a coping mechanism, it can be very destabilizing for them if the frequencies are suddenly and irreversibly changed.

We therefore urge extreme caution in this situation. Even if the person assures you they feel ready for change and they enthusiastically welcome it, they may still find the results difficult to live with.

If you decide to go ahead, at the very least we advise completely excluding the person's room from the ceremony and doing the space clearing when they are not present. If they spend a lot of time in communal areas of the home, it may be best to exclude those areas too.

Then wait a week or two and see what happens. If they have a favourable response to the effects of the space clearing, consider doing the space clearing again, this time for the entire home.

There are no hard and fast rules here. Each person's mental health issues and their relationship to their environment will be unique to them, so the suitability of space clearing will need to be assessed on an individual basis.

In the case of a pet that has anxiety or other behavioural issues, space clearing is usually very beneficial. Just be sure to make arrangements for them to be taken care of outside the home during the ceremony.

If a person or pet in your home is unwell

Never do space clearing in a room where there is a person or pet who is physically unwell. In their weakened condition, they will be vulnerable to picking up some of the energies that are being cleared, which will make them feel worse, not better.

It's ideal if you can do the ceremony when the person is not in the home at all (when they are attending a medical appointment, for example). If a pet is unwell, you may be able to put it in the garden for a while, if you have one, or have it taken care of elsewhere by a friend or a professional pet carer.

If a person or pet is too sick to leave the home while you do the ceremony, keep the door to their room closed and exclude their room completely. Then move them to one of the freshly space-cleared rooms while you do a second ceremony just for their room.

If a sick person is physically fit enough to take part in the harmony ball infusion and frequencing part of the ceremony, it's fine for them to do so and it can be very enjoyable for them too.

For more detailed information, see the chapter about space clearing for health in Part Four of *Space Clearing, Volume 2*.

If your home is so cluttered that it's impossible to walk around the inner perimeter of the rooms

Space clearing can sometimes be the best way to kick-start clutter clearing a home because it removes the stagnant energies that have accumulated around all the stuff, which makes it easier to sort through it and let things go.

This only works if the clutter is at reasonable levels. If there are rooms you can't enter because they are stacked to the ceiling with junk, or if there are so many things piled up that you can't get to the walls to walk around the inner perimeter of some of the rooms, then you will not be able to do space clearing until you've cleared the clutter in those areas first.

Public buildings (unless you are renting the space)

We want to make it very clear that it is NOT OK to space clear public buildings, however much you may convince yourself that it will be for the greater good of humanity.

To give an example, suppose you have excellent space clearing skills and you decide to clear out a tourist attraction that has centuries of grisly history contained in its walls. This may make the place feel much better, but if you don't own or rent the property, you have no more right to change its energy than to put graffiti on the walls.

Meeting rooms

If you hire a public room to conduct a meeting of some kind, that's a different matter. There's no need to seek permission, although if you do an Essential or Full Space Clearing, you will need to check that it's OK to burn candles.

Space clearing to set the space for a workshop or seminar can make a huge difference to the event. We have a great deal of experience in this area, having conducted workshops, seminars, and talks in many different meeting rooms around the world. We have also used space clearing to set the space for boardroom meetings, other types of business meetings, meditation groups, and so on. There are many such situations where space clearing is invaluable.

If you are conducting a meeting in a borrowed space, you will need to get permission to space clear. It's preferable if the person you borrow the space from has already personally experienced space clearing in their own home, so they know what they are agreeing to.

Note that the method for space clearing a meeting room is substantially different from that for a residential space. We have included a chapter about it in Part Five of *Space Clearing, Volume 2*.

Hospitals, hospices, and other places where sickness or death are common

Even with our depth of experience, we would never attempt to space clear a hospital or hospice that is in active use because of the sheer quantity of perverse energies and entities (astral fragments from deceased people) in such places.

Hospitals

A question we are often asked is how to help when someone you know is admitted to hospital. Is it possible to space clear their room?

From an energetic standpoint, a very unfortunate paradox is that hospitals, where sick people go to get well, are generally some of the most energetically toxic environments. The buildings are full of the etheric excretions and astral imprints of sickness and trauma of all the patients who have ever been there. They are also, to varying degrees, swarming with perverse energies and entities that remain in the space after someone has died, looking for a new host. These can literally number in their thousands.

If you are admitted to hospital as a patient, you are likely to be weak and vulnerable, and probably fearful of what may happen. The odds are truly stacked against you getting well in such a place. It takes a great deal of energy to hold all these unwholesome types of energies at bay, leaving very little for your own healing. For anyone with energetic discernment, the last place on earth they would want to go if they were sick is a hospital. They may reluctantly have to, but they certainly wouldn't want to.

The information in this book will not equip you to space clear the homes of people you don't know very well or at all. The many things that can go wrong in that situation are bad enough. Attempting to space clear a hospital room presents a far greater risk. It's an absolute no-no, even for an experienced professional space clearing practitioner.

In Karen's first space clearing book, she said that it was her fondest hope that one day teams of space clearers would be commissioned to go into the hospitals of the world to regularly clear the energies that accumulate in such buildings. She had some ideas at that time about how to develop the techniques for this. However, after much research, we have concluded that the only way space clearing could ever be incorporated into hospitals, care homes, and hospices would be if all patients have private rooms and space clearing is included as standard practice from the first day the facility is opened, so that toxic levels never build up. To achieve this, all rooms would need to be cleared between patients, and long-stay patients would regularly need to be moved to a bed in another room while their room and bed are cleared. The space clearers doing this work would need to have very advanced skills to do this safely and effectively, and they would need to be capable and experienced entity clearers too.

Sadly, the cost of training people to this level of competence and hiring them to perform this service will never be accepted unless it is recognized as being as essential to hospital maintenance as physical cleaning. And since there is hardly any possibility of that ever happening, it is not something we have ever trained any space clearers to do.

If you ever have to go into hospital, the best advice we can offer is to do your best to get a private room so that you can at least minimize the energetic traffic moving through your space and have more control over levels of noise, light, and the electromagnetic fields generated by equipment. If possible, get a room with windows that open so that you can have fresh air circulating in the space. A room with a view of nature is the best of all to support healing. It's often wise to avoid eating the hospital food, if you can. Have someone bring you freshly prepared organic food of the kind your body needs and wants instead of the nutritionally deficient meals that many hospital kitchens dish up.

Hospices

Hospices are for people who have a terminal condition. It's where they go to be cared for until they die. Every patient who enters a hospice is expected to die there, so the death rate is very much higher than in hospitals. This, of course, means the density of entities is correspondingly greater.

We believe it would be possible for regular space clearing by trained professionals to be incorporated into the schedule of a hospice, providing all the patients have individual rooms and space clearing is done from the first day the facility is opened. However, we have never received a request for this, so we have never trained any practitioners to do it.

Churches or temples that are consecrated to a particular religion or spiritual stream

While it would be highly unusual for anyone to want to do this, it's a topic that has come up a few times since Karen's first book was published, so we have decided to include some information about it here.

Churches and temples are usually consecrated to the religious or spiritual stream they are affiliated with, using rituals that have been created for that specific purpose. Space clearing is non-denominational, so it's compatible with them all, but doing space clearing in such places requires skills that are beyond what you will learn by reading this book. You would also have to be personally invited by the head of the church or temple to space clear the building, otherwise you may come up against occult forces that have been put in place to prevent energetic interference.

For all these reasons, if you ever find yourself in the situation of wanting to space clear a consecrated space, we strongly advise against it unless you are authorized to do so and it has already been ritually deconsecrated so that it can be used for other purposes.

A place where there has been a suicide, murder, violent crime, or traumatic event

When you meet the kind of people whose job it is to physically clean up places where a suicide, murder, or other traumatic event has taken place, you're likely to notice they have a particular kind of mettle. They are usually non-reactive and very etherically robust.

Space clearing such a place after the physical clean-up has been done requires similar qualities. The space clearer also needs to have an awareness of the types of energies that can be picked up during the process, such as entities and pancakes, and know how to clean themselves up after. In other words, this type of space clearing needs an experienced professional who is also a trained entity clearer. It involves multiple skills that are far beyond the scope of this book.

A place where someone you knew has recently died, and you are still grieving their loss

Space clearing is not something to rush into in this situation. There needs to be a grieving period, and the length of time that takes will be different for each person.

You also need to be aware that it's not just a person's physical body that dies and disintegrates. Their astral body also goes through a process of shattering, and their etheric body gradually dissolves, eventually leaving just the person's Higher Self, which is the eternal part that is not earthbound.

In fact, it's not that simple because there are crystallized parts of the astral body that can survive death in the form of astral fragments that can form entities. This is far too big a topic to go into here, although it's one that anyone who is on a path of personal development will benefit hugely from exploring. If you are interested to learn more about it, we highly recommend reading Samuel Sagan's book *Entities: Parasites of the Body of Energy* (published in the United States as *Entity Possession: Freeing the Energy Body of Negative Influences*).

The reason we mention this here is because during the astral shattering that takes place after someone's death, there is a very strong risk of picking up astral fragments. The risk is heightened if you are grieving the loss of the person, and it becomes even greater if you space clear the place where they lived. This is a situation where it is best to enlist the help of a professional space clearer rather than attempt to do a space clearing yourself. A certain objectivity, robustness, and degree of energetic awareness is needed.

The space clearers we have trained have this skill and know how to energetically hold a client while the ceremony is in progress so that they can feel their feelings and find their own pathway to moving forward. This is a wonderful gift for any bereaved person to aid their grief recovery process.

If the deceased person was sick before dying, a skilful space clearer can also clear out the astral imprints from that time and remove any residues of grief or other emotions that have accumulated since their death, while leaving the higher and happier frequencies intact.

You can find more information about this in the chapters about space clearing for major life events in Part Four of *Space Clearing, Volume 2*.

A business you do not own

If you own a business, you may want to space clear your workplace after you've gained some experience of space clearing your home. The specific techniques for this can be found in Part Five of *Space Clearing, Volume 2*.

However, we strongly advise against space clearing the business premises of a relative or friend, if they ask you to do so. One reason for this is the complex superastral aspects that need to be taken into account. Another is that if the business runs into trouble after you have space cleared it, and especially if it loses money, then it's likely you will get blamed for this. Even if it's not your fault, it can cause rifts in a friendship that will be hard to repair.

We recommend you do not put yourself in this position. Simply tell your relative or friend that you do not have the skills to do it.

The guest room of a friend you are visiting (unless they give their permission)

Being invited to stay in the guest room of a friend does not include the right to space clear it unless they invite you to do so, or you ask their permission and they happily give it. For more information, see the chapter about space clearing when travelling in Part Four of *Space Clearing, Volume 2*.

Outdoor areas

Space clearing is not effective in outdoor areas. You can clap in corners and ring bells all you like in your garden, and it will have no effect at all, except perhaps to alarm your cat or annoy your neighbours. It's a complete waste of time.

Nor is it necessary. In outdoor areas, there is a constant etheric cleansing of the space by the elements – the sun, wind, rain, and so on.

The land energies of outdoor areas can, however, become astrally imprinted by repetitive behaviours or traumatic events. There is a way to remove the imprints in such places, although it's a very different technique to space clearing, and it would also be unethical to do so.

The reason is that if you clear an area of land in this way, you must then take custodianship of it and maintain it energetically, as the Balinese have done, generation after generation, with their hundreds of thousands of daily purification ceremonies conducted all over the island. To clear an area of land and just walk away is irresponsible and risky. It creates an energetic void that low-level elemental forces and undesirable astral beings can move into and fill. However well-meaning your intentions, if you clear land energies and don't make arrangements to maintain the space after, including if you move away or die, then it will almost certainly create a much worse situation than before.

Fortunately, very few people in the world can operate clearings of this depth, so this is not a common problem. And those who can clear land energies generally only do so for a specific purpose, such as building a temple. If the temple is entrusted to a spiritual community who are taught effective purification skills to energetically maintain the building for generations to come (as is the case in most religions), that's absolutely fine.

PART FIVE

How to prepare to do a space clearing ceremony

24

Why it's vital to prepare to do space clearing

There are some essential preparations that need to be made in the weeks and days before doing a space clearing ceremony. The better you prepare, the better your results will be.

An analogy we often make is that if you decide to redecorate an area of your home, it's very tempting to just open a can of paint and begin. However, if you take the time to carefully prepare the surfaces first, you'll get a much better and more enduring finish.

It's the same with space clearing. The better you prepare, the deeper and more long-lasting the effects of the ceremony will be. Since the purpose of space clearing is to create a better-quality environment, it therefore makes no sense at all to take shortcuts.

If you're the kind of person who never reads manuals and likes to jump straight in, please make an exception and read this part of the book instead of skipping it!

Checklist of preparations
- Clarify the focus of the ceremony
- Decide which rooms to include
- Choose a date and time for the ceremony
- Practise the main space clearing techniques

- Clear your clutter
- Clean and tidy your home
- Buy space clearing materials
- Clean and polish your space clearing kit

25

Clarify the focus of the ceremony

If we were to come to your home to conduct a space clearing ceremony without you being present and with no knowledge of what you or any of the other occupants of your home need help with at this time in your lives, the best we would be able to do is to clear out the energy of any previous occupants to give you a fresh start and reset the space at a higher level. In fact, in the early days of space clearing other people's homes, that's exactly what Karen did.

However, it didn't take her long to realize that being more specific about the reason for doing the ceremony makes it much more effective. We now always advise taking some time to clarify the focus for space clearing so that you can hold it in your awareness while doing the ceremony, in a specific way that we will explain.

This is especially important in a home that you have already lived in for some time, where you will be clearing out the energies of previous occupants, as well as your own energies and those of anyone you share your home with.

Clarifying the focus will help you to consciously take more energetic ownership of the space and avoid filling it again with the same frequencies you just cleared.

How a focus is different to a wish list

Some of the clients we've worked with have written a long wish list of everything they want, thinking that a space clearing ceremony will magically make it all happen.

One person Karen remembers sent her three long pages of things she was hoping the ceremony would fix in her life, ranging from helping her cat to get rid of its fleas to being personally gifted a large country mansion to live in rent-free. When Karen met her in person, it soon became apparent that the thing she most needed help with was regaining her self-confidence after leaving a demoralizing relationship, so that she could make her own decisions and move forward in life. Karen helped her to realize that all the other things on her list were unimportant compared with regaining control of her own life. The large rent-free mansion, for example, only symbolized her need to re-establish her own self-respect and feel respected by others. She was actually perfectly happy to continue to live in the modest home she rented after she felt better about herself.

So, a space clearing focus is not a wish list. The difference is that a wish list is a bottom-up approach that will take you off in all kinds of directions and still never get to the most important issue. A focus that is arrived at top-down gets to the core of what you truly need. When you find the key issue to address at any particular time and work with that, it will bring about changes in many other aspects of your life too.

How to clarify your focus for a space clearing ceremony

We recommend you take some time to clarify your focus for a space clearing ceremony. It's not a snap decision to make a few minutes before you begin or something to arrive at intuitively without knowing why. Consciously put some vision* on it for a few days. At the very least, make a decision about the focus the evening before the space clearing so that you can sleep on it and allow higher levels of your consciousness to work on it during the night. Often when you do this, you'll wake up with more insights about it than you had the previous day.

Use a pen and paper

Find a quiet time when you can sit down with a pen and paper. You can use a digital device if you really want to, although most people find they can go deeper if they use pen and paper rather than typing. Using a keyboard may be faster and more convenient, but writing by hand allows you to slow down, be in the moment, and connect to what's important to you in your life.

There is also something about holding a pen or pencil in your hand and moving it across the paper. You pour yourself through the movement of forming letters when writing. The shape of the individual characters flows through you, which allows you to connect more with the essence of the words you write and gain greater clarity. This is very different to tapping keys on a keyboard, where all the letters feel the same.

Clarify why you want to do space clearing

Think back to the moment you decided you wanted to do a space clearing ceremony. What were you hoping it could help you with? Write that down.

If several other reasons seem relevant and it's not immediately clear to you which is the most important, list them all. Then circle the three that will most change your life, and the lives of anyone you share your home with, for the better. Finally, choose the most important of those three at this time. Usually, it is possible to see that if one aspect were given priority then it would facilitate all the other aspects you need help with too.

If you've done space clearing before, don't assume the focus will be the same the next time you do it. It's very unlikely it will. Life moves on. Approach it from a fresh perspective each time.

Sum up your focus in seven words or less

Aim to sum up your focus for the ceremony in seven words or less. This is important because you need to be able to hold it in your conscious awareness throughout the ceremony as a packed thought* above your head instead of as an unpacked thought* in your mind. If your focus is too long or convoluted, or includes too many ramifications, you won't be able to do that.

A packed thought is the seed or archetype* of a thought before it reaches your mind. It's the essence of a thought before it is coated in words. This means it can be held in your consciousness *above* your head instead of the usual way that thoughts happen inside your head.

For example, consider a glass of water. Without you needing to think it through, you immediately know certain things about it:

- Water is a naturally colourless, transparent liquid
- The glass is likely to feel cold to the touch if you pick it up
- Providing there are no cracks in the glass, it will hold the water without leakage
- If you turn the glass upside down, all the water will pour out, and anything it comes into contact with will become wet
- If you drink some of the water, the level of water in the glass will go down
- If you drink some of the water, it's unlikely to kill you or make you sick
- If you drink some of the water, it will help to quench your thirst

You have learned all these things about a glass of water from all your previous experiences of handling one. Now, when you think about a glass of water, all that information is stored in packed form without you having to recall it in words. You already know it.

In a similar way, you can hold the focus for a space clearing ceremony in packed form so that you don't have to think it through. You hold awareness of the essence of the focus, not the details.

This, by the way, is a wonderful ability to cultivate in any aspect of your life. If you've ever seen a top-end programmer, chef, or racing car driver at work in their field of accomplishment, this is how they operate so fluidly. It's a superastral*, top-down engagement.

If you tend to overthink, you may find it challenging to limit yourself to seven words when defining your focus or holding a packed thought of any kind. You will probably want to include subclauses to cover every eventuality you can think of. This will make the focus less, not more, effective, so please resist the urge to add word clutter. Make the focus of the ceremony as succinct as you can.

How to clarify the focus of a ceremony if you share your home with other people

If you share your home with others, you will need to take their needs into account too, which can make the process more complicated. In this situation, it is even more vital to stick to core issues instead of getting distracted by rambling wish lists.

Active participation by others

If the people you share your home with wish to actively participate in the space clearing ceremony, guide them through the process of how to establish their own focus for it in seven words or less. Don't share each of your individual focuses until you've all finished. Each person needs to be able to determine what's important to them without being influenced or compromised by the wishes of others.

This is a wonderful process to do at least once a year, whether you're about to do space clearing or not. It's especially good for partners to do, to see how on track you are as a couple. And it's good for families and house-sharers to do too, to re-establish what you have in common and how you can best help each other in your individual journeys through life.

Taking the time to do this can intercept many problems you wouldn't otherwise see coming. It's all too easy to get bogged down in the details of everyday life and fail to see the bigger picture. It often takes something like a health crisis or relationship breakdown for someone to fully comprehend what they value and adjust their lifestyle accordingly, by which time it can often be too late.

Setting the focus for a space clearing ceremony is an opportunity for you to view your life from the highest and most visionful* perspective you can access, to clarify what's truly important to you. When those you live with take the time to do so too, it can move you all to a completely new level of interaction, allowing you to support each other's highest aspirations, rather than enabling and supporting each other's weaknesses, as so often happens by default in relationships. Holding a clear focus throughout the ceremony, and actively infusing new, higher frequencies into the energetic structure of your home during the final part of a ceremony, takes this a stage further and adds new levels of possibilities for everyone.

Passive participation by others

If you share your home with other people who do not wish to be involved in the space clearing ceremony, you can still go ahead, providing you are the head of the household, or one of the joint heads of the household, and they have given their permission for you to clear any areas of the property they have use of. It will work best to do the space clearing when they are not at home.

If they don't give this permission, or you decide not to even ask them, then the only areas you can clear are those that you solely occupy and use yourself (you can find more information about this in the next chapter).

Space clearing always needs to be done for the benefit of everyone who lives in a place, not just the person doing the ceremony or those who decide to participate in it. However, don't try to guess what the focus of non-participating household members might be. That would be a bottom-up, not a top-down approach. Always do a space clearing ceremony for each person's highest good, without specifying what you think that might be.

Children

There is no need to invite children under 8 years old to clarify their focus for a space clearing ceremony. This is because they will generally not be able to see the bigger picture at such a young age, so they are more likely to come up with a personal wish list.

Note that the age of 8 is only intended as a general guideline. There may be exceptions to this, depending on the maturity of the child, so use your own discretion.

26

Decide which rooms to include

Space clearing works best if you include all the rooms in your home. It may sometimes not be possible to do this, though, so you will need to keep the doors to any excluded rooms closed while the space clearing is in progress. You will need to know in advance if this applies to any rooms in your home so that you can calculate the quantities of flowers and candles you will need.

The main situations this applies to are:

- Any parts of your home that are difficult to access
- Any parts of your home that are rented to a tenant
- Any parts of your home that are occupied by someone who does not want those areas to be space cleared
- Any parts of your home that are occupied by someone who has mental health issues
- Any parts of your home where a person or pet is physically unwell
- Any parts of your home that are used for business and you want to keep those areas energetically separate

If any of these apply to you, please read the relevant information below.

Any parts of your home that are difficult to access

Exclude inaccessible basements and attics, as well as any rooms that are too cluttered or dangerous to easily walk around.

Any parts of your home that are rented to a tenant

It would be an invasion of a tenant's privacy to include their room in the ceremony without their permission. You must, therefore, exclude it unless they understand what space clearing is, voluntarily ask you to include their areas, and you are willing to do so.

Be aware, though, that this will cause the energies of your part of the home and your tenant's part of the home to be mixed, so this will only work well if you are on very good terms with them and they are like family. We do not recommend it otherwise.

Any parts of your home that are occupied by someone who does not want those areas to be space cleared

If you share your home with an adult (a spouse, for example) who has the same rights of occupation you have and does not want the areas they use to be included in the space clearing, you can only space clear the areas you have sole use of. This means you will have to exclude all communal areas, as well as their rooms (see Chapter 22 for more information).

If you are the parent or caregiver of a teenager or an adult child who does not want their areas to be included in a space clearing, that's different because they live under your auspices. You will only need to exclude the areas they have sole use of. It will be fine to include the communal areas.

Any parts of your home that are occupied by someone who has mental health issues

It may or may not be advisable to include these areas. Please read the section about this in Chapter 23.

Any parts of your home where a person or pet is physically unwell

In this situation, the room the person or pet is in must always be excluded from the space clearing unless they can temporarily be moved to another location during the ceremony. See Chapter 23 for more information about this.

Any parts of your home that are used for business and you want to keep those areas energetically separate

If you use some rooms of your home exclusively for work and it's important to you to keep your work life and your home life separate, space clear the home areas first, then do a separate ceremony for the rooms you use for your work, either on the same day or a day or two later.

27

Choose a date and time for the ceremony

This chapter will help you to estimate how long it will take you to space clear your home so that you can schedule the best date and time to do it.

How long does it take to do a space clearing ceremony?

There are a number of factors that need to be taken into account when estimating how long it will take you to do a space clearing:

- The size of your home
- The number of people who live in your home
- The amount of clutter in your home
- The history of what has happened in your home
- Your space clearing knowledge and skills

Here's the information you need to know about each of these.

The size of your home

The larger your home, the longer it will take to space clear it. Here are some rough estimates.

Basic Space Clearing

- Studio apartment: 15 minutes
- 2-bedroom apartment: 30 minutes
- 3- or 4-bedroom house: 1.5–2 hours

Essential Space Clearing

- Studio apartment: 30 minutes
- 2-bedroom apartment: 1 hour
- 3- or 4-bedroom house: 2–3 hours

Full Space Clearing

- Studio apartment: 1 hour
- 2-bedroom apartment: 2 hours
- 3- or 4-bedroom house: 3–4 hours

If your home has several floors, you will need to allow a bit of extra time for going up and down the stairs on each circuit.

If you generally prefer to do things at a slower pace, you will need to allow extra time for that too. However, please be aware that intentionally doing the ceremony slowly will usually not mean you'll get a better result. It will work best to do most of the steps at a lively, awakened pace.

The number of people who live in your home

The more people you share your home with, the greater the variety of energetic frequencies there will be in the space, which can often mean that the ceremony will take a bit longer.

The amount of clutter in your home

It always takes longer to space clear a home that has clutter. This is because stagnant energies accumulate around clutter, and the astral imprints in the space tend to be more densely embedded too. If the home is full of furniture, you will need to allow extra walking time too.

The history of what has happened in your home

It is much quicker and easier to space clear a new home that no one has ever lived in before than a deeply imprinted property that has had many prior occupants.

Your space clearing knowledge and skills

Expect it to take longer to do the ceremony the first time you do it, simply because it's new to you and you're learning the techniques as you go. This is why we recommend practising the main techniques ahead of time (see Chapter 28) so that you'll be more familiar with them.

The best time to do space clearing

Most people find it's easiest to do space clearing in the early part of the day, when they are at their freshest.

Some other factors to take into account when choosing a time are:

- When you will be able to stay at home for the rest of the day after the ceremony
- When you will be sleeping at home for at least a week after the ceremony
- When you can turn off your phone and not have any other interruptions or distractions
- When you can make arrangements for any children under 8 years old to be taken care of away from the home
- When you can make arrangements for any pets that need to be taken care of away from the home
- When only the people who live with you and wish to participate in the ceremony will be at home
- When all activities in your home can come to a complete standstill
- When no people or pets will be asleep in any of the rooms being space cleared
- Not on the day of a full moon, or two days before or after a full moon
- During daylight hours

Here's more information about each of these aspects.

Choose a time when you will be able to stay at home for the rest of the day after the ceremony

The hours after a space clearing are a very special time when the energies in your home feel fresh. You have the opportunity to fine-tune the new trajectory of your life in keeping with the focus of the ceremony. You will therefore get the most from an Essential or Full Space Clearing if you schedule to do the ceremony at a time when you can be at home for the rest of the day, enjoying the space and integrating the changes.

You can spend the time alone or with anyone you live with. Just don't invite any visitors to your home or any guests to sleep in your home that first night because that will introduce their frequencies into the space, which can impede the effectiveness of the changes brought about by the space clearing.

Choose a time when you will be sleeping at home for at least a week after the ceremony

After an Essential or Full Space Clearing ceremony, it usually takes about a week for all the changes to integrate. Much of this happens during the hours of sleep, so to receive the full benefit, choose a time when you will not be going on vacation or sleeping away from your home during the following week. It's fine to go out during the day, and it's fine for other people who live with you to go away. However, as MC of the ceremony, it will work best if you sleep in the home each night for the first week to hold the space. The effects of the space clearing will be deeper and will last substantially longer that way.

Of course, an exception to this would be if your reason for space clearing is because you are moving to a new home in the next few days (this version of the ceremony is explained in Part Four of *Space Clearing, Volume 2*). In that situation, no integration time is needed.

Choose a time when you can turn off your phone and not have any other interruptions or distractions

Space clearing your home is a giving to and an honouring of yourself, so don't skimp on it. Find a time when you can turn off your phone and let the world get on without you for a while. Also, do your best to avoid any interruptions. An unexpected phone call or visitor arriving will mean you have to stop the ceremony to deal with it. This will usually cause the momentum of the space clearing to fall flat, so it will need to be postponed until another time.

Choose a time when you can make arrangements for any children under 8 years old to be taken care of away from the home

Young children, and especially babies, are very susceptible to picking up energetic debris that is dislodged during a space clearing ceremony. They are also usually more sensitive to energy shifts than adults or may act up simply because the focus of attention is no longer on them. If they become unsettled during the ceremony, you will have to stop what you are doing to attend to them.

You will therefore need to make arrangements to have any children under 8 years old taken care of elsewhere for a few hours at the home of a relative or friend, or do the ceremony when they are at school. If you can't find someone to take care of your children for the entire duration of the ceremony, then at least make sure they are not present during the activation of flower offerings, when the greatest degree of stillness is required, or during the clapping and belling circuits, when the major clearing work is done.

Of course, 8 years old is only a guideline. Some older children may have no interest in space clearing and could cause havoc if they were present during a ceremony. Conversely, some younger children may have a deep wish to be present and have the maturity to do so. You know your own children best, so make your own decision about this accordingly.

There are also certain parts of the ceremony that young children can participate in. It usually works very well for children who are 3 years old or older to come back into the home for the harmony ball part of the ceremony, near the end. Providing they are able to sit quietly, they can be present while you're infusing the harmony ball. If you have an extra neutral harmony ball that you can give to them to use, they can join in the circuit where you go from room to room, following behind you and shaking out the new frequencies into the space. You, the adult, must be the one who does the actual frequencing. It won't work to give that level of responsibility to a child. They can follow around behind you, though. Most children really enjoy this, and because they're smaller than adults, they can get into places you wouldn't think of, such as under tables and in closets. It's very cute to see.

Choose a time when you can make arrangements for any pets that need to be taken care of away from the home

Most animals are a lot more sensitive to energy changes than humans. Some like to be around during a space clearing. Others prefer not to be there. You won't know how your pet will react until you do the ceremony, so it's wise to make some preparations beforehand.

If your pet has a way of leaving if it wants to (to a garden or balcony, for example), then simply make sure that the exit route is available throughout the ceremony.

If your pet is caged or has no way of exiting, it will be best to make arrangements for it to be taken care of elsewhere during the ceremony. Or you can put it in your garage or shed, if you have one, providing it will not be too hot, too cold, or unsettling. If none of these suggestions are practical or desirable then proceed very carefully, checking from time to time that your pet is OK, and be prepared to abandon the ceremony if it becomes distressed. It's unlikely, but it can happen.

Some pets may also need to be taken care of elsewhere if they will be too disruptive during the ceremony (a noisy or attention-seeking dog, for example).

Choose a time when only the people who live with you and wish to participate in the ceremony will be at home

Never space clear when you have guests staying with you or people present who do not usually live in your home. This is because their energies will become woven into the space, which can feel very odd and create a whole range of problems. If you have adult children who have a room in your home but no longer live with you most of the time, do the ceremony when they are not present. If you employ staff, schedule the ceremony for a time when they will not be there.

It's also important to make sure that everyone present understands what you are doing. Space clearing moves energies in people as well as in the space. If someone starts to feel unfamiliar shifts of energy and they don't know why, they can react with fear, distress, irritation, or a whole range of other emotions. If you attempt to reassure them by explaining how space clearing works, this will interrupt the flow of the ceremony. Until you are very experienced, it is best to work alone and only invite other occupants of the home to be present who have read this book and understand what you are doing and why.

Choose a time when all activities in your home can come to a complete standstill

For space clearing to be effective, all activities in the home need to come to a stop, including children or pets running around the space. All computers, tablets, phones, TVs, radios, and other gadgets need to be turned off so that the focus of everyone present is exclusively on the ceremony. It is therefore usually best for anyone who is not actively participating in the space clearing to leave for a few hours while it is in progress.

One exception to this would be where an adult member of the household has specifically asked for their room to be excluded from the space clearing and they have agreed to stay in that room throughout the ceremony, engaged in a silent activity of some kind.

Choose a time when no people or pets will be asleep in any of the rooms being space cleared

During sleep, there is an opening of a person's etheric body that can make them vulnerable to picking up some of the energies that are being cleared. If someone needs to take a nap while you are preparing to do the ceremony (Steps 1 to 14), that's fine. Just make sure no one is asleep in the entire area you are space clearing after you start Step 15. That includes pets, too.

Choose a time that is not on the day of a full moon, or two days before or after a full moon

Even the professional space clearers we train, who can get great results at any time, never do space clearings on the day of a full moon. Global energies can be much too chaotic at that time. When space clearing your own home, we also recommend you don't schedule doing it during the two days before a full moon or two days after.

If the emphasis of the ceremony is more about making a fresh start than on clearing out old energies, it can work very well to do it on the first day of a new moon.

Choose a time during daylight hours

Some spiritual practices work best during the day. Some work best at night. Space clearing has a strong affinity with solar forces, so it's most definitely a daytime ceremony.

If you live in a part of the world where it gets dark in the afternoon during the winter months, then it may not be possible to conduct the entire ceremony during daylight hours. That's fine, providing you start while there is still some sunlight and you switch on lights in all the rooms as the daylight fades.

In parts of the world, such as the northern regions of Canada and Scandinavia, where there is continuous daylight for some months of the year and continuous darkness for the other months, do the ceremony during what would normally be daytime hours, not at night-time. There is a tangible energetic difference between the two.

28

Practise the main space clearing techniques

You will need to practise the main space clearing techniques before doing a ceremony so that you can do them without referring to this book. If you try to learn them while doing your first ceremony, it will only be minimally effective or may not work at all.

The main techniques are:

- Breathing and throat friction
- Hand sensing
- Belling
- Making space clearing water
- Activating a flower offering
- Clapping

We have included a brief description of each technique here. You can find more detailed information later in the book and more in-depth information about how each technique works in *Space Clearing, Volume 2*.

Breathing and throat friction

The breathing and throat friction techniques used during space clearing are described in Chapter 10. Throat friction is very simple to learn, yet it is one of the most powerful spiritual techniques there is, with many applications.

When you first learn to do throat friction, it will probably sound quite loud (a bit like Darth Vader breath). With practice, you can achieve the same results silently.

Hand sensing

The hand-sensing technique is described in Chapter 33, Step 12. To start developing this skill, it is much easier to hand sense the etheric energies that emanate from living beings than to feel the subtler vibrations of buildings and objects in your home. It's therefore a good idea to practise on plants, pets, and any friends who willingly volunteer for this.

Cats are generally the easiest to work with and the most receptive. If you stroke a cat just above its fur, it will feel it and will usually respond by arching its back in the same way it does when being physically stroked. Be sure to energetically stroke from head to tail. They are likely to become annoyed if you do it the other way around, just as they do if you physically stroke them against the lie of their fur.

Belling

There's a lot more to ringing a Balinese bell than just picking it up and shaking it.

How to hold a Balinese space clearing bell

The correct way to hold a Balinese bell is to pick it up by the handle between your thumb, forefinger, and middle finger of your dominant hand. Hold it firmly enough that you don't drop it but not so tightly that your hand is tense. If you hold the bell too far down or too far up the handle, you will have less control of the sound it makes. The large and small bells have both been designed so that there is a narrow, comfortable spot to hold them halfway up the handle.

After picking up the bell in this way, pull your shoulders back, align your head vertically with your spine, raise your elbow to shoulder level, and bend your elbow so that your forearm is at a 90-degree angle to your body. This is the position to hold during the entire belling circuit to create minimal strain and maximum effectiveness.

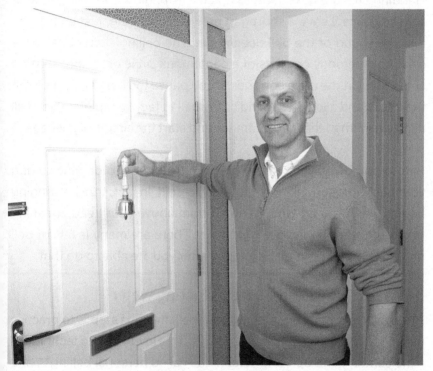

How to hold a Balinese space clearing bell

How to ring a Balinese space clearing bell

The first time you try to ring a Balinese bell, the clapper will probably circulate inside the dome instead of moving from side to side, which will cause the bell to make a discordant, jarring noise. The most likely reason for this is that you are trying to ring the bell by moving your arm. You will need to learn to keep your elbow and shoulder perfectly still while rotating your wrist from side to side so that the clapper inside the bell moves smoothly and precisely from side to side. This will produce the clear, resonant sound that is needed to do space clearing.

After you have learned to control the sound of the bell while you are standing still, the next thing to practise is ringing it while walking at a steady pace. Leave a short gap between each ring, just enough so that the sound of the bell doesn't die. The belling circuit in a space clearing ceremony consists of a continuous circle of sound, starting and ending at the main entrance. If you pause too long at any point in the circuit and allow the sound of the bell to fade completely, you will need to return to the main entrance and start the circuit all over again.

Before doing your first space clearing, you need to be able to ring your bell without thinking about how to do it. In fact, true bell ringing begins when you are able to ring it from above your head, meaning from verticality*, not from your mind. There are many levels of bell ringing skills that can be developed after you are able to do that.

Making space clearing water

After you have practised ringing your bell, the next step is to practise using it to make space clearing water**. This involves two techniques – the centring and uplifting* technique called personal belling**, and presencing* the water. You can find detailed information about both techniques in Chapter 33, Step 15.

For personal belling to be effective, you will need to learn to ring your bell and keep it perfectly vertical as you raise it in front of your body, following the energetic line of the central channel of energy that runs up the centre of your body and the central thread of your column above*. Be careful to avoid any extra accidental ringing of the bell as you do this. We recommend practising this a few times in front of a mirror to check that you do not tilt the bell or slant it off to one side when you lift it above your head, which many people make the mistake of doing, usually because of gripping the bell too tightly.

Presencing the water needs even more practice because it involves several techniques that need to be done simultaneously.

Activating a flower offering

You can find instructions in Chapter 33, Step 16 for how to light a flower offering, sprinkle it with space clearing water, and activate it. You will need to practise this many times, until you are able to do it confidently and fluidly, without referring to this book or your own notes.

Clapping

Clapping sounds very easy. It's something we all do without thinking when we applaud someone on stage. But the clapping technique used in space clearing is very different and will need to be practised, if you want it to be effective. The technique is described in Chapter 33, Step 17.

***

Please return to this chapter after you have read the rest of this book and gained a better understanding of how these techniques fit into the ceremony.

29

Clear your clutter

One of the most important steps to prepare for space clearing is to clear out any clutter you have accumulated. The more thoroughly you do this, the better your space clearing results will be.

Restoring integrity

Clutter clearing is the art of restoring integrity to your life, one item at a time. It's the process of sorting through all your belongings and letting go of all the things that no longer fit with who you are or where you are headed. Until you do that, you don't own your stuff – it owns you. And you will only be able to live life bottom-up, which is the exact opposite of the changes that space clearing is designed to bring about – to own your space top-down.

Some people feel dismayed to learn that they will need to roll up their sleeves and tackle the very mundane level of clutter clearing first. They want to get straight to space clearing, hoping it will fix everything else. What they don't realize is how spiritually disconnecting clutter is and how spiritually awakening clearing it out can be. We warmly encourage you to change your attitude and embrace clutter clearing with enthusiasm.

Clutter is stuck energy

Never underestimate the effects of clutter on your life. Your home is a reflection of you. Whenever you feel stuck in some way, there will always be a corresponding stuck energy of some kind in your home.

Healthy energy in a home is moving energy. Clutter accumulates when energy stagnates, and likewise, energy stagnates when clutter accumulates.

Think what happens when a pool of water becomes stagnant. It quickly becomes murky and starts to smell. This is similar to what happens energetically when you live surrounded by clutter. When we visit someone's home, we can smell clutter, even if it's stashed away out of sight. The musty odour that surrounds it is unmistakable. It's not a physical smell, although it can sometimes be accompanied by one. And this doesn't only apply to a person's home. The energetic frequencies and odour of clutter also accompany them wherever they go.

> **Karen**: After a talk I once gave about the frequencies of clutter, a woman queuing to get her copy of my book signed asked me, "Can you tell what kind of clutter I have at home?" The ears of everyone waiting in line immediately pricked up to listen to my reply.
>
> "Yes," I replied, after taking a few moments to tune into her energy. "You like soft things – fabrics, clothing, cuddly toys, that kind of thing. And you love stationery. Stationery shops are a magnet for you."
>
> Her adult son, standing next to her, was so impressed that he jumped in too. "What about me?" he asked. I could tell that he had hardly any physical clutter, but he loved to collect digital apps. The way his mother rolled her eyes at what I said was all the confirmation I needed.

On another occasion, a journalist who was interviewing me asked if I thought she had any clutter at home. "You have a thing about sexy underwear," I told her. "Not just the odd item. You have a whole drawer full of it."

"Enough!" she said. "That's far too much detail!"

For the reassurance of anyone who may one day meet either of us, we don't tune in this way to everyone we spend time with. It's a skill we can turn on or off as we choose, according to the requirements of a situation. It's certainly not something we do automatically. There is far too much clutter in the world for us to want to do that.

Why there's very little point doing any kind of personal development work if you haven't cleared your clutter first

Karen remembers the moment it first dawned on her what an uphill battle it is to do any form of personal development work without clearing your clutter first. It was at a self-help workshop she attended in 1990, when she took a minute to look around the audience.

As she moved her gaze from person to person and tuned in to their energy, she could easily see who had clutter at home and who did not. And she realized that the people who were going back to a clutter-filled home really wouldn't get much benefit from the workshop at all because there was no space in their life for anything new. Their time would have been better spent staying at home for the weekend and sorting through their stuff. Or rather, their time would have been better spent the previous weekend (or previous week, month or year, in some cases) sorting through their belongings so that they could attend the workshop and be ready to put into action what they learned.

The benefits of clutter clearing

Most people who have a lot of clutter say they can't find the energy to begin to clear it. They constantly feel tired. That's because we are energetically connected to everything we own. Living surrounded by clutter is like dragging the weight of your past around with you everywhere you go. Of course that will make you feel tired.

Clearing clutter releases huge amounts of energy. You will feel lighter and freer as you let each load go. And when you only have things around you that are useful and meaningful to you, you can live in present time instead of being anchored in the past.

Karen explains in *Clear Your Clutter with Feng Shui*:

> The higher purpose of clutter clearing is to help to clear the debris that prevents us from connecting to the high spiritual realms from whence we came and to which we will return. It is all too easy to lose the plot down here, get immersed in materialism, and come to believe that this world is all there is, when in fact being here is only a short interlude in the spiritual journey each of us is on.

> Clutter clearing in all its forms helps to restore clarity and simplicity. When you keep around you just the things you need for your personal journey instead of burdening yourself with things that obscure your way and hold you back, it makes it much easier for you to connect with your spiritual path. And when you have the sense of peace and purpose that comes with that, you will never feel the need for clutter again.

Getting the right balance

It continually amazes us how people invest time, money, and effort in doing spiritual work for years and yet still have clutter at home. Their spiritual progress will always be limited by the stuff they are holding on to. Clearing it is much more important than most people realize.

This is not to say that you have to relinquish all your possessions and live an ascetic way of life. That was a popular method in times gone by. What is needed now is to be able to engage a spiritual path while still being part of the world.

History abounds with tales of people who renounced all worldly possessions in their quest to find enlightenment. After much self-deprivation, even the Buddha discovered that The Middle Way was a more wholesome approach – having enough to satisfy one's needs but not so much as to be self-indulgent.

Our approach to this is similar. It's only over-attachment to material things that causes imbalance. Each person is here on earth for a purpose, so the possessions you keep around you need to reflect this – not so few that you can't do what you're here to do, and not so many that you are burdened or held back. Keep around you the things that you need for your daily life and a few possessions that bring joy to your heart, and let the rest go.

The inescapable fact of life is that no one can take any of their belongings with them when they die. We are born with nothing, and we die with nothing. The things we acquire while we're here can help or hinder us in our journey, but they are all stripped away at the end. Forming too much attachment to material things is spiritually disconnecting and ultimately futile.

Understanding the underlying reasons for clutter

The important thing to understand about clutter is that it is only ever a symptom of underlying issues. Decluttering is not really about clearing physical items at all. It's about working through the mental, emotional, and spiritual issues that caused it to accumulate in the first place.

If you have a lot of clutter at the moment, it will be because, for some reason, you have felt you needed it. Understanding the reasons for this will help you to begin to let it go and not need to accumulate more of it again in the future.

In our experience, any method of helping people to clear their clutter that does not address this deeper level of sourcing emotions means it will only be a matter of time before new clutter appears to replace the old.

> **Karen**: Twice in my life I have let go of everything I owned and started again. Both times it was a scary yet incredibly revitalizing experience, a real turning point in my life.
>
> The first time I radically decluttered was when I was 19 years old and living in England. I had just ended a relationship with a boyfriend and decided to move from one end of the country to the other. I didn't own a car at that time, so I packed a change of clothes and left everything else with him to use or dispose of as he wished. He was fine with this arrangement, and many years later he turned up at one of my clutter clearing talks in London and told me he liked my stuff so much that he still had some of it.
>
> The second time was when I was 37 and owned a whole apartment full of things. I decided to move from the UK to

Bali and not take anything with me. I sold all my furniture to a friend, sold everything else at a market, and got on a plane the next day.

In both cases, the decluttering was accomplished within a week of deciding to do it, and I never looked back. By the time I left for Bali, I no longer owned a single possession from my childhood, teenage years, twenties, or thirties, and was as free as a bird.

I've also been fortunate to find a husband who shares the same attitude to possessions. In fact, Richard is the only person I know who has let go of everything and started a new life even more times than me.

Richard: My relationship to physical belongings has always been very different to that of most of the people I know. I enjoy the things I have but have never held on to stuff. My approach has been to open and embrace each new opportunity in my life, to discover and explore. I believe that's the way we're designed to be. Trying to hold onto things is holding on to the past, which is nearly always rooted in fear.

When I was 16, I decided to become a chef. I knew I had chosen a profession that would involve a lot of travel. I moved from job to job around Australia and later to various locations around the world. Each time, I let go of everything I owned and took only a suitcase or two with me.

The same thing happened when I met Karen and moved to Bali to live with her, and again five years later when we sold everything in Bali and moved to the UK. The only items I still have from the early years of my life are a handful of photos, 12 books, and some of my best-quality chef's knives, which Karen and I still use each day.

Such radical clutter clearing is certainly not for everyone, we know. It only feels purposeful and liberating if you have a very clear idea of the next important step to take in your journey after you've lightened your load.

A lovely analogy for this can be found in Brian Tracy's book *Eat That Frog!* It comes from an experience he had of crossing a bleak 500-mile stretch of the Sahara Desert, where over 1,300 people had lost their way and died. Then someone had the bright idea to place a 55-gallon oil barrel every 5 kilometres (3 miles) to mark the route. After that, all anyone had to do was drive from one oil barrel to the next. The last oil barrel and the next one would always be in sight, so no one ever got lost again.

The concept of "one oil barrel at a time" can also be applied to navigating through life. Get clear about your next step, and off you go. If you can't yet see the next step, wait until you can. But wait proactively, not passively. Research, explore, and be relentless in your quest until you get that next oil barrel in your sights. Clutter clearing to let go of anything you no longer need and space clearing to clear and revitalize the energies in your home will both help enormously to bring more clarity and integrity to your life.

Is it always best to do clutter clearing before space clearing?

The ideal order is to do clutter clearing first, then space clearing. However, if you find it difficult to get started with clutter clearing, it is possible to do space clearing first, providing there's enough physically clear space to be able to walk around the inner perimeters of the rooms in your home. Space clearing will revitalize the stagnant energies that have collected around your clutter, which will make it much easier to clear.

If you do space clearing before clutter clearing, we recommend doing space clearing again after you finish clutter clearing, with the focus on what you aspire to in your life now that you are no longer burdened by all your stuff. It takes a bit more work to do it this way around, it's true, but it's better than being immobilized by your clutter and not being able to move forward at all.

How to clear your clutter

There are four categories of clutter:

- Things you do not use or love
- Things that are untidy or disorganized
- Too many things in too small a space
- Anything unfinished

If you have so much clutter you feel you don't even know where to begin, then we suggest you put a bookmark in this book right now and read Karen's *Clear Your Clutter with Feng Shui* book first, which will explain these four categories in depth and take you through the entire clutter clearing process, step by step. That book was written in response to the vast numbers of people who contacted her to say they purchased her first book about space clearing and never got past the chapter about clutter clearing.

If you prefer a more interactive approach, check our website for a range of other types of clutter clearing help, including online courses, personal sessions, and our directory of certified clutter clearing practitioners.

30

Clean and tidy your home

When preparing to do a space clearing, the next step after clutter clearing is to clean and tidy your entire home from top to bottom.

This would be too daunting a task for most people to do and then do space clearing the same day, so aim to do this on the day or days before a ceremony.

If the reason for doing space clearing is to help you to declutter and you can't face doing a major clean-up first, then at least take the time to clean all the floors and tidy up as much as possible.

Cleaning

The best type of cleaning before a space clearing is the equivalent of a major spring clean.

As well as cleaning all the surfaces where dust and grime gathers, clean all the awkward bits too – under beds, on top of cupboards and picture frames, behind wardrobes, sofas, and other large items of furniture, inside bathroom cabinets, inside your fridge, your dishwasher, and so on.

If you want to be really thorough, clean the types of equipment that have ventilation grilles where dust and fluff accumulate over time, computer keyboards that can fill with all kinds of debris, and any other small areas that need attention because they are rarely cleaned. Go this extra mile, not as a chore but because the object is a part of your life and you wish to honour yourself. Everything in your home reflects an aspect of you.

The most effective way to clean is in keeping with the laws of gravity. If your home occupies more than one floor, start at the top of the house and work down. Then start with the highest places first in each room, such as the tops of cupboards, door frames, and pictures hung on the wall. Finish by sweeping, mopping, or vacuuming the floors, using whatever method works best for the type of floor surfaces you have.

It's necessary to understand that high-level energies collect in high places and low-level energies collect in low places. Our experience of people who live in mountainous regions is that they are often more optimistic than people who live in valleys, where the energies tend to collect and stagnate. It is much easier to feel elated on top, looking down, than at the bottom, looking up.

This is also why penthouse suites are so sought after, because the people living there have an energetic advantage over people living at lower levels. Living in a basement apartment can be challenging, partly because of the gloomy quality of daylight they tend to have and partly because of the quantities of dust and low-level energies that gather there.

In all rooms, low-level energies collect at floor level, so sweeping, mopping, and vacuuming immediately helps to remedy this. In fact, if your home needs a quick pick-me-up, doing a once-around with a vacuum cleaner works wonders. Don't get obsessive about vacuuming, though. One woman Karen knew used to vacuum her entire home several times a day, which left the energy of the space feeling raw. She became so touchy that she would get angry with anyone who said a word (or put a foot) out of place.

In most Asian cultures it is common practice to remove your shoes before entering a home. This is because it's well understood that footwear picks up low-level energies from the ground and becomes imprinted with the emanations of the feet. All footwear is strictly forbidden in most indoor temples, in order to preserve the purity of the space.

If you've always worn outdoor shoes inside your home, there will be a gunky layer of energy at floor level that probably feels normal to you, so it won't change much if you stop wearing shoes indoors. If you make a fresh start by cleaning your carpets and washing your floors, and especially if you space clear your home too, then a no outdoor shoes rule will make a very noticeable difference. You'll wonder why you never thought of it before.

Tidying and organizing

The art of tidying and organizing is about giving everything you own a place where it lives and putting it back where it belongs after each time you use it. This creates a structure in the space that your consciousness can rest on.

Some people find this very easy to do. But if you were never taught how to tidy and organize things when you were young, "a place for everything and everything in its place" might as well be words from an obscure language for all the sense they will make.

No place for anything and nothing in its place

If you have no laundry system, a wet towel left on the bathroom floor is "in its place". If you have no method of storing items in closets and drawers, things left out in the open are "in their place". And if you have no filing system for paperwork, documents are "in their place" wherever they happen to end up after they enter your home or wherever you place them to remind you to take an action of some kind.

The problem is that piles of things will grow if not tended to. Soon you'll have a heap of used towels on the bathroom floor and none you can use to dry yourself. Eventually, you have so many things scattered around your home that it will sometimes be easier to go out and buy a new item than to find the one you know you have. And paperwork will become such a jumbled nightmare that you'll do your best to ignore it and carry on as best you can.

Without a daily tidying routine and organized storage systems, life very quickly gets out of control.

Three steps to tidying and organizing your home

The three steps to tidying and organizing a messy home are:

- Group items into categories
- Store similar categories together
- Have a daily tidy-up to keep everything organized

The best way to explain this is by giving an example. Suppose you decide to tidy your kitchen utensils. Most people have at least a few unnecessary items hiding in their kitchen drawers.

First, group them into categories, such as all the peelers together, all the graters together, and so on. This helps you to see how many of each item you have and weed out those you don't need.

Then store similar things together. For example, if you have four drawers in your kitchen, you may divide your utensils into four groups, like this:

- Food preparation utensils such as peelers, graters, slicers, and knives
- Cooking utensils such as spatulas, wooden spoons, whisks, and mashers
- Serving utensils such as large spoons, ladles, and tongs
- Gadgets such as can openers, corkscrews, timers, and measuring tools

This makes it much easier to find things when you need them. And to make it easier still, use drawer organizers to split each drawer into separate areas, such as one section for peelers, one for graters, and so on (do an internet search for "drawer organizers" to find what options are available in your part of the world).

The final step is to understand that tidying is never just a one-time event. Each time you use a utensil, you'll need to wash it, dry it, and put it back where it belongs, ready for the next time. This is a cornerstone habit to develop.

The best way to develop any new habit is to link it to something you already do so that it becomes automatic. In this example, it might be that each time you finish eating, you straight away wash up, dry, and put away everything you used for the preparation and serving of that meal. If you have a dishwasher, you can stack everything in there, and get into the habit of running it when it's full and unloading it before you cook the next meal. At the very least, aim to clean and tidy your kitchen at the end of each day so that you start the next morning fresh.

31

Buy space clearing materials

A day or two before a space clearing ceremony, buy any materials you need (see Chapter 18 for more detailed information).

Basic Space Clearing

- Brass cleaner and two soft polishing cloths
- Unscented hand cream (if needed)

Essential Space Clearing

- 5–6 flower heads, approximately the same size
- A mini carnation (white or pastel coloured)
- An unscented tealight candle in a holder
- Long matches
- An unopened bottle of still spring water
- Brass cleaner and two soft polishing cloths
- Unscented hand cream (if needed)

Full Space Clearing

- Flower heads (quantity determined by the size of your home)
- A mini carnation (white or pastel coloured)
- Unscented tealight candles in holders
- Long matches
- An unopened bottle of still spring water
- Brass cleaner and two soft polishing cloths
- Unscented hand cream (if needed)

32

Clean and polish your space clearing kit

Space clearing is about purification, so of course you need to cleanse yourself before doing a ceremony and cleanse the equipment you will be using too.

When using ritual items, the respectful way you handle them and the care you put into cleaning them all counts. When you take this approach instead of doing the rushed minimum you think you can get away with, the result is very different. It will help to open the space for you to conduct the ceremony at a higher level.

This is why we recommend preparing your space clearing kit the evening before the ceremony, or if that's not possible, the morning before. Don't stop part of the way through a ceremony to do it.

It's also why we advise keeping the cloths you use for cleaning your space clearing equipment separate from any you use for household cleaning or other mundane purposes, in order not to mix frequencies.

Space clearing equipment

Your space clearing bell and harmony ball(s)

The dome of a space clearing bell is made of a special type of bronze. Harmony balls are made of electroplated brass. Both will become tarnished over time, so it's usually necessary and always desirable to polish them before a space clearing ceremony. It only takes a few minutes, and the resulting shine makes the effort very worthwhile.

You can find information about how to clean a Balinese bell in Chapter 14 and how to clean harmony balls in Chapter 15.

If needed, from time to time the wooden handle of your bell and the wooden harmony ball stand or plate can be cleaned with a damp cloth.

To reduce tarnishing, store your bell and harmony ball(s) in their boxes between space clearing ceremonies.

Space clearing water pot and saucer

Make sure your space clearing water pot and saucer are sparking clean by washing them and then drying them with a paper towel or tissues.

Household items

A white tablecloth

Check that your white tablecloth is clean, ironed, and ready to use.

Small plate(s) or saucer(s)

Check that these items are clean and ready to use.

PART SIX

How to do space clearing

33

The 21 steps to space clearing your own home

Please read this entire chapter and any additional chapters that are referred to if they are relevant to your situation. Do this at least a few days before your first ceremony so that you will know in advance what is involved.

If you are space clearing someone else's home, you will also need to read Chapter 36.

Choose which level of space clearing to do

The three levels of space clearing described in this book are:

- Basic Space Clearing
- Essential Space Clearing
- Full Space Clearing

Basic Space Clearing

This is the quickest and easiest version of space clearing there is, and the best one to start with. The only equipment you'll need is a Balinese space clearing bell and stand, a harmony ball and stand, and a small white tablecloth.

Essential Space Clearing

Essential Space Clearing takes a bit longer to do and requires more equipment than Basic Space Clearing, but it's quicker and easier than doing a Full Space Clearing ceremony because there is no need to create a full altar and you only need one flower offering.

Full Space Clearing

This is the most effective version of space clearing. It requires a Full Space Clearing kit, so it's usually not the level most people start with.

Space clearing ceremony checklists

You can find a checklist for each version of the ceremony on the following pages so that you will know which steps to include and which to omit.

Be sure to do the steps in the prescribed order and don't add any extras. Doing so will weaken the effectiveness of the ceremony, not improve it.

Basic Space Clearing

☐ Step 1:   Do not attempt space clearing if you feel any fear or apprehension

☐ Step 2:   Check that you are in integrity

☐ Step 3:   Check your personal fitness to do space clearing

☐ Step 4:   Check that any people or pets present are in good health

☐ Step 5:   Remove any metal you are wearing

☐ Step 6:   Take a bath or shower and put on clean clothing

☐ Step 7:   Do the ceremony barefoot, if it is practical to do so

☐ Step 8:   Put food and drinks away

☐ Step 9:   Open at least one window on each floor

☐ Step 10: Bring the space to a standstill

☐ Step 11: Roll up your sleeves, and wash your hands and forearms

☐ Step 12: Do a circuit of hand sensing (optional)

Step 13: (Omit this step)

Step 14: (Omit this step)

Step 15: (Omit this step)

Step 16: (Omit this step)

☐ Step 17: Do a circuit of clapping

☐ Step 18: Wash your hands and forearms

☐ Step 19: Do a circuit of belling

☐ Step 20: Do harmony ball infusion and frequencing

☐ Step 21: Resense the energy (optional)

Essential Space Clearing

☐ Step 1: Do not attempt space clearing if you feel any fear or apprehension

☐ Step 2: Check that you are in integrity

☐ Step 3: Check your personal fitness to do space clearing

☐ Step 4: Check that any people or pets present are in good health

☐ Step 5: Remove any metal you are wearing

☐ Step 6: Take a bath or shower and put on clean clothing

☐ Step 7: Do the ceremony barefoot, if it is practical to do so

☐ Step 8: Put food and drinks away

☐ Step 9: Open at least one window on each floor

☐ Step 10: Bring the space to a standstill

☐ Step 11: Roll up your sleeves, and wash your hands and forearms

☐ Step 12: Do a circuit of hand sensing

☐ Step 13: Create one flower offering

☐ Step 14: Create a space clearing altar

☐ Step 15: Make some space clearing water

☐ Step 16: Activate the flower offering

☐ Step 17: Do a circuit of clapping

☐ Step 18: Wash your hands and forearms

☐ Step 19: Do a circuit of belling

☐ Step 20: Do harmony ball infusion and frequencing

☐ Step 21: Resense the energy

Full Space Clearing

- ☐ Step 1: Do not attempt space clearing if you feel any fear or apprehension
- ☐ Step 2: Check that you are in integrity
- ☐ Step 3: Check your personal fitness to do space clearing
- ☐ Step 4: Check that any people or pets present are in good health
- ☐ Step 5: Remove any metal you are wearing
- ☐ Step 6: Take a bath or shower and put on clean clothing
- ☐ Step 7: Do the ceremony barefoot, if it is practical to do so
- ☐ Step 8: Put food and drinks away
- ☐ Step 9: Open at least one window on each floor
- ☐ Step 10: Bring the space to a standstill
- ☐ Step 11: Roll up your sleeves, and wash your hands and forearms
- ☐ Step 12: Do a circuit of hand sensing
- ☐ Step 13: Create flower offerings
- ☐ Step 14: Create a space clearing altar
- ☐ Step 15: Make some space clearing water
- ☐ Step 16: Activate the flower offerings
- ☐ Step 17: Do a circuit of clapping
- ☐ Step 18: Wash your hands and forearms
- ☐ Step 19: Do a circuit of belling
- ☐ Step 20: Do harmony ball infusion and frequencing
- ☐ Step 21: Resense the energy

Step 1
Do not attempt space clearing
if you feel any fear or apprehension

☑ Basic Space Clearing

☑ Essential Space Clearing

☑ Full Space Clearing

Always use discernment when deciding whether to do space clearing.

Most people can safely do space clearing in their own home using the information in this book, especially if they have already lived in it for some time. If this is your situation, you will already be immersed in the energies of the place where you live, so you will not be exposing yourself to anything new.

However, there are some cautions that always need to be observed, and one of the most important is to check if you feel any fear or apprehension about doing the ceremony. This is particularly important if you are moving into a new home or have been asked by a close friend or relative to space clear their home.

There are unsavoury energies that can be found in houses, such as entities and the residues of violent, abusive, and traumatic events. If you feel any fear or apprehension about doing space clearing, listen to those feelings and do not override them. It usually means you will need to get professional help instead of attempting to space clear it yourself. This kind of situation rarely happens, but it's important to be aware that it can.

Energetic protection

In case you are thinking of using energy protection techniques you may have heard of, we have included a chapter about this topic in *Space Clearing, Volume 2* to explain why most of these methods have no effect at all.

It's possible to develop the ability to open and close your energy, and if you're interested to learn how to do this, the techniques are described in detail in Chapters 17 to 21 of *Awakening the Third Eye* by Samuel Sagan. This is not something you can learn in a few minutes, of course. It takes most people years to develop the ability to seal their energy at will, and even so, the protection it offers will never be complete.

Your best protection when doing one of the three levels of the space clearing ceremony described in this book is to carefully follow all the guidelines and steps, observe all the warnings, do not take shortcuts, and do not add techniques you have invented yourself or learned elsewhere.

Step 2
Check that you are in integrity

☑ *Basic Space Clearing*
☑ *Essential Space Clearing*
☑ *Full Space Clearing*

Space clearing is about restoring integrity to spaces, so the first thing to check is that you are fully in integrity yourself.

- Do not use the information in this book to do professional space clearings
- Make sure you have no personal agenda
- Check your level of involution
- Check the suitability of the place for space clearing

Here's more information about each of these aspects.

Do not use the information in this book to do professional space clearings

This book contains so much information that it may give the impression it can be used as a manual to conduct a professional space clearing.

Please don't make that mistake.

It is much more detailed than Karen's first space clearing book (*Creating Sacred Space with Feng Shui*), but still only contains, at most, about 20% of the knowledge and skills needed to do space clearing safely and effectively at practitioner level, as we explain in Chapter 39. It would therefore be completely out of integrity to use it to conduct space clearings for paying clients.

Make sure you have no personal agenda

If you share your home with other people, make sure before doing space clearing that you have no personal agenda about the outcome. You must want to do the ceremony for the highest good of all the occupants of your home, with no ulterior motive to manipulate the results for your own purposes, no bias to create benefits for one person more than another, and no intention to fix anyone you perceive as needing to be fixed.

These agendas can arise if you try to conduct a space clearing ceremony at the level of ordinary mental consciousness, where it's all too easy to get embroiled in relationship dynamics and your own likes and dislikes. The best way to avoid this is by being involuted.

Check your level of involution

The entire space clearing ceremony needs to be done at a more involuted level of consciousness than that of everyday life. Being involuted will help you to hold awareness of the focus as a packed thought above your head instead of as a stream of unpacked thoughts or an intention of your mind. It will also enable you to do the techniques from a higher level of consciousness.

If you meditate, the best time to schedule a space clearing is straight after your morning practice, at a time when there will be no interruptions or distractions and you can bring all activities in your home to a standstill. At the very least, allow some time to wind down from your everyday activities before starting a space clearing ceremony.

Please reread Chapter 11 about involution and Chapter 25 about clarifying the focus of a ceremony if you need to refresh your memory about either of these aspects.

Check the suitability of the place for space clearing

The three levels of space clearing ceremonies described in this book are designed to be done in a home where you are the head of the household or a joint head of the household (see Chapter 22 for more information about this). It can also be used to space clear the homes of close friends and relatives (see Chapter 36), if they request it and you have already successfully space cleared your own home at least once and ideally several times, so that you are very familiar with the ceremony.

It may not be advisable to do space clearing in any of these situations

- If someone in your home has mental health issues
- If a person or pet in your home is unwell (see Step 4)
- If your home is so cluttered that it's impossible to walk around the inner perimeter of the space

Do NOT do space clearing in any of these places

- Public buildings (unless you are renting the space)
- Hospitals, hospices, and other places where sickness or death are common
- Churches or temples that have been consecrated to a particular religion or spiritual stream
- A place where there has been a suicide, murder, violent crime, or other traumatic event
- A place where someone you knew has recently died and you are still grieving their loss
- A business you do not own
- The guest room of a friend you are visiting (unless they give their permission)
- Outdoor areas

If any of these situations apply to you, please reread the relevant information in Chapter 23 before proceeding.

Step 3
Check your personal fitness to do space clearing

☑ *Basic Space Clearing*

☑ *Essential Space Clearing*

☑ *Full Space Clearing*

You need to be fit to do space clearing and free from the influence of any psychoactive drugs.

For ease of reference, we have included here a summary of the information earlier in the book about when not to do space clearing. If any of the situations listed here apply to you, please read the more detailed information in Chapter 21 before going any further.

Do NOT do space clearing in any of these situations

- If you are unwell
- If you are mentally or emotionally unstable
- If you feel tired or energetically depleted
- If you are pregnant or breastfeeding
- If you are menstruating
- If you have any gynaecological health problems
- If you have any open wounds or weeping eczema
- If you have recently taken any psychoactive drugs, including alcohol, sleeping pills, or tranquilizers; it's also advisable not to consume any sugar or caffeine before or during the ceremony

Step 4
Check that any people or
pets present are in good health

☑ *Basic Space Clearing*

☑ *Essential Space Clearing*

☑ *Full Space Clearing*

Make sure that only the people or pets who normally live in your home are present and that they are all in good health.

People and pets

Before space clearing, be sure to:

- Check that only the people who normally live in your home and wish to participate in the ceremony are present, except for babies and children under 8 years old
- Check that any people or pets who are present are in good health
- Check that there will not be any people or pets asleep in any of the rooms being space cleared

Check that only the people who normally live in your home and wish to participate in the ceremony are present, except for children under 8 years old

Don't do space clearing if you have any guests staying with you or any visitors, tradespeople, or staff in your home during the ceremony. You will also need to make arrangements for any children under 8 years old to be taken care of elsewhere. See Chapter 27 for more information about why.

Check that any people or pets who are present are in good health

If a person or pet is likely to be sick for only a few days, wait until they are better. If they have been physically or mentally unwell for some time, please be sure to read our advice about this in Chapter 23. It may only be possible for you to space clear certain rooms, or, in some cases, you may not be able to do space clearing at all.

Check that there will not be any people or pets asleep in any of the rooms being space cleared

Do not do space clearing while any people or pets are asleep in any of the rooms you are clearing. See Chapter 27 for an explanation.

Special precautions if you have pets

In many countries, around 50% of homes have a pet of some kind. Some pets love to be present during space clearing, and others really don't. If you have a pet, please read the relevant section of this chapter for guidance. Here's a list of the topics covered:

- Place flower offerings carefully to avoid any fire risk
- Place flower offerings where pets can't eat them
- Don't allow pets to climb up onto the altar
- Pets must be able to leave during the ceremony if they wish to
- Special precautions with dogs
- Special precautions with cats
- Special precautions with caged animals
- Special precautions with birds
- Special precautions with fish

Place flower offerings carefully to avoid any fire risk

When positioning each flower offering, choose a location that is a safe distance from any materials that could catch fire. If you have pets, take care not to place a flower offering where your pet could brush past it and set itself on fire or knock it over and set your home alight.

Place flower offerings where pets can't eat them

Some flowers are toxic to animals. If you have a curious pet who might decide to try eating a flower offering, either be sure to put offerings well out of its reach or keep your pet out of the rooms where flower offerings are placed.

Don't allow pets to climb up onto the altar

Cats, in particular, sometimes like to involve themselves in the ceremony by climbing up onto the altar. While it can seem very endearing, it will detract from the effectiveness of the altar, can be a fire hazard after the flower offering on the altar has been lit, can cause your bell, harmony balls, and other items to get knocked over or fall onto the floor and get damaged, and can generally mess up the altar.

Pets must be able to leave during the ceremony if they wish to

Most pets are more sensitive to energies than humans, so an important consideration is that they must be able to make their own decision about whether to stay or leave while a ceremony is in progress.

If you have a cat and your home has a cat door that it can use to come and go, that's ideal. If you have a dog that will bark to let you know it wants to be let out and you have a garden it can go to, that's fine too. If there is no easy exit route for your cat or dog, or you have a caged animal that is normally kept inside your home, you will need to keep a close eye on them during the ceremony to look out for signs of distress and be prepared to stop if this happens. Better still, make arrangements for them to be taken care of elsewhere for a few hours.

Special precautions with dogs

Most dogs are fascinated by space clearing and enjoy being present during a ceremony. They are able to feel the energy changes, and they appreciate them.

If they are of a nervous disposition, some dogs may run away during the clapping circuit. Most enjoy being present for the belling circuit, providing it's done with a Balinese bell. Other types of bells may hurt their ears and can make them howl piteously or send them running.

Some dogs can be very disruptive. They may bark, howl, get in the way, or demand attention in some other way. If you know your dog can be like this, make arrangements for it to be taken care of elsewhere while you do the space clearing ceremony.

> **Richard**: I once space cleared a home where there was a dog that was very territorial. As soon as I started the belling circuit, he started howling. This wasn't because the sound of the bell was causing him any pain. It was his way of competing for ownership of the space by making his own kind of noise. There was a kind of beauty to it that made me smile, but I couldn't do the space clearing with him howling along, so I had to ask the owner to put him outside for a while. He continued to howl from afar, then eventually quietened down.

> **Karen**: One dog I remember very well was a lovely Golden Labrador called Maysie that lived with a family in their house in Ireland. She came out to meet me when I arrived, and while stroking her, I took the opportunity to casually hand sense her too. I could feel how impacted by stagnant energies she was, and this gave me a very accurate preview of what I would find in the house.

> Maysie faithfully followed me around during the initial tour of the home as the owners showed me their property. She then went to the back door, which was made out of glass, and

barked to be let out. She was getting on in years, and I got the impression she had made the decision that I knew what I was doing and she didn't need to be involved. Someone opened the door for her. She went out, curled up on the back doorstep, and fell asleep.

It was a large property, so the space clearing took about five hours. The house was deeply imprinted, so clearing it was really hard work. At various points, I clapped and rang bells in the vicinity of the back door. Even though Maysie must have heard this, I could see through the glass that she never moved or even twitched an ear, which was very unusual for a dog.

Some part of her was paying attention, though, because as soon as the ceremony was over, she barked to be let in. While I was packing up my space clearing kit, I noticed her going around each of the rooms of the home, as if she was inspecting the changes.

The biggest surprise of all was when I walked out of the front door to put the final pieces of equipment in my car. I had left the car boot open, and there was Maysie, sitting in it, with an imploring look on her face that seemed to say, "Please take me home with you!"

The owners were astonished and called for her to come to them. Maysie took no notice and resolutely sat there. She had to be coaxed out of the boot so that I could close it and drive away. I remember the expression on her face and her determination to this day.

Special precautions with cats

Cats can be unpredictable about space clearing. Some love to be involved in the ceremony and will follow you around from room to room. Others make it perfectly clear they have no wish to be involved and leave at the first opportunity.

> **Richard**: If you have the kind of cat that likes to sit on your keyboard while you are typing or generally make themselves the centre of attention much of the time, don't be surprised if they show a special fascination if you set up a space clearing altar in your home.
>
> In one consultation I remember, the cat jumped up as soon as I spread the white tablecloth on the table, then again as soon as I placed the altar cloth on top, and she kept jumping up as I continued to add my space clearing equipment and flower offerings. This soon stopped being cute and started being a problem when she began to trample over things and nearly knocked my bell off its stand. Each time she jumped up, I lifted her off, but eventually the only solution was to ask the owner to put her outside for the duration of the ceremony.
>
> **Karen**: In one home I space cleared, there was a cat who climbed to the top of a wardrobe and stayed there throughout the entire ceremony, watching everything I did from on high. I had some space clearing water left over at the end and decided to throw it over the family's front doorstep to bless the front entrance area. I was just about to do this when a furry being made itself known to me, winding itself around my ankles.

Cats generally don't like water, but this one seemed to want some. So I dipped a flower head in my space clearing water pot, gently sprinkled a few drops on its head, and then rubbed the water in. It purred with delight, so I did it again. And a third time. The owner was as amazed as I was.

Since then, I've noticed that if a family has a cat or a dog, it will often make an appearance during the final stage of a ceremony, wanting to be included, so I often sprinkle some space clearing water on the animal's head. I've tried doing this with ordinary tap water, as an experiment, and cats always run away. It's only when I use space clearing water that they stand perfectly still and want more.

Special precautions with caged animals

We don't recommend doing space clearing with rabbits present in the home. They are very sensitive to energy movements and loud noises and will freeze and breathe rapidly when scared. It's best to move their cage elsewhere during the ceremony.

Other caged animals, such as guinea pigs, gerbils, mice, rats, hamsters, tortoises, lizards, and snakes are generally more hardy. Do keep an eye out for signs of distress, though, such as running away and hiding, or moving excessively around the cage as if trying to find a way out. If it's easy to pick these types of pets up in their cages and move them outside the building during space clearing, it's best to do so, weather permitting. Do take care to put them in a shady spot, though, not in bright sunlight or a place that can become hotter as the hours go by.

Special precautions with birds

Parrots and other large birds are usually fine during space clearing. Smaller birds can become frightened during clapping and belling.

We even know of an occasion when a canary died of fright during a space clearing. We hasten to add that this was not during a ceremony conducted by either of us or any of the practitioners we have trained. It was a feng shui consultant who had read Karen's book and decided to "have a go" at space clearing for a client. She'd had no professional training at all.

The client was so shocked to discover her canary dead in the bottom of its cage at the end of the ceremony that she contacted Karen to ask if this was normal. "Of course not," Karen said, and asked for the feng shui consultant's phone number. "I know why you're calling," the consultant said immediately when Karen said who she was. "I've learned my lesson and will never do space clearing for clients again."

Special precautions with fish

Water is a great purifier, so it will absorb some of the energies being cleared during a ceremony. If you have fish, this won't be good for them. If it's not possible to seal your fish tank while doing space clearing, be sure to change the water as soon as possible after the ceremony.

Step 5
Remove any metal you are wearing

☑ *Basic Space Clearing*

☑ *Essential Space Clearing*

☑ *Full Space Clearing*

Take off your watch and remove any metal jewellery, piercings, and other metal objects.

Why metal is a problem

In our modern world, we live in a sea of electromagnetic smog created by the electrical wiring and appliances in our homes and workplaces, as well as the microwave radiation and other radiofrequencies from Wi-Fi, Bluetooth, radio, TV, and radar that surround and permeate us.

Metal is a wonderful conductor of electricity, which is why it is used so effectively in wiring. However, metal anywhere on the body can amplify electromagnetic radiation from electrical equipment and Wi-Fi-enabled devices. This can create significantly higher local concentrations of electromagnetic radiation in the surrounding soft tissues of the body, which can affect us in a number of ways, from inhibiting DNA repair processes to interfering with melatonin production and cellular communication.

Before the invention of electricity, it was fine to wear metal close to the skin. It's not a good idea now.

In times gone by, spiritual schools would site their temples on mountaintops to have the best access to high spiritual forces. Today most of these locations are bombarded by such an onslaught of electromagnetic frequencies from communication masts and other sources that they no longer offer the levels of stillness required for spiritual practices. Deep valleys that radiofrequencies cannot penetrate, and specially shielded buildings, are now much better options.

One man Karen knew became extremely electrosensitive after accidentally falling into a sheep dip (a chemical bath used by some farmers to cleanse sheep of external parasites). The toxins he absorbed in the few minutes he was in there changed his life forever because he discovered he was no longer able to tolerate the electromagnetic fields we all live with. To get some relief from the emissions of the electrical wiring and equipment in his house, he moved out and lived in a tent in his back garden. He once described visiting a valley in a remote location and the utter peace he experienced as he descended to the bottom of the gorge, where no microwave signals or other types of radiofrequency radiation could penetrate. He said he never wanted to leave. We are now so drenched in these frequencies that we no longer know what this normal state of being he described feels like.

In our modern world, metal in any form is counterproductive to spiritual practices, as experienced meditators will tell you. A beautiful example of this level of awareness is a magnificent Hindu temple in the surprising location of Neasden (an unremarkable London suburb that does not have a reputation as a spiritual destination for any other reason).

Known as the Bochasanwasi Shri Akshar Purushottam Swaminarayan Sanstha Shri Swaminarayan Mandir London (or BAPS Shri Swaminarayan Mandir for short), the temple was opened in 1995. It consists of 26,300 pieces of Bulgarian limestone and marble from Italy and India, expertly carved by 1,526 stonemasons in India, then shipped to England and assembled without any structural steel at all. It's unique in that it embodies ancient sacred principles of Indian architecture while conforming to the building regulations of the UK. The purity of the structure, and the daily devotional rituals that are performed to maintain the energetic integrity of the space, make it conducive to hosting the high-level spiritual presences that reside there. It's well worth a visit.

Metal jewellery and piercings

Jewellery

Jewellery was worn in ancient cultures not only for decoration or as a status symbol, as it is worn today, but also to enhance a person's energy field. If someone wanted to attract the vibrant frequency of silver, they would wear silver jewellery to help them do that. If they were doing a sacred dance that rested on frequencies of gold, they would wear gold jewellery to attune themselves to that. You can see many examples of this in ancient art and echoes of it in sacred dances that are still performed today in places such as Bali and Thailand.

If you wear metallic jewellery while space clearing, however, it won't have an enhancing effect at all because we live in very different times. It will cause your body to act as an antenna for the electromagnetic fields around you. By the end of the ceremony, you are likely to feel tired rather than energized, and you will need to do extra work to cleanse your own energy and the jewellery you have been wearing. Jewellery worn on your wrists and fingers can also interfere with your ability to do the space clearing techniques, especially hand sensing, flower offering activation, and clapping. Professional space clearers are very aware of this and never wear metal jewellery while space clearing.

A wedding ring that won't come off is the most common problem that people ask us about in relation to this. The best way to purify such a ring after space clearing is to immerse your hand for a few minutes in a bowl of warm water mixed with Epsom salt (magnesium sulfate). Use the organic, food-grade variety, not the kind widely available in supermarkets, which often has added chemicals. Providing you are in good health, are only space clearing your own home, and only do so once or twice a year, this is all you'll need to do.

Metal piercings

Be sure to remove any metal body piercings before doing space clearing. If you have any health problems, you may also want to review the wisdom of having piercings at all. We have yet to meet any experienced acupuncturist who recommends them. They can play havoc with the flows of energies through the body's meridians, especially if placed on or close to the centre line of the body, such as in the navel, nose, tongue, or chin. Even wearing a necklace with metal components can cause health issues.

Other metal objects

Metal implants

We have found it impossible to train anyone to practitioner level who has a metal implant in their body such as a plate, rod, pins, screws, or wires. Those who have tried always report extreme pain in the area of the implant as they become more sensitized to energies.

If you are only space clearing your own home once or twice a year, this is usually not a problem. If you feel any aches and pains after the ceremony, take an Epsom salt bath and practise the etheric excretion technique described in Chapter 8 of Samuel Sagan's book, *Awakening the Third Eye*. If the pain continues, seek medical advice to check if there is a more serious reason for your discomfort.

Dental amalgams

Dental amalgams are usually made of 50% mercury with varying quantities of silver, copper, tin, and sometimes zinc. Reports of people having recovered from debilitating health issues as a result of having amalgams removed are well documented.

Experienced acupuncturists and dentists we have talked to believe that the main reason for this is that each tooth is connected to a meridian that runs through the body. Removing the metal from a tooth allows the meridians to regain their full function, which restores health to all the body parts that are located along that meridian.

Karen had a personal experience of this when she was able to cure an ingrowing toenail by tracing the meridian line up to a tooth in her mouth and asking her dentist to check it. Externally, the tooth looked fine, and it was not giving her any pain. Yet, sure enough, an X-ray revealed substantial internal decay. After dental surgery to repair the tooth, her ingrowing toenail very quickly corrected itself.

Anyone who takes our Professional Space Clearing Practitioner Training has either already had all metal amalgam fillings in their teeth removed and replaced by non-metallic compounds or soon decides to do so because they can feel the aggravation caused by the metal when doing space clearing. If you're only space clearing your own home from time to time, this won't be an issue because the effect will be negligible.

Pacemakers

Pacemakers are usually made of the metal titanium. We therefore strongly advise against doing space clearing if you have such a device fitted.

Watches

Never wear a watch while space clearing. Watches have metal components that can cause the same issues as jewellery, and quartz watches emit electric pulses that will create waves of disturbance in your etheric body. Hand sensing and other parts of the ceremony will also be easier to do without anything on your wrists. Neither of us owns or has worn a watch of any kind for decades.

This advice, of course, includes smart watches and other similar gadgets, even if the exterior casing is not made of metal. The radiofrequency signals generated by such devices will create interference at the cellular level, which will impact your etheric sensitivity and create astral interference.

Metal-framed glasses

If you can manage without them, it is best not to wear metal-framed glasses while space clearing, especially if the frames have a metal piece across the nose. The study of acupuncture shows that this can short-circuit the energy meridians of the head, which can cause tiredness, confusion, and headaches, even in normal, everyday circumstances.

Metal buckles

It's usually fine to wear a belt with a metal buckle while space clearing. Just avoid wearing any clothing with metal components such as zips that are directly in contact with your skin.

Metal coins

Empty any coins out of your pockets before starting a space clearing ceremony. This has nothing to do with the fact that they are made of metal. If they are in your pocket, they are not directly in contact with your skin, so they will not affect you in the same way that wearing jewellery, piercings, or a watch will.

The problem with coins is that they can randomly jingle and create unwanted noise. Another issue is they have usually been handled by many people, so they are often imprinted with unwholesome astral frequencies that will hinder rather than help you during a space clearing ceremony. It's therefore best not to have any money in your pockets, including notes.

Step 6
Take a bath or shower and put on clean clothing

☑ *Basic Space Clearing*

☑ *Essential Space Clearing*

☑ *Full Space Clearing*

A vital preparation for any purification ceremony is to first cleanse yourself and put on clean clothing.

Take a bath or shower

For best results, take a full bath or shower immediately before the space clearing, including washing your hair and brushing your teeth. If it's not practical to do this for some reason, be sure to take a bath or shower some time earlier in the day.

It's best to use unscented soap and shampoo, and a freshly laundered, unscented towel to dry yourself. Scents, especially synthetic types, will inhibit your ability to access high-level frequencies during the ceremony, so do not put on any scented deodorant, perfume, or cologne after bathing.

Also, do not put on any skin creams or make-up, as this will clog the ethericity* of your skin. If you normally wear skin creams or make-up, choose a date and time for the ceremony when you can be at home without needing to wear any.

After bathing, put on clean clothing.

Wear natural fabrics

Pure cotton is best because it facilitates healthy circulations of energies around the body and a free-flowing exchange of energies with your environment. It allows your etheric to breathe.

Wearing garments made of synthetic blends or lined with synthetic materials will affect you energetically and will also affect the quality of the space clearing results you will be able to obtain. They will dull your etheric, causing your life force energy and the interchange of energies with the environment to be diminished. In other words, they will make you feel less present and less alive.

There's some scientific evidence for this too. Medical researcher Ahmed Shafik won an Ig Nobel Prize in 2016 for studying the effects on rats, dogs, and male humans of wearing underpants made of cotton, wool, polyester, or a polyester/cotton blend (we're not making this up). In all cases, he found a lower sperm count in males who wore polyester underpants and, most notably, he recorded that the men who wore these for an average of 140 days stopped producing viable sperm at all (they recovered after they stopped wearing them).

These studies pose the important question: Could modern fertility problems be helped by everyone simply going back to wearing cotton underwear?

The closer to the body the fabric is, the more it will cause physical overheating and affect energy circulations, which is why cotton has been the universal fabric of choice for underwear for centuries. Dressing in layers so that only natural fabrics are in contact with your skin can mitigate the effect of synthetics to some extent. However, your etheric extends beyond the physical layer of the skin, so wearing any garments made of synthetic fabrics will still have an effect.

Sensitive people intuitively know that wearing cotton is better for them than synthetics, which is one of the reasons why manufacturers add some cotton so they can call a fabric "cotton-rich" or "cotton blend". It's a psychological marketing trick that has become commonplace. We mention it here so you can avoid falling for it.

There are other natural fabrics to choose from that are etherically compatible, fully biodegradable, and ethically sound. The main ones are wool, linen (made from flax, not linen viscose), and hemp. Be sure to check labels to make sure they aren't synthetic versions or haven't been blended with synthetics. Acrylic, polyester, and nylon are the most etheric-depleting fabrics you can wear and also the cause of massive environmental pollution worldwide.

What colour to wear

White is traditionally associated in many cultures with purification practices and cleanliness. You certainly *can* wear white to do space clearing if you want to, but it's not necessary. You can wear any colour you like, except black.

Black is not actually a colour. It's the absence of all colours. Its most defining quality is absorption, both physically and energetically. If you wear black clothes on a hot, sunny day, it will make you feel hotter. This is because black so readily absorbs heat from the sun. It also absorbs all wavelengths of light and reflects none.

If you wear black while space clearing, you will be more likely to pick up stagnant energies and etheric debris.

Don't wear a hat while space clearing

In case you are in the habit of wearing a hat indoors, we want to mention here that you'll find it will work best to take it off while space clearing.

The reason is that wearing a hat will make it more difficult to access the subtle body structures above your head, which in turn will make it more difficult to access the higher levels of consciousness that the ceremony is designed to connect to.

Step 7
Do the ceremony barefoot, if it is practical to do so

☑ *Basic Space Clearing*

☑ *Essential Space Clearing*

☑ *Full Space Clearing*

Take off any shoes, slippers, or socks you are wearing.

You will be able to feel and connect to the energies of a space much better barefoot than if you wear shoes, slippers, or socks. Foot coverings of any kind have a numbing effect on the etheric, which is why people who spend a lot of their time barefoot are usually more sensitive to energies than those who do not.

If you have highly developed etheric awareness, there's a lot of information that can be accessed through the soles of the feet during space clearing. Shoes will insulate you from that, especially the type with soles made of artificial materials. If there are areas of your home where it's more practical to wear shoes, put them on for that section and take them off when you come out (slip-on shoes work best for this).

If you are doing space clearing in winter, wear cotton socks or leather-soled slippers to keep your feet warm. There's no point being barefoot if your feet become like blocks of ice and you can't feel them.

Step 8
Put food and drinks away

☑ *Basic Space Clearing*

☑ *Essential Space Clearing*

☑ *Full Space Clearing*

Put food and drinks away in a fridge, or in sealed glass or plastic containers.

Water is a natural purifier, so any food substances or drinks that contain water may absorb some of the energies that are shifted during space clearing. If you then eat or drink them, they won't harm you, but they usually won't taste good, and your body will have to do extra work to process the energies. It's much better to take a minute to put these items away before you begin the ceremony.

Fresh foods

Most fresh foods will need to be stored during a space clearing ceremony, especially the type that go mouldy over time (mould is an indicator of water content because it can only form when water is present). This includes most kinds of vegetables and any type of fruit that you usually eat the skin of, such as apples, grapes, stone fruit, and so on.

It's not enough to put these food items in a wooden cupboard or a cardboard box because energies can easily pass through those types of materials. You will need to put them in a fridge that has a rubber seal around the edge, or in sealed glass or plastic containers.

There's no need to put away any fruits that have a thick, water-repellent skin that is removed before eating, such as citrus fruits, avocados, and bananas, or nuts that are still in their shells.

Canned and bottled foods and drinks

These items also do not need to be stored away, unless they have been opened.

It's good to drink a lot of water while you are space clearing to keep yourself hydrated, so we recommend using a sealed container rather than an open glass. If you forget and accidentally drink a fluid that has been left open during the ceremony, drink plenty of water from a fresh supply to flush it through.

Pet food and drinks

Put away any pet food or drinking water before you start the ceremony. If you forget, at the end of the ceremony throw away anything that has been left out and replace it with fresh pet food and water.

Step 9
Open at least one window on each floor

☑ *Basic Space Clearing*

☑ *Essential Space Clearing*

☑ *Full Space Clearing*

Open at least one window on each floor so that there is a gentle flow of fresh air through the space.

Why fresh air is important

It's important to have a flow of fresh air while space clearing because it contains life-giving oxygen and etheric vitality. The etheric aspect can't be measured by any scientific equipment, but it can be felt, even by people who have no spiritual background or energetic sensitivity. A good example of this is the difference between how a room feels when it has been closed up for some time, and is filled with stale air, and how it feels after it has been opened up and aired. A freshly aired room has more oxygen, which makes it feel easier to breathe. It also has more etheric vitality, which makes the space feel more alive.

For space clearing, it's important to get the right balance. Don't have so much air rushing through that it makes it difficult to do hand sensing or keep the candles of your flower offerings alight. Opening one or two windows on each floor of a property is usually enough.

If the weather is very still or humid, open the windows as widely as feels comfortable. If it is cold or windy, open them just enough to allow a small amount of air to circulate, but not so much that it feels draughty.

It's fine to leave fly screens in place, if your home is fitted with these.

What to do if the windows in your home cannot be opened

Some modern buildings, usually in very hot locations, are built with completely sealed windows that can never be opened. They rely entirely on air conditioning for cooling.

Other common scenarios are homes where the windows have been painted shut, where they do not open because they are in need of repair, or where there is so much clutter that it's impossible to get to the windows to open them. Any of these situations will make it very difficult to do more than a superficial level of space clearing because there will be no etheric vitality in the space at all.

The main entrance to your home will need to remain closed throughout the ceremony because that's where each of the circuits begins and ends. However, if you have a back door or a side door, to compensate for all the windows being closed, it would be good to keep one of them at least partially open to let some air in, providing you are in a safe enough area to do so.

If you only have air conditioning and no opening windows, the best we can suggest is that you keep it turned on while doing the preparations and for most of the ceremony, but briefly turn it off during the parts where fresh air and stillness are essential (making the space clearing water, activating the flower offerings, and doing the belling circuit).

If you live in a home that relies on air conditioning to keep it cool and *does* have opening windows, a good compromise can be to open at least one window on each floor and also keep the air conditioning on, except when you are making the space clearing water, activating the flower offerings, and doing the belling circuit. This will help a bit.

The problem with air conditioning

Having air conditioning permanently turned on with no fresh air ever entering your home is problematic in several ways. Firstly, there is the constant drone of machinery, which can exhaust you at deep etheric levels because you never fully rest. Next, there's the drying effect on your eyes, nose, and throat. There are also air-borne microorganisms that can cause a range of respiratory problems if the air conditioners are not regularly cleaned and the filters changed every few months.

Many studies have found an association between working in an air-conditioned environment and a greater incidence of ear, nose, and throat problems, respiratory and dermatological ailments, headaches, fatigue, and a general feeling of malaise.

More worrying still is the effect that living in a completely air-conditioned environment has on our etheric. This type of air lacks life force energy. It contains enough oxygen to keep someone alive but does not have the etheric vitality that we need to thrive.

Experienced meditators know that there is a massive difference between meditating in a room that has a circulation of fresh air and one that does not. This isn't so noticeable if you are doing the kind of technique that simply aims to help you to centre yourself or relax. It becomes very noticeable if you want to access higher states of consciousness. The etheric quality of the air in a room is crucial for that.

If you are new to meditation, by the way, we need to point out that it does not follow that meditating in the open air is therefore better. Yes, the air will be more vital, but there will be too many destabilizing draughts and influences passing through the space for you to be able to deeply internalize. There may also be disturbances caused by weather fluctuations, passing insects, animals, people, and so on.

The alluring photos in magazines and social media of people posing to meditate in the open air are not examples to follow. Meditating in a closed space is much better, as the ancients who meditated in caves or temples knew.

While we are on this topic, we'll also mention the problem of sleeping in an air-conditioned room or a room with closed windows. This is fine once in a while in conditions of extreme heat, extreme cold, or because you are travelling and have no alternative but to stay in a hotel that has sealed windows. However, if you sleep like this every night, it will affect you in ways you may not realize.

Sleep has profound spiritual aspects that most people know nothing about. What needs to be understood is that it's not the physical body that runs low on physical stamina and makes us need to sleep. It's the etheric body, which permeates the physical body, that runs low on etheric vitality.

What is supposed to happen during sleep is that the subtle body structures that constitute our upper complex* (the astral body and Higher Self) lift out of the lower complex* (the physical body and the etheric), allowing the lower complex to be refreshed, revitalized, and repaired, and the upper complex to access higher realms. The degree to which this happens is determined by a number of factors, such as the trajectory you take as you fall asleep and the energetic environment you sleep in. To maximize energetic revitalization during sleep, it works best to sleep with a window open to provide a circulation of fresh air. Even opening a window a tiny crack is better than not opening one at all.

Step 10
Bring the space to a standstill

☑ *Basic Space Clearing*

☑ *Essential Space Clearing*

☑ *Full Space Clearing*

Space clearing is most effective when done in complete silence and stillness. Turn off any equipment that can interfere with the ceremony and bring all activities in the area being space cleared to a stop.

This means it will work best to:

- Turn off phones and any other connected devices
- Turn off your home Wi-Fi
- Turn off your TV, radio, podcasts, and so on
- Turn off any background music
- Turn off any air-churning equipment, such as fans and air conditioning
- Turn off any equipment that makes a loud or droning noise
- Eliminate external noises as much as possible
- Bring all other activities to a standstill

Turn off phones and any other connected devices

Think of a space clearing ceremony as high-quality "me" time, where you let the world get on without you for a while. This means scheduling it for a time when you are not likely to be interrupted by personal callers or other distractions, and when you can turn off all digital devices such as computers, tablets, phones, personal digital assistants, and other gadgets.

By this, we mean completely turning the devices off, not just putting them in sleep mode. When you leave a device in sleep mode, a part of your superastrality* will still be engaged with it, and this can influence the effectiveness of the space clearing. To be fully available for the changes that space clearing can bring about, you need to totally disengage from all external influences for a few hours.

We know some people will be horrified by this advice. It will seem unnecessary, annoying, or even risky because you may miss an important call or message during that time. However, previous generations managed to run their lives perfectly well without mobile phones or even landlines. Feeling the need to be on call at all times is a modern worry.

If you feel really uncomfortable being voluntarily disconnected from the outside world for a few hours to give yourself time to do space clearing, the best we can suggest is that you quickly turn on your chosen device to check for messages once an hour and tell anyone who needs to know that you will be doing so. This method will require some self-discipline because in order to check if there has been a genuine emergency that needs your immediate attention, you will probably need to scan other messages that are far from urgent. This will draw your attention away from the space clearing ceremony and allow mundane influences to flood the space. If you get distracted by this after activating the flower offering(s), you may as well stop the ceremony right there because there will be no point continuing. You will need to start the ceremony again from Step 16, or better still, reschedule it for another day when you will be able to stay focused.

Turn off your home Wi-Fi

To obtain the best space clearing results, if you use Wi-Fi in your home we recommend turning off your router while doing space clearing. Wi-Fi uses radiofrequency electromagnetic fields to communicate between devices. You may not be sensitive enough to feel how this affects you, but your etheric and higher parts of you will feel the interference it creates.

When meditating or conducting a high-level ceremony such as space clearing, Wi-Fi frequencies have a disruptive effect that make it impossible to access deep levels of stillness. There may be nothing you can do about Wi-Fi signals from your neighbours. However, you can turn your own router off and that will at least remove the strongest signals that permeate your home.

Most cordless DECT (digital enhanced cordless telecommunications) phones also emit Wi-Fi radiation continuously, so if you have any of these devices in your home, be sure to unplug them at the power outlet during space clearing too.

Turn off your TV, radio, podcasts, and so on

Space clearing is not just about clearing energies. It is also about raising the frequencies in your home to higher levels. It will therefore be counterproductive to have the everyday babble of a TV, radio, podcasts, or anything similar in the background during any part of the ceremony, even at the preparations stage. It will pull the energy of the space down and make it impossible for you to obtain good results.

Turn off any background music

Some of the most crucial parts of the space clearing ceremony involve listening to the way the sounds of clapping and belling change as energies are revitalized and cleared. The entire ceremony works best without any background music. It will hinder rather than enhance the process.

Turn off any air-churning equipment, such as fans and air conditioning

Fans and air conditioning churn the air, the energy of a room, and the energy field of anyone in the vicinity of the machinery. Fans, in particular, create large movements of air. This will make it impossible to sense energies during the hand-sensing circuits, challenging to activate the flower offerings, and difficult or impossible for the candle flames to stay alight and burn vertically. The turbulence will also make it more difficult for you to stay centred while you are doing the ceremony.

Air conditioning is generally less intrusive than fans, although its effect can be more insidious, as explained in Step 9.

Turn off any equipment that makes a loud or droning noise

The droning noise emitted by fans, air conditioning, and forced-air heating can also be a problem. If you are used to having these types of equipment running in your home, you may have learned how to tune out the noise from your conscious awareness. However, it will still be affecting you in ways you don't realize. During space clearing, all sounds become accentuated and much more noticeable. Loud or droning equipment will feel disruptive and, like background music, will make it difficult or impossible to hear the energetic changes that happen during the clapping and belling circuits.

Fridges can be particularly bothersome. Most people are completely unaware of how much the noise of their fridge affects them. If you have a silent one, that's ideal. If you have the kind that emits a continuous drone, or one that shudders and starts up every so often and then cuts out, it could be a significant source of stress in your life, especially if it emits a high-pitched sound instead of just a low hum. If you have a noisy fridge, you may want to consider getting it repaired or replacing it with one of the near-silent models that are now available.

If you have a noisy fridge, it's fine to keep it turned on while you are doing the preparations during Steps 1 to 14. From Step 15 on, we recommend that you turn it off. Be sure to write yourself a note and place it somewhere you'll be sure to see it at the end of the ceremony to remind yourself to turn it back on so that your food won't spoil.

Eliminate external noises as much as possible

It can sometimes happen that you are just about to begin a space clearing when a thunderstorm suddenly brews up, or your neighbour decides to noisily mow their lawn or start up a hedge trimmer, leaf blower, or chainsaw. These harsh sounds will intrude into your home and affect your ability to achieve good space clearing results. In these types of situations, it's best to delay the ceremony for a few hours until silence has resumed. If it persists, reschedule for another day.

If you live near a busy road or under a flight path, there will be nothing you can do about external noises except to choose a time when traffic is likely to be at its least intrusive. If you live near a public building that has a lot of events or footfall, choose a time when the area is relatively quiet.

Bring all other activities to a standstill

Before moving to the next step of the ceremony, any other activities in the space will need to come to a complete stop, so that the focus of everyone present can be placed on the ceremony.

If someone present does not wish their room to be included in the space clearing, they will need to keep the door to their room closed from this point on so that you can completely exclude it from the ceremony. They can then continue with whatever activity they are engaged in, providing it does not make any noise that can be heard in the rest of the home.

Step 11
Roll up your sleeves, and
wash your hands and forearms

☑ *Basic Space Clearing*

☑ *Essential Space Clearing*

☑ *Full Space Clearing*

Roll your sleeves up to above the elbow. Wash your hands and forearms with soap and water, then dry them on a clean towel.

Roll up your sleeves

If you are wearing a garment with long or three-quarter-length sleeves, roll both sleeves up. Not just a little bit. Roll them all the way up to above your elbows and secure them in some way so they will stay up throughout the entire ceremony without you needing to continuously adjust them. Better still, if the temperature of your home is warm enough, wear a short-sleeved top instead.

The main reasons why it's so important to do space clearing with your sleeves rolled up are explained in Chapter 8:

- To improve sensitivity
- To prevent stagnant energies from becoming entangled in your clothing
- To engage MC-ship
- To enhance your etheric awareness

If you skipped reading that chapter or don't remember it very well, please take a moment to read it now.

Wash your hands and forearms

The next step of the space clearing ceremony involves hand sensing. It's therefore essential to wash your hands and forearms with soap and water first. Use a freshly laundered towel to dry yourself, if one is available, or paper towels or tissues.

For the best results, wash your face too, and don't use any skin creams or cosmetics. Any products you put on your skin will block levels of functioning of your etheric, which will inhibit your ability to do hand sensing.

Step 12
Do a circuit of hand sensing

☑ *Basic Space Clearing (optional)*

☑ *Essential Space Clearing*

☑ *Full Space Clearing*

Starting at the main entrance to your home, walk around the entire inner perimeter of the space, sensing the energy of the walls, furniture, and other items with your hand.

The purpose of hand sensing

There are four good reasons to include the hand-sensing circuit in each type of space clearing you do, whether it's a Basic, Essential, or Full Space Clearing ceremony:

- Discerning the energies in the space
- Perceiving the flow of energies around the space
- Establishing the area to be space cleared
- Starting to take energetic ownership of the space

Discerning the energies in the space

The main purpose of hand sensing is to read the energies of a place at the start of a space clearing ceremony and again at the end, to gauge how effective it has been.

Most people can feel some energy differences in their home through hand sensing. Even if you are not able to feel anything, or if you have space cleared your home before and are not expecting the energies to have changed much since then, this circuit is still worth including for all the other reasons listed.

Perceiving the flow of energies around the space

During the hand-sensing circuit, you will gain a better appreciation of how energy flows around your home. If you have to clamber over obstacles or pick your way through piles of clutter to make your way around, for example, you will appreciate that energies circulating your home will have the same difficulties you do. This will hopefully inspire you, after the ceremony, to make some changes to improve that.

Establishing the area to be space cleared

It usually works best to space clear your entire home. However, there are some situations where this won't be possible, in which case the hand-sensing circuit is vital to establish the area you will be space clearing and which rooms will be excluded from the ceremony.

The main situations this applies to are any parts of your home that are:

- Difficult to access
- Rented to a tenant
- Occupied by someone who does not want those areas to be space cleared
- Occupied by someone who has mental health issues
- Occupied by a person or pet who is physically unwell
- Used for business and you want to space clear those areas separately

See Chapter 26 for more information about this.

Starting to take energetic ownership of the space

Physically walking the inner perimeter of your home, as close to the walls as possible without moving furniture, is a dynamic way to start taking energetic ownership of your space. It has some similarities with how a cat owns its territory when it first arrives in a new place.

If you have lived somewhere for many years and never done this, you're likely to be pleasantly surprised by how good it feels. If you've only recently moved in, this simple technique can help you to feel at home very quickly. Each time you do this circuit at the beginning of a space clearing ceremony, it will help you to forge a deeper level of energetically owning the space of your home.

The hand-sensing circuit

The hand-sensing circuit begins and ends inside the main entrance door to your home, with the door firmly closed.

This is very straightforward if your home has a front door that everyone uses when entering or leaving. You simply start the circuit inside the front door and go around the inner perimeter of the property until you arrive back where you started.

If your home has more than one front door, or your front door is not the one that is used most often by people entering or leaving, you will first need to read the information in Chapter 6 about how to determine the main entrance.

Example: Suppose you live in a three-storey house that has a basement, a ground floor, and a first floor, and your main entrance is on the ground floor. The circuit you would take is to start at the main entrance and follow the inner perimeter of the wall until you reach the first staircase. If it leads to the basement, go down. If it leads to the floor above, go up.

Suppose the first staircase goes down to the basement. You would then go around the inner perimeter of the basement, come back up, continue around the ground floor until you reach the stairs going up to the first floor, go around the inner perimeter of the first floor, then back down the stairs, around the remainder of the ground floor, and finish back at the main entrance.

If the first staircase takes you up to the first floor instead of to the basement, go up those stairs and follow the wall wherever it leads.

If your home has other floors above the first floor, go up and down each staircase as you come to it and continue to follow the wall until you arrive back at the main entrance.

More than one staircase

If your home has a second staircase connecting any of the floors, the route is a bit more complicated. To create a coherent inner perimeter that you follow during each space clearing circuit (hand sensing, clapping, belling, and harmony ball frequencing), use the staircase that is used the most during everyday life. Include the secondary staircase in each of the circuits but treat it as if it is a corridor that leads nowhere. In other words, each time you come to a secondary staircase, go up it and straight back down it, doing the relevant circuit of the ceremony as you go. (Note that it's usually only necessary to clap a staircase if its design includes corners where stagnant energies can collect.)

Rooms with multiple doors

If any room in your home has more than one door, close the door or doors that are least used so that you only enter and exit each room through the door that is used the most. Treat the secondary doors as if they are walls.

Islands

In some homes, if you follow the inner perimeter all the way around, it's possible to arrive back at the main entrance without having hand sensed some walls. That's because the property has an independent structure that we call an island**, such as a freestanding floor-to-ceiling fireplace in the centre of a living room or, in a large property, it could be an entire room within a room.

In order to include the walls of an island, after you complete the initial circuit and arrive back at the main entrance, splice the energies into the etheric layer of the door, then continue walking with your hand still raised. Go to the area that has been missed, hand sense the walls you have not yet sensed, then return to the main entrance and splice the energies into the door a second time to complete the circuit. (Splicing is explained later in this chapter in the section about how to do hand sensing.)

Basements

Stagnant energies often tend to accumulate in basements, so if you have one in your home, do include it in the space clearing ceremony, if you can. If it's too cluttered or precarious to walk around, or is too damp or foul-smelling for you to want to go down there, you may have to omit it from the first space clearing ceremony you do, then take steps to remedy the situation so that you can do it on another day or at least include it in future space clearings.

Attics

Include the attic in the hand-sensing circuit if there is easy access to it and you can walk around it.

Garages

If your garage is only used to store your car and does not have any clutter, there's no need to include it in the space clearing ceremony, although you can if you want to. If it is used for other purposes, and especially if it's full of clutter, include it in the main ceremony if it is connected to your home by an internal door, or do a separate ceremony for it after you have space cleared your home if it has a separate entrance.

Outbuildings

Include any areas that are connected to your home by a door. If they are not connected, space clear your home first, then do separate space clearing ceremonies for any outbuildings such as an annex, home office, or garden room. You can also do separate ceremonies for sheds, garages, and other types of outbuildings, if you want to and it would not be a fire hazard to use lit candles in those spaces.

A very large property

If you have an unusually large home, it may be too tiring to space clear the entire property in one go. See Chapter 35 for how to adapt the ceremony in this situation.

Furniture and fittings

In a room that has furniture in the centre, such as sofas and a coffee table, a dining table and chairs, or a fixture such as a kitchen island with a countertop, find a convenient point to break off from hand sensing the walls to hand sense these items too, then return to the wall and continue from where you left off.

If you have so much stuff you can't reach the walls to hand sense them

You don't have to move furniture away from the walls to do hand sensing. Just switch to sensing the furniture wherever you come across it, then go back to sensing the walls after that.

However, if your home is so full of clutter that you can't get to the walls to do hand sensing without clambering over piles of things, then you're not going to be able to do hand sensing or space clearing. You will need to declutter first.

Which direction to take

When it comes to healing, the general principle is the same as for opening and closing a bottle top. To close a bottle, you turn it clockwise. To open it, you turn it anticlockwise. Similarly, for most healing techniques, a clockwise movement puts energy in and an anticlockwise movement draws it out.

This does not apply to the direction you take when doing a space clearing ceremony, though, because on some circuits you will be putting energies in, on others you will be clearing energies out, and during the hand-sensing circuit you will simply be sensing energies.

What determines the direction you take is what allows you to most easily use your most dextrous and etherically sensitive hand. If you're predominantly right-handed, do the circuits of the space clearing ceremony in an anticlockwise direction around the inner perimeter of your home so that your right side is nearest the wall. If you're predominantly left-handed, do each circuit in a clockwise direction. If you happen to be ambidextrous, you can choose whichever direction you prefer, providing you do all the circuits in the same direction.

If you do the ceremony with the assistance of a partner who happens to be left-handed and you are right-handed (or vice versa), it won't work for the MC to do some of the circuits of the ceremony in one direction and the partner to do some circuits in the opposite direction. As MC, you will determine the direction that all circuits take. Your partner will need to follow that, even if it feels a bit awkward for them to do so.

How to sensitize your hands

To prepare to do hand sensing, first check that your sleeves are fully rolled up above your elbows.

Begin by massaging your palms and fingers. It's also a good idea to bend your fingers back to help to loosen the joints, release astrality*, and make your hands more etherically alive and supple.

To bring more awareness to the palms of your hands, briskly rub them together for a few seconds, as if you are trying to get them warm. Then let your hands go limp and shake them a few times from the wrists, which will help to release more astrality.

How to begin the hand-sensing circuit

Go to the main entrance of your home. Stand sideways to the door, facing in the direction you will be walking. Don't look at the door. That's a mistake a lot of people make, and it won't help because it will keep you in your mind. Hand sensing is an etheric technique, so look straight ahead of you in the direction you will be walking and adjust your vision so that it is soft and peripheral rather than focused on anything.

Stretch your hand out toward the centre of the door at heart level. Bend your hand at about 45 to 90 degrees to your wrist (depending on how flexible your wrist is), with your palm facing toward the door and your fingers pointing up. During the entire hand-sensing circuit, keep your hand and your arm supple and relaxed, with your palm slightly curved. Any tension in your hand will block your ability to read energies, so don't try to bend it back at the wrist more than feels comfortable for you to do.

In most homes, the ideal distance to hold your hand is about 3–5 cm (1–2 inches) from the door. If your home is very old or has had many previous occupants, the layers of energy may be thicker, so you may need to position your hand farther away.

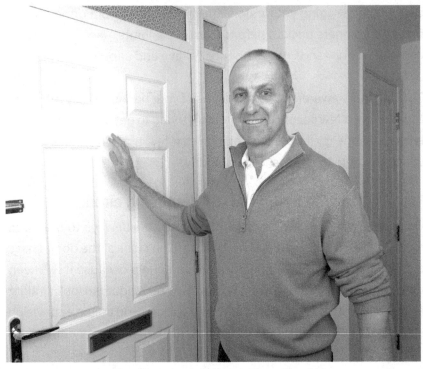

Starting the hand-sensing circuit

Breathe in. Then, on the out-breath, gear into the etheric layer of your home by moving your hand forward a few times, keeping it near to, but not touching, the door. The movement is similar to gently stroking a cat. Engage throat friction as you do this (see Chapter 10), which will help you to go deeper into cognizing the layers of energy embedded in the door.

This technique will work best if your main entrance door is made of wood. The denser the wood, the better. A solid wooden door is a much more effective anchor for energies than one made of fibreboard, which is one of the reasons why wood has been the material of choice for front doors for centuries. Having a solid partition between you and the outside world also makes you feel more secure in your home.

If the door is made of metal, glass, plastic, or other synthetic materials, you may not feel very much when you engage hand sensing. These types of materials do not allow the deep anchoring of energies that a solid wooden front door provides.

If the door has a glass panel at heart level or is entirely made of glass, it will work better to start and end the hand-sensing circuit at a solid part of the door or the door frame, rather than the centre of the door.

How to do hand sensing

Walk around the entire inner perimeter of your home, hand sensing the walls as you go and any furniture that is next to the walls, such as cupboards and bookcases. If there are items of furniture in the middle of the room such as sofas or tables, momentarily break away from the walls to sense these items, then return to where you left the wall and carry on.

When sensing walls, it generally works best to hold your hand at heart level. When sensing other objects, you can move your hand up and down or from side to side, as necessary. If you come across something that has interesting energies, it's fine to make several passes over it, engaging throat friction and tuning into it more deeply each time.

As you go from room to room, wedge the doors open and turn on any lights that need to be turned on in order to see where you are going. It will interrupt the flow if you have to keep opening and closing doors or turning light switches on and off, so leave the doors open and the lights turned on until the end of the ceremony.

It's not necessary to open all your cupboards and drawers to hand sense the items stored in them, although you can if you want to be very thorough. If you decide to do this, leave them open too so that you can continue to give these areas extra attention during the other circuits of the ceremony.

How to read energies

When you first start doing hand sensing, you may not feel very much. Don't worry if that happens. While it's crucial for professional space clearing practitioners to be able to read the energies in clients' homes with a high degree of accuracy, the space clearing techniques in this book will still work in your own home even if you can't feel anything.

There are two levels to hand sensing – etheric and astral. The etheric level is about sensing the stagnant energies that build up daily. These can be a problem because they tend to cause you to feel stuck.

The astral level is about reading and interpreting astral imprints that have been created by repetitive actions or traumatic events, either by the current occupants of the home or previous occupants. The entire history of everything that happens in a building gets imprinted in the walls, floors, ceilings, fixtures, furniture, and other objects in the space. This can be a problem because the imprints can affect you in many ways, without you realizing it.

Be as fluid as possible while hand sensing. Relax any tensions in your body. Don't hold your breath. Don't think. Don't try too hard. And don't react to anything you discern. Remain neutral and sense the impressions, as if you are a radio receiver and your hand is an antenna.

It's about learning to feel from a different part of yourself. It will work best if you breathe through your nose, rather than your mouth, and use the throat friction technique.

Some energies will feel cool and some will feel warm. Some sensations will be pleasant and others not so pleasant. You may feel dull aches in your bones or shimmering tingles in your palms. Some layers of energy may feel as smooth as honey or as lumpy as gravel. They may feel dense or buoyant, prickly or soft, and so on. In some buildings, it can feel like you are putting your hands into the energetic equivalent of fine cobwebs. In others it may feel like thick, sticky treacle.

The most important thing to look for is whether each area feels stuck or flowing, stagnant or vibrant, stale or fresh. If you start to feel confused by the flood of impressions, or if you find you are not feeling much at all, break off from the circuit for a few seconds, shake your hand to refresh its sensitivity, then resume.

How to finish the hand-sensing circuit

At the end of the circuit, when you arrive back at the main entrance, use your hand to splice back into the etheric of the door to seal and complete the circuit.

Splicing means etherically weaving the beginning and end of the hand-sensing circuit together, in a similar way to how the strands of a physical rope can be interwoven by splicing to form a rope circle. If your etheric is not sufficiently awakened to be able to do etheric splicing, it will still help a lot if you take care to start and finish the hand-sensing circuit in exactly the same area of the main entrance door.

How to improve your hand-sensing skills

With a bit of practice, most people can develop etheric sensing* enough to feel some sensations. Accurately perceiving and reading astral imprints is much more advanced because it involves first developing the subtle body structure above the head known as verticality* as an organ of perception. If you're interested to learn more, we've included more information about both aspects in Part Two of *Space Clearing, Volume 2*.

Step 13
Create flower offerings

☐ *Basic Space Clearing*

☑ *Essential Space Clearing*

☑ *Full Space Clearing*

Create flower offerings consisting of a saucer or plate, a tealight candle, and fresh flower heads.

The purpose of flower offerings

The flower offering on the altar creates an anchor for energies during the ceremony and facilitates taking energetic ownership of the space. The additional flower offerings of a Full Space Clearing ceremony are used to create an energy matrix in your home that high spiritual forces can gear into.

How many flower offerings do you need?

For Essential Space Clearing, you will only need one flower offering on the space clearing altar.

For a Full Space Clearing, you will need a flower offering on the altar, one for each room, and a matrix flower offering for each floor of your home. If some rooms have more than one function, each area in that room will need to have its own flower offering too. For example, an open-plan kitchen/diner will need two flower offerings. A studio apartment that has a kitchen, living area, and sleeping area will need three flower offerings plus a matrix flower offering.

It's not usually necessary to put a flower offering in any of the following rooms, although you can if you really want to.

Attics

There is no need to place an offering in an attic if it is hardly used, if access to it is difficult, or if there is so much clutter up there that a lit offering would be a fire risk.

Bathroom and toilets

Flower offerings are not needed in bathrooms or toilets, unless you have the type of bathroom that is like a small living room because creature comforts have been added, such as a TV, armchair, some carpet, and so on.

Utility rooms

These functional rooms also do not usually need a flower offering, except if they are in what we call an "orphaned" position in the house. This means a utility room that feels isolated from the rest of the home, such as one that is in its own wing or at the farthest end of an L-shape. It can be helpful to place a flower offering in such a room in order to include the wing or the entire leg of the property in the ceremony.

Garages

If your garage is only used to store vehicles, there's no need to put a flower offering in there.

If you use your garage primarily to store things and it can be accessed through an internal door that is connected to your home, include it in all the circuits of the ceremony and place a flower offering in it, unless it is so cluttered that a tealight candle could be a fire risk. Also be very careful not to put a flower offering near any flammable liquids.

If your garage is used primarily to store things and is not connected to your home, do a separate ceremony for it after you have completed the main ceremony for your home, observing all the cautions already mentioned.

Garden sheds

There's no need to put a flower offering in a garden shed that is used for storing garden equipment and the like. However, if you have a garden room with four walls and a roof that is used as a living or working space, do a separate ceremony for it after you have space cleared your main home.

Types of flower offerings

There are two types of flower offerings used in space clearing:

- Classic flower offerings
- Rose-petal flower offerings

You can find detailed information in Chapters 17 and 18 about the types of flowers, saucers/plates, and candles to use. For both types, always use the freshest flowers you can find because they will have the most vibrant ethericity.

The best flower colours to use are pink, orange, yellow, white, purple, or bright red. Don't use dark colours, artificially dyed flowers, or the type that have been sprinkled with glitter or other synthetic materials.

Pick the flower heads so that there is no stalk remaining. The flower head is the essence of the flower. The stalk is not required. You will be able to engage much more with the ethericity of the flowers if you pick the heads by hand. If you find this difficult, or if you have a very large home that needs a lot of flower offerings, you can use scissors, if you prefer.

How to create a classic flower offering

Classic flower offerings are the easiest to create, so we recommend you start with this type.

Materials

- A small saucer or plate
- A tealight candle in a holder
- 5–6 flower heads, approximately the same size

Method

Place a candle in the centre of a small plate or saucer and arrange five or six flower heads around it, radiating out. Make the contrasting colours and arrangement of the flowers as beautiful as you can.

Use a variety of flower head shapes that are approximately the same size, and colours that go well together. The best flowers to use are chrysanthemums, carnations, alstroemerias, freesias, orchids, and small roses. Don't use tulips, large carnations, irises, or large-headed flowers such as gerberas or sunflowers.

Don't put any water in the saucer or plate. It's not needed and can lead to spills when you are carrying the flower offerings from the altar to the various rooms in your home.

Examples of classic flower offerings

Examples of how NOT to create classic flower offerings

Can you spot what's wrong with each of these?

These flower heads are pointing in, not out

These flower heads are much too large

This offering does not have enough flower heads

The stalks have not been removed from these flower heads

You can find more examples of classic flower offerings on our website at www.clearspaceliving.com/flower-offerings

How to create a rose-petal flower offering

Creating rose-petal flower offerings requires more artistic talent than classic flower offerings, and you will also need roses of a particular size, shape, and freshness.

Materials

- A small saucer or plate
- A tealight candle in a holder
- Medium-sized rose petals
- 3 or 4 flower heads (assorted or all the same type)

In places such as the United States, where roses are often bred to be very large, the petals can be droopy and lacking etheric vitality. If medium-sized roses with petals that are no more than 4–5 cm (1.5–2 inches) long are not available in your area, create classic flower offerings instead. Never use crinkled, torn, or wilting rose petals because they will not be effective as offerings.

Method

Place a candle in the centre of the saucer or plate. Remove the rose from its stem by breaking it cleanly at the base of the flower head. Place your thumbs inside the base of the flower head and gently pull it open to release a cascade of rose petals without tearing any of them.

Take some of the rose petals and arrange them around the candle, taking care not to place any petals underneath the candle or draping over the edges of the saucer or plate. Then place three or four flower heads of a similar size on top of the bed of petals, radiating out from the candle.

When creating this type of offering, it's essential to use a combination of rose petals and flower heads, not just rose petals.

For situations where you need more order or stability in your life, use the same type and colour of flower heads on each offering. For situations where you need more possibilities to open in your life, use a variety of types and colours of flower heads.

Examples of rose-petal flower offerings

Examples of rose-petal flower offerings

Examples of how NOT to create rose-petal flower offerings

Can you spot what's wrong with each of these?

This offering does not have enough rose petals and has no flower heads

The candle is not centred, only one flower head has been used, and it's far too big

The flower heads are pointing inward, not outward

These flower heads are too large

You can find more examples of rose-petal flower offerings on our website at www.clearspaceliving.com/flower-offerings

Step 14
Create a space clearing altar

☐ *Basic Space Clearing*

☑ *Essential Space Clearing*

☑ *Full Space Clearing*

Use your space clearing kit and flower offerings to create a space clearing altar.

Basic Space Clearing

No altar is needed for a Basic Space Clearing ceremony. Simply place your space clearing equipment on a white tablecloth.

Essential Space Clearing

The altar for an Essential Space Clearing is a simplified version of the type used for a Full Space Clearing.

Full Space Clearing

The altar for a Full Space Clearing requires a Full Space Clearing kit, including an altar cloth and colourizers.

How to choose the best location for your altar

Whichever version of the space clearing ceremony you do, you will need a clean, clear, horizontal raised surface to place your space clearing equipment on. It's best to use a table. If you don't have one, use another type of surface, such as a kitchen countertop, a desk, or a low chest of drawers or dresser. It can be square, rectangular, or circular.

Each circuit of the space clearing ceremony begins and ends at the main entrance of the area being cleared, so it's very helpful to locate your altar within easy reach of this, if you can. It will also work best to create it in a quiet area of your home, away from any traffic or other external noises.

Unless your home is a studio apartment that has only one room, always set up your altar in a communal area such as a living room, dining room, kitchen, or entrance hall, rather than a bedroom. Never set up a space clearing altar in a child's bedroom or a junk room. Choose a room that already has vibrant energy in preference to one that feels stagnant or stuck.

For Essential Space Clearing and Full Space Clearing, it will work best if you can position the altar in a location that will facilitate you taking energetic ownership of the space you are clearing. To help with this, point the top of the altar toward the home rather than away from it.

Also check there is a clear headspace above the spot where you'll be standing to activate the flower offering on the altar (don't stand under an exposed beam, for example).

If you already have an altar of some kind in your home, don't attempt to adapt it for space clearing use. Mixing frequencies in that way won't work at all.

Equipment and materials needed to create a space clearing altar, in order of placement

Essential Space Clearing

- A white tablecloth
- A Balinese altar cloth (optional)
- A Balinese space clearing bell and bell stand
- A Balinese harmony ball and stand
- A space clearing water pot and saucer

- A mini carnation flower head (white or pastel coloured)
- One flower offering

Full Space Clearing

- A white tablecloth
- A Balinese altar cloth
- Balinese colourizers
- A Balinese space clearing bell and bell stand
- A Balinese harmony ball and stand
- Up to three neutral Balinese harmony balls on a plate (optional)
- A space clearing water pot and saucer
- A mini carnation flower head (white or pastel coloured)
- Flower offerings, with a coaster beneath the main flower offering

How to create an Essential Space Clearing altar

An example of an Essential Space Clearing altar

The main difference between the two types of altars is that a Full Space Clearing altar involves the creation of a specific design using an altar cloth and colourizers, with multiple flower offerings. The Essential Space Clearing ceremony only needs a simple altar with one flower offering.

1. Place a white tablecloth on the table

A clean white tablecloth is the first step to transform an ordinary table into a space clearing altar. Ideally, use a brand-new tablecloth that has never been used for anything else before. If that's not possible, at least use one that has been freshly laundered.

Remove any objects that are on the table and any chairs that are normally placed near or around it. Wipe the surface of the table with a clean, wet cloth and use another clean cloth to dry it. Then lay your tablecloth on it and smooth it out.

2. Place a Balinese altar cloth on top of the tablecloth

Handwoven gold-threaded Balinese altar cloths are extraordinarily beautiful. It's optional to use one for Essential Space Clearing but highly recommended. It will substantially enhance and add definition to the altar.

Place the altar cloth in the centre of the table, on top of the white tablecloth. If you discover that the size of altar cloth you have chosen hangs over the edges of the table, then you will either need to use a bigger table or a smaller altar cloth.

Altar cloths are available in three colours. Choose the colour that fits best with your overall reason for doing the space clearing:

White: Clarity, simplicity, and purity
Purple: Prosperity and empowerment
Red: Motivation, action, and accomplishment

You can find more information about these colours in Chapter 16.

3. Place your space clearing equipment on the altar

Begin by placing your space clearing bell and stand in the exact centre of the altar. You can decorate the bell stand with a few flower heads, if you would like to.

Place a flower offering in front of the bell and stand, with a coaster beneath it to prevent the surface of the table from scorching when the candle burns down.

Place your harmony ball and stand in front of the bell and stand or behind it, if you prefer (in which case, leave enough room to place your space clearing water pot and saucer behind it after you have finished using the space clearing water).

Adjust the positions of all the items to form a straight vertical line up the centre of the altar.

If you decide to use two personal harmony balls because there are two joint heads of household in your home and you prefer to use one each rather than sharing, to preserve the symmetry of the altar, place the two harmony balls next to each other on the centre line (known as the central vertical axis and explained in more detail later in this chapter), or put one harmony ball and stand on either side of the altar, in line with the bell stand.

4. Place your space clearing water pot and saucer on the table

Place your space clearing water pot and saucer below the lower edge of the altar cloth, in line with the central vertical axis of the altar, and place a mini carnation on the saucer, next to the water pot.

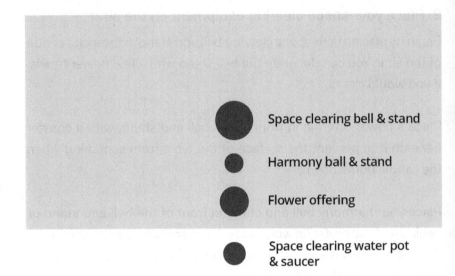

How to position space clearing equipment on an altar

What does NOT belong on a space clearing altar

We've learned from experience that people who have a lot of clutter tend to want to clutter their altar too, so if this applies to you, please resist the urge to do this. The simplest altars are usually the most profound. Do your best to make it as tidy, symmetrical, and uncluttered as possible.

Don't put any personal items on the altar, such as photos, trinkets, symbols, decorative objects, photos of gurus, or text of any kind. These types of things may serve a purpose on other types of altars, but they will detract from the archetypal integrity of a space clearing altar and weaken its effectiveness, not enhance it.

Matches are needed for the ceremony, but they do not belong on the altar. Keep them nearby.

Additional features of a Full Space Clearing altar

An example of a Full Space Clearing altar

An altar is used in a Full Space Clearing to create a symbolic representation of the focus for the ceremony and an anchorage for the frequencies of change it is designed to facilitate. It's a way of unpacking archetypal and superastral levels of the ceremony, and greatly increases its effectiveness.

Karen didn't include this information in her first space clearing book because at that time she was only teaching altar design skills to professional practitioners. Since then, many people have purchased altar cloths and colourizers from our online shop, so we want to include detailed information in this book about how to use them.

The best size of altar cloth to use

The size of altar cloth you need for a Full Space Clearing will be determined by how many flower offerings you'll be placing on it. This, in turn, will be determined by how large your home is. Put simply, if you have a large home or a home with lots of rooms, you'll need a large altar cloth. If you have a small home, a smaller altar cloth will be fine, although it's also fine to use a large altar cloth if you prefer to.

Colourizers

Choose according to the focus of the ceremony, using the following guidelines:

White: Clarity, simplicity, and purity
Purple: Prosperity and empowerment
Red: Motivation, action, and accomplishment
Pink: Passion and love of life
Orange: Creativity and confidence
Yellow: Hope, joy, and happiness
Green: Harmony, healing, and vibrancy
Blue: Truth, integrity, and purpose
Turquoise: Ancient resonance and inner calm

You can find full information about each of these colours in Chapter 16.

Harmony balls

If you opt to use neutral harmony balls in the ceremony, place them on a plate on the altar, on one side of the bell and stand, and place your personal harmony ball(s) on the opposite side, instead of on the central vertical axis.

Altar design elements

Each time you do a Full Space Clearing ceremony, you will need to create a new altar design that fits with the focus of that ceremony. If you find yourself tempted to use the same altar design repeatedly, we recommend you reread this chapter to get fresh inspiration.

The two most important elements of any space clearing altar are:

• The central vertical axis
• The horizontal base line

Not every altar will include both elements. In those that do, it works best to place the central vertical axis first, then the horizontal base line, then any other elements after that.

The central vertical axis

The central vertical axis of an altar is the line that runs vertically up the centre. Anything placed in this position is accentuated and represents the direction you wish to move in. It's the best position for a colourizer that relates to the core focus of the ceremony.

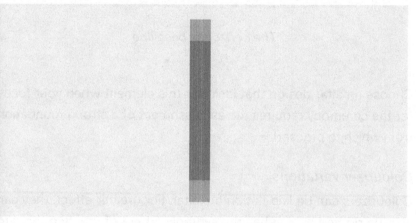

The central vertical axis

The horizontal base line

The horizontal base line of an altar is formed by placing a colourizer in a horizontal position next to the lower edge of the altar cloth.

The horizontal base line

Choose an altar design that includes this element when your focus for the ceremony requires the establishment of a strong foundation from which to proceed.

Colourizer variations

Colourizers can be laid flat on the altar. For greater effect, they can also be rippled, which has the symbolic effect of creating forward momentum.

- Single ripple – mild effect
- Double ripple – stronger effect
- Triple ripple – maximum effect

It's also possible to space the ripples along the colourizer according to the pace at which you feel ready for change to happen:

- Spaced ripples – slow engagement
- Packed ripples – fast engagement

How to ripple a colourizer

Suppose you have an altar design that has a vertical colourizer in the position of the central vertical axis and you want to create two ripples along it. The best way to do this is to lay the colourizer vertically on the altar with its lower edge in the correct position. Then hold the bottom part of the colourizer while you slide the upper parts toward you, forming the lower ripple first and then the upper ripple. Leave enough space between the two ripples to place your bell stand and bell.

Note that this is only possible with large colourizers. Small colourizers are not long enough to be rippled.

Examples of spaced ripples

Examples of packed ripples

When creating ripples on a vertically or diagonally positioned colourizer, always follow the direction *away* from the base of the altar to give the effect of a wave of energy that takes you up and out.

It's less common for horizontal colourizers to be rippled, although this can sometimes work well on the horizontal base line. When used in this way, the ripple on the left side of the colourizer will need to flow out from the centre toward the left of the altar and the ripple on the right side of the colourizer will need to flow out from the centre toward the right of the altar.

Dynamic corners

Dynamic corners create a three-dimensional effect that adds emphasis and depth. They can be used in altar designs that include corners, such as The Stabilizer.

To create a diagonal corner, place the ends of two colourizers at a right angle to each other. At the point where they meet, fold the ends of both colourizers back at a 45-degree angle to create a diagonal crease in each, then press the two diagonals together so that they point vertically up.

Example of a dynamic corner

The 12 archetypal altar designs

The main altar designs are:

- Single Focus
- Dual Focus
- The Accelerator
- Establishing Foundations
- Establishing Levels
- Crossroads
- Incarnation
- The Facilitator
- New Beginnings
- All Possibilities
- The Stabilizer
- Spiritual Aspirations

Here's how to create each of these designs, using a small or large altar cloth.

Single Focus

Form

A single central vertical axis.

Use

The beauty of this altar design lies in its profound simplicity. It is for moving forward with a single purpose or goal, with no distractions.

Design

Small

- 1 small altar cloth
- 1 small colourizer, or 1 large, rippled colourizer

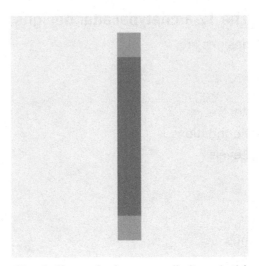

Single Focus (using a small altar cloth)

Large

- 1 large altar cloth
- 1 small colourizer, or 1 large, rippled colourizer

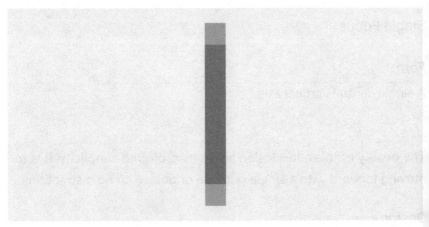

Single Focus (using a large altar cloth)

Dual Focus

Form

A dual central vertical axis.

Use

This altar design is used when there are two equally important focuses (for example, if you share your home with a partner and each of you has very different priorities). Note that there needs to be a slight gap of about 0.5 cm (about 1/5 inch) between the two vertical colourizers so that there is a clear delineation of each focus rather than a merging together.

Design

Small

- 1 small altar cloth
- 2 small colourizers, or 2 large, rippled colourizers

Dual Focus (using a small altar cloth)

Large

- 1 large altar cloth
- 2 small colourizers, or 2 large, rippled colourizers

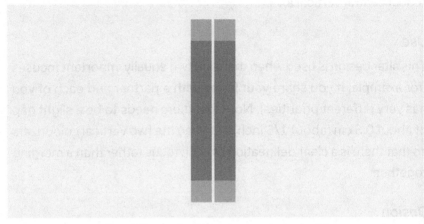

Dual Focus (using a large altar cloth)

The Accelerator

Form

Three parallel vertical lines.

Use

The three vertical lines are symbolic of moving forward, so this altar is best used when you feel stuck in life and want to get moving. This is also one of the best altar designs to add ripples to, according to the speed at which you feel ready to change.

To move forward at a moderate pace, use three small colourizers. If you're ready to get moving quickly, use long colourizers with one, two or three ripples, depending on how fast you want to go.

This altar is also excellent for anyone who has clutter they want to clear. For this purpose, use a small red altar cloth with the colourizers of your choice to create a small altar design, or a large white altar cloth with a red colourizer in the central vertical position and two other colourizers of your choice to create a large altar design.

Design

Small

- 1 small altar cloth
- 3 small colourizers, or 3 large, rippled colourizers, or a combination of small and large rippled colourizers

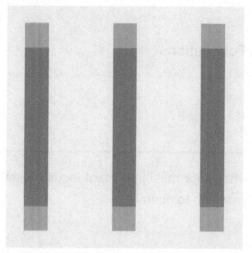

The Accelerator (using a small altar cloth)

Large

- 1 large altar cloth
- 3 small colourizers, or 3 large, rippled colourizers, or a combination of small and large, rippled colourizers

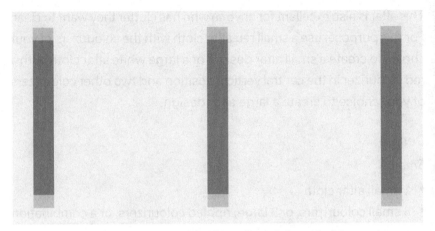

The Accelerator (using a large altar cloth)

Establishing Foundations

Form
A horizontal base line.

Use
Use this altar when your most important focus is establishing a firm foundation from which to operate.

Design
Small

- 1 small altar cloth
- 1 small colourizer

Establishing Foundations (using a small altar cloth)

Large

- 1 large altar cloth
- 1 large colourizer

Establishing Foundations (using a large altar cloth)

Establishing Levels

Form

Three parallel horizontal lines, spaced an equal distance apart.

Use

Use this altar design when you need to put your life in order by separating out the various levels such as work life, personal life, and spiritual life.

Design

Small

- 1 small altar cloth
- 3 small colourizers

Establishing Levels (using a small altar cloth)

Large

- 1 large altar cloth
- 3 large colourizers

Establishing Levels (using a large altar cloth)

Crossroads

Form

A physical cross.

Use

The physical cross symbolizes the four elements meeting at the centre in the alchemical melting pot of transformation. This altar design can be used when you are at a crossroads in your life or when you are engaged in creating a new physical environment for yourself.

Design

Small

1 small altar cloth
2 or 4 small colourizers, or 2 large, rippled colourizers, or 4 large colourizers folded in half, or combinations of these

Crossroads (using a small altar cloth)

Large

- 1 large altar cloth
- 2 or 4 small colourizers, or 2 or 4 large colourizers, flat, folded, or rippled, or a combination of these

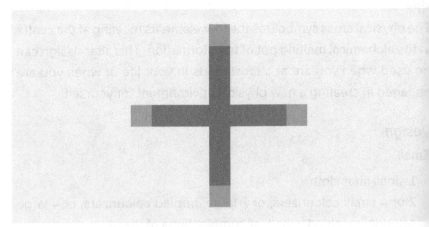

Crossroads (using a large altar cloth)

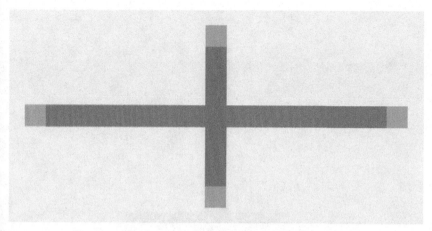

Crossroads (a variation using a large altar cloth)

Incarnation

Form

A base horizontal line with a central vertical axis.

Use

This altar design can be used at times when you need to return to basics to regain clarity and simplicity for the next phase of your life. It is called Incarnation because it facilitates landing in the world and engaging your purpose in life.

Design

Small

- 1 small altar cloth
- 2 small colourizers, 2 large, rippled colourizers, or 1 small colourizer in the base horizontal position and 1 large, rippled colourizer in the central vertical axis position

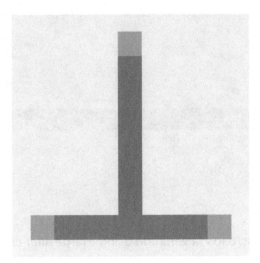

Incarnation (using a small altar cloth)

Large

- 1 large altar cloth
- 1 large colourizer and 1 small colourizer, or 1 large colourizer in the base horizontal position and 1 large, rippled colourizer in the central vertical axis position

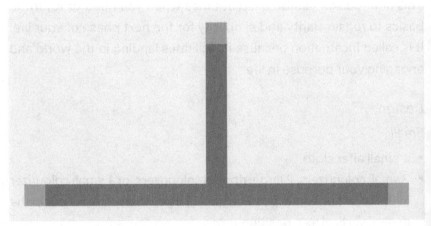

Incarnation (using a large altar cloth)

The Facilitator

Form

Three parallel vertical lines with a horizonal base colourizer.

Use

The purpose of this design is moving forward from a firm foundation. It is similar to The Accelerator and is used when more support to move forward is needed.

Design

Small

- 1 small altar cloth
- 1 small colourizer in the base horizontal position
- 3 small colourizers, or 3 large, rippled colourizers, or a combination of small and large rippled, vertical colourizers

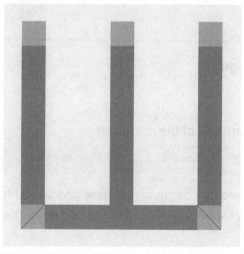

The Facilitator (using a small altar cloth)

Large

- 1 large altar cloth
- 1 large colourizer in the base horizontal position
- 3 small colourizers, or 3 large, rippled colourizers, or a combination of small and large rippled, vertical colourizers

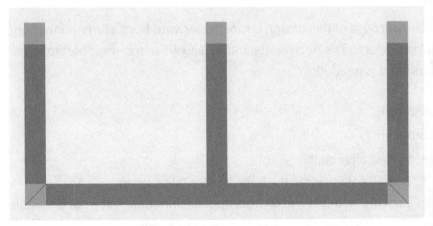

The Facilitator (using a large altar cloth)

New Beginnings

Form

A fan shape, symbolic of the rising sun.

Use

This altar is used for beginning a new phase of life from a solid foundation. It is reminiscent of a sunrise and is uplifting in nature.

New Beginnings is the altar design that is most frequently used because it can apply to so many situations, such as a new home, a new job, a new relationship, a new phase of life, or any other new beginning. It is for any situation where change is welcomed and embraced.

The fan represents the different aspects involved, with the most vital quality placed in the position of the central vertical axis and the supporting quality placed in the horizontal base position.

Design

Small five-fold fan

- 1 small altar cloth
- 1 small colourizer in the horizontal base position
- 3 small colourizers, or 3 large, rippled colourizers, or a combination of small and large rippled colourizers forming the fan

New Beginnings (using a small altar cloth)

Large five-fold fan

1 large altar cloth
1 large colourizer in the horizontal base position
3 small colourizers, or 3 large, rippled colourizers, or a combination of small and large rippled colourizers forming the fan

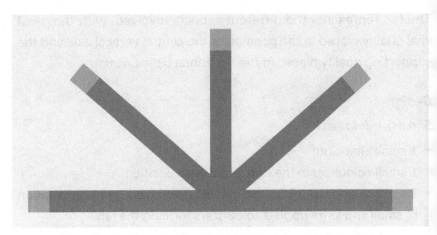

New Beginnings (a five-fold fan on a large altar cloth)

Large seven-fold fan

- 1 large altar cloth
- 1 large colourizer in the horizontal base position
- 5 small colourizers, or 5 large, rippled colourizers, or a combination of small and large rippled colourizers forming the fan

New Beginnings (a seven-fold fan on a large altar cloth)

All Possibilities

Form

An eight-pointed star.

Use

This altar design is for enhancing all aspects of life simultaneously. It's only recommended if you already have all aspects of your life working well and are ready to move to the next level.

Design

Small

- 1 small altar cloth
- 4 or 8 small colourizers

All Possibilities (using a small altar cloth)

Large

- 1 large altar cloth
- 8 small colourizers, 4 or 8 large, rippled colourizers, or combinations of these

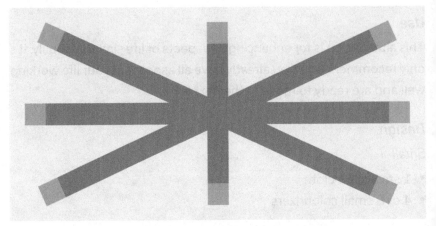

All Possibilities (using a large altar cloth)

The Stabilizer

Form

A square or rectangle.

Use

This altar design can be used when you need a period of stability in your life. It's about creating order from chaos. The square or rectangular formation creates a containment for taking stock and regrouping before moving forward. It's an excellent altar design for a period of reinventing yourself.

The Stabilizer differs from all the other altar designs because it's about staying still, not moving forward. All the changes happen on the inside, not the outside.

Design

Small

- 1 small altar cloth
- 4 small colourizers, connected by dynamic corners

The Stabilizer (using a small altar cloth)

Large

- 1 large altar cloth
- 2 large colourizers and 2 small colourizers, connected by dynamic corners

The Stabilizer (using a large altar cloth)

Spiritual Aspirations

Form
An upward-pointing triangle.

Use
This altar design can be used when the primary focus of a space clearing ceremony is progressing your spiritual path. It's a fiery configuration to increase the voltage, if you're ready to step up your spiritual practices.

Design
Small

- 1 small altar cloth
- 3 small colourizers, connected by dynamic corners

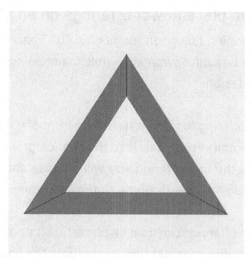

Spiritual Aspirations (using a small altar cloth)

Large

- 1 large altar cloth
- 1 large colourizer in the base horizontal position
- 2 large, rippled colourizers, or 2 small colourizers forming the upper sides of the triangle, connected by dynamic corners

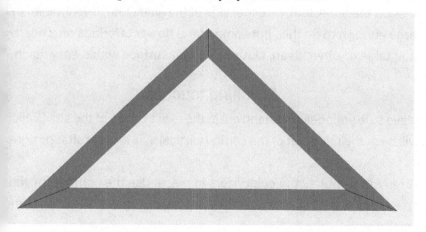

Spiritual Aspirations (using a large altar cloth)

How to place flower offerings on an altar

The art of positioning flower offerings on a Full Space Clearing altar lies in creating a beautiful symmetry while maintaining the structural integrity of the design.

The first flower offering to place is directly in front of your bell and bell stand, on the central vertical axis (see the altar diagram earlier in this chapter). This is the first offering you will activate and the only one that will remain on the altar throughout the ceremony.

The other flower offerings can then be placed at strategic points along colourizers, in such a way that they accentuate the lines of the altar design and bring the altar to life. To preserve symmetry, if you place a flower offering on a colourizer on the left-hand side of the altar, be sure to place one in a mirror position on the right-hand side too.

If your altar is small or you have a large number of flower offerings because your home has many rooms, don't clutter the altar by trying to crowd all the offerings onto it. Instead, put some of them in vertical lines on the tablecloth, on either side of the altar cloth. If your table isn't large enough to do this, put some of the flower offerings on a nearby side table or other clean, clutter-free, flat surface within easy reach.

Finishing touches

Make sure your bell and stand are in the exact centre of the altar, which will be at the midpoint of the central vertical axis in most altar designs.

After you've put all the colourizers in place, use the comb from your space clearing kit to straighten any exposed fringes at the ends of the colourizers.

To complete your altar design, make any small adjustments that are needed to create clean lines and precise symmetry. Take a few moments to take a step back and appreciate its beauty.

Step 15
Make some space clearing water

☐ *Basic Space Clearing*

☑ *Essential Space Clearing*

☑ *Full Space Clearing*

Make some space clearing water using a Balinese space clearing bell and some spring water.

Water is a unique substance that has the remarkable quality of being able to be infused with the presence of high spiritual forces. This is extraordinary because it provides us with the clearest and most tangible proof of the existence of those forces. Anyone with a sufficiently awakened etheric can feel the difference between ordinary water and water that has been spiritually presenced.

Of course, most people these days do not have an awakened etheric. It has to be cultivated, and it's not easy to find someone who can teach you how to do that. Making presenced water is also not easy, which is why the holy water-making process has been in the exclusive domain of priests and priestesses for thousands of years.

This step of the space clearing ceremony has been one of the most challenging for us to write about because we need to teach you an effective way to make space clearing water that won't require you to spend several decades doing the subtle bodybuilding* and spiritual practices we have done. It also needs to be easy for anyone to do, yet not so simplified that it becomes an empty ritual.

What you are about to learn is therefore very different to the way we make space clearing water for ourselves and for our certified practitioners. However, it will still make a huge difference to any space clearing you do. It's a method we have specifically designed for anyone reading this book who wishes to conduct a space clearing ceremony in their own home or in the homes of close friends and relatives. It's not suitable for professional space clearing.

Why it's essential to use a Balinese space clearing bell

You can use a large Balinese space clearing bell or a small one, but it won't work to use any other type of bell.

The reason for this lies in understanding that humans don't make presenced water. Spiritual connections* do. Balinese bells have a distinct sound that is invitational to a specific high-level spiritual connection known as White Gold**. If you follow the method described here exactly, it can open a space for the connection to ride on the sound of the bell to presence the water.

The White Gold connection is non-denominational, which is why the space clearing ceremony you are learning is compatible with all religions. It's also why space clearing water is deliberately *not* called holy water and why it doesn't work to use holy water from a religious source instead of space clearing water. We've done extensive research using holy water from many sources to test this.

How to make space clearing water

Fill your space clearing pot with water

Open your bottle of still spring water and fill your space clearing water pot about three-quarters full. Take care not to splash any water on your altar cloth or colourizers, as they can easily become water stained.

Do personal belling

Personal belling is a technique that can be used for a number of purposes. In this context, you will be using it to centre and uplift yourself, in preparation for making space clearing water.

Stand facing the altar with your head and spine vertical, and your legs slightly apart so that you are stable.

Pick up your bell by the handle. If you are right-handed, use your right hand. If you are left-handed, use your left hand.

Hold the bell in front of you, with the dome at the same level as your root charge* (just below your genital area). Keep it a few centimetres/ inches away from your body and far enough away from the table that you will not accidentally knock the bell against it.

Close your eyes and take three conscious breaths to centre yourself. Breathe in and out through your nose, not your mouth. On each exhalation, completely relax and let go, emptying your mind of all thoughts as you do so.

At the end of the third exhalation, ring the bell and then move it vertically up past your navel, then past the centre of your chest, your throat, and the centre of your forehead. Breathe in as you raise the bell and receive the sound in your central channel of energy, which runs up the centre of your body.

Finish by stretching your arm up as far as it will reach above your head, keeping the bell perfectly vertical as you do so. Hold your breath briefly in that position and, before the sound of the bell fades, still holding the bell vertical, twist the handle horizontally 90 degrees in a clockwise direction, as seen from above, which will have the effect of sealing and reinforcing the effects of the belling.

Then relax your arm, breathe out, and bring the bell back to the root charge position. Do this by moving the bell out to the side of your body in a wide semi-circular arc. Don't lower it vertically back down because you'll undo the uplifting effect that you just created in your central channel.

Repeat the technique two more times (three times in all), taking a few deep breaths between each ring of the bell.

The sound of the bell needs to last long enough for you to be able to hear it when it is above your head, so be sure to ring it loudly enough for that to happen on each of the three passes.

Presence the water

Cradle your bell between your hands, using one hand to hold the handle of the bell and the other hand beneath the dome, palm facing up, to support it. Keep your eyes closed and take a few more breaths as you involute into the central thread of your column above*, which extends vertically up from the centre of the top of your head.

Involution is essential to this technique. Being involuted is the natural state of a human, with our consciousness turned inward rather than out. Involuting into the central thread is a technique used by experienced meditators who do not need to rely on methods such as guided instructions, mantras, sounds, or awareness of the breath. It will help you to silence the usual chitter-chatter in your mind.

After you have stabilized yourself in a more involuted state, open your eyes and position your Balinese space clearing bell about 5 cm (2 inches) above the centre of the water in the bowl. If necessary, adjust your position by moving forward or backward so that you can see the rim of the water pot and your bell while keeping your head vertical.

- Ring your bell vigorously above the centre of the water pot, then immediately move it in a clockwise circle above the water. Engage throat friction as you do so and consciously direct the sound of the bell into the water.
- After completing the first circle, ring the bell again above the centre of the water pot and do a second circle.
- Then ring the bell again and do a third circle.
- End by lifting the bell vertically up over the centre of the water pot, as high as your arm will comfortably stretch, until the sound of the bell fades. Keep your bell vertical as you do this so it does not ring.
- Then place your bell back on its bell stand.

The water is now ready to be used in the space clearing ceremony you are about to do. You can expect it to retain its potency for a maximum of 24 hours.

Step 16
Activate the flower offering(s)

☐ *Basic Space Clearing*

☑ *Essential Space Clearing*

☑ *Full Space Clearing*

To activate a flower offering, light the candle in the centre, then perform the space clearing flower offering mudra using a mini carnation and space clearing water.

Basic Space Clearing

No flower offering is needed.

Essential Space Clearing

Only one flower offering on the altar is needed.

Full Space Clearing

Multiple flower offerings are needed for this version of the ceremony. The first flower offering to be activated is always the one in the centre-front position on the altar. Then follow the instructions in this chapter about how to take the other flower offerings from the altar, one by one, and activate them in the various parts of your home. Place a coaster under each flower offering, except the one that is placed on the kitchen stove, where no coaster is needed because there is no danger of scorching the surface.

How to activate a flower offering

Flower offerings are merely flowers and candles on plates until they are activated. For anyone with the vision* to perceive what happens energetically, this is the most profound part of the entire ceremony. It can be an extraordinarily moving experience.

Learning how to do this on behalf of a client is one of the most challenging parts of the ceremony professional space clearing trainees have to learn. That's why we can only train those who have already spent many years developing the subtle body structures that are needed to be able to do this effectively.

Activating flower offerings in your own home is much easier to do but, even so, your first attempts are likely to be insubstantial and you may feel that not much happens. That's not surprising since this requires a know-how that goes far beyond the level of ordinary mental consciousness that life is generally lived at. It will take some practice, and we can't guarantee that everyone will be able to do it.

If you have taken our online course The Seven Levels of Consciousness, it may be helpful to know that activating flower offerings is ultimately a very advanced Level 3 skill. Fortunately, all that is needed to experience the benefits of space clearing in your own home is to be able to activate the flower offerings at Level 5, which is one level up from the level of everyday life (Level 6). This is more easily achievable, even though it is likely to be a substantial stretch for many people.

There are three steps involved in activating a space clearing flower offering:

1. Light the candle with a match
2. Use a flower head to sprinkle the flower offering three times with space clearing water
3. Do the space clearing flower offering mudra**

The technique is very simple, but there's much that needs to be understood about each of these steps for the flower offering activation to work.

1. Light the candle with a match

The remarkable thing about a candle flame is that it is always vertical. No matter which way you tilt it, it will always adjust to burn vertically. It is the epitome of spiritual aspiration, always pointing upward. That's why we humans have such a great affinity with candle flames. They resonate with the principle of cosmic fire that is an innate quality of our Higher Self.

This special vertical quality is what makes a candle flame so spiritually connectable. Whenever you light a candle, it will always connect to unseen forces of some kind. In everyday life, it doesn't really matter what it connects to. However, whenever you light a candle that is used in any kind of spiritual practice, it needs to be done consciously to ensure it connects to the forces you intend it to connect to. This is especially important when lighting the candles of flower offerings in a space clearing ceremony.

Before lighting the candle of the first flower offering on the altar, all activities in your home need to come to a complete standstill, and you need to become very still and involuted yourself (see Chapter 11).

Follow these steps to light the candle.

Check your sleeves
Make sure your sleeves are securely rolled up above the elbow.

Check your posture
It works best to activate a flower offering from a standing or sitting position, keeping your head and spine vertical while maintaining eye contact with the candle. Activating a flower offering from a kneeling position is usually not very effective. Only use it when an offering has to be placed on a low piece of furniture such as a coffee table.

Take out a match

Pick up your box of long matches, take one out, close the matchbox, and hold the match against the striker strip, ready to ignite it.

Centre yourself

Before striking the match, close your eyes and take a few conscious breaths, in and out through your nose, to centre yourself.

Involute

With your eyes still closed and your head vertical, move your awareness vertically upward from inside your head to above your head. Rest your consciousness in your column above and involute. Still your mind as much as possible. No thoughts.

Light the candle

Open your eyes, strike the match, and light the candle from the space of involuted stillness above your head, holding eye contact with the candle flame as you do so. Rest in the integrity of your own verticality and consciously connect it to the verticality of the flame. If you do this correctly, it will feel as if time stands still and nothing else exists in the world except you and the flower offering.

Put the matches down

Blow out the match and put the match and matchbox down on a nearby surface (not on the altar).

2. Use a flower head to sprinkle the flower offering three times with space clearing water

Pick up your space clearing water pot and flower head

Take your space clearing water pot in one hand and pick up a flower head with your other hand (the one you normally use to write with).

The best type of flower to use for this is a white or pastel-coloured mini carnation, with no remaining stalk attached. Hold the base of the flower head between the inner tip of your thumb and the inner tips of your forefinger and middle finger.

How to hold a flower head to sprinkle the flower offering

Maintain eye contact with the flame

From this point on, maintain eye contact with the candle flame while keeping your head and spine vertical.

Sprinkle space clearing water on the flower offering three times

Dip the flower head into the water and gently sprinkle a few drops from the flower head onto one section of the flower offering. Repeat this twice more, sprinkling water drops on different sections each time.

The three sections need to be roughly equidistant. If you accidentally sprinkle water on the flame and cause it to go out, replace it with a fresh tealight candle and start again (don't worry, this does sometimes happen).

3. Do the space clearing flower offering mudra

Change the way you hold the flower head

As soon as you've done the third sprinkling of space clearing water, smoothly make the transition from holding the flower head between your thumb, forefinger, and middle finger to holding it between your forefinger and middle finger, with the flower head now pointing away from your palm rather than toward it. There is no need to use your other hand to help you do this. It's a very easy and natural movement that can be done using one hand only.

How to hold a flower head while doing the space clearing mudra

Rest in your root charge

Keep your awareness above your head while simultaneously resting energetically in your root charge (located just below your anus and perineum), as if you are sitting on a dense, immovable rock.

Engage throat friction

Engage throat friction (see Chapter 10) while breathing slowly and steadily in and out through your nose.

Engage the starting position for the space clearing flower offering mudra

Breathe in as you raise your hand to throat level, with the flattened palm of your hand facing toward your throat, the flower head pointing away from you, your arm bent at the elbow, and your forearm extended horizontally to the side of your throat area, parallel to the floor. Position your hand so that the flower head is about 5 cm (2–3 inches) away from your larynx. Keep your head vertical and your eyes focused on the candle flame.

Perform the space clearing flower offering mudra

Continue to hold eye contact with the flame as you move your hand vertically down, following the midline of your body. Keep your palm facing toward you, a few centimetres/inches away from your body, and the flower head between your fingers pointing away from you.

At the bottom of the downsweep, when your hand is close to the flower offering, twist your wrist through 180 degrees so that your flattened palm now faces away from you and toward the offering, and the flower head now points toward you. Then move your hand up in a wide loop about 30 cm (12 inches) away from your body, back up to chin level, offering up the essence of the flower offering as you do so. Twist your wrist through 180 degrees again to return to the mudra starting position at the larynx.

Pause a few seconds, then repeat the mudra a second time, exactly the same as the first.

Pause a few seconds, then do a third and final downsweep. At the bottom of this downsweep, twist your wrist through 180 degrees so that your flattened palm now faces away from you, toward the flower offering, and instead of doing an upsweep, do a small circle in the air close to the flower offering, ending the loop with an almost imperceptible side-to-side motion of your hand that has a densifying, sealing effect. Hold this position for a few seconds, then smoothly and gently withdraw your hand and place the mini carnation back on the saucer.

Where to place your space clearing water pot

If you are doing an Essential Space Clearing ceremony, you won't need any more space clearing water, so you can place your space clearing water pot and saucer at the top of the altar, behind the harmony ball and stand.

If you are doing a Full Space Clearing ceremony, wait until after you have activated all the other flower offerings around your home to do this. For now, leave your space clearing pot and saucer in front of the flower offering so that you can easily access it.

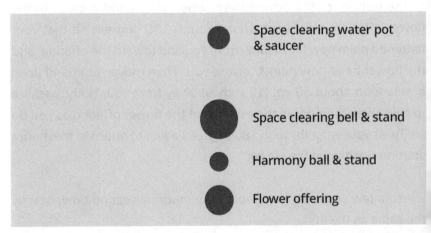

Space clearing water pot
& saucer

Space clearing bell & stand

Harmony ball & stand

Flower offering

The final positioning of space clearing equipment on the altar

Points to remember

- Maintain eye contact with the flame throughout the mudra. Don't be tempted to tilt your head forward. Stay vertical. If you can't easily see the flame, change your position or move the flower offering so that you can.
- Take a breath before starting the mudra. On the downsweep, breathe out, using throat friction. On the upsweep, breathe in, using milder throat friction.
- The downsweep of the mudra needs to be done slowly, taking about 10 seconds. The upsweep is faster and takes about 5 seconds. If you are not able to sustain an out-breath during the downsweep for 10 seconds, it's fine to quickly take an in-breath halfway and continue with the out-breath.
- Your palm will always be facing toward you on the downsweep and always away from you on the upsweep.
- Throughout the mudra, hold your awareness above your head. You will need to practise the mudra before doing a space clearing ceremony so that you know it well enough to do it without thinking.
- On each downsweep, feel how the mudra movement resonates with your central channel of energy and highlights your heart area and pelvic region as it passes over them.
- At the bottom of the downsweep, as you turn your palm out toward the flower offering, connect to the ethericity of the flowers so that you can offer up their essence on the upsweep.
- On the third downsweep, when doing the small circle at the end of the mudra, breathe quickly in and out using strong throat friction. It only takes one or two seconds. Then hold your breath at the bottom of the out-breath, while holding your flattened hand completely still in the final position close to the edge of the flower offering for about 2 seconds before doing the seal.
- Don't move the flower offering after it has been activated.

Very important: A common mistake that people make is to visualize pulling energies down into the room during the downsweep of the mudra. Don't do this. It's ineffectual at best and energetically venomizing at worst (high-level forces need to be held above the head – they can be toxic if pulled down into the physical body). If you do the mudra correctly, the space around the flower offering will become noticeably stiller and denser. If this doesn't happen each time, don't worry or try to force it or visualize it. It does take practice.

How to remove flower offerings from the altar

At the start of a Full Space Clearing ceremony, all the flower offerings are placed on the altar, accentuating the lines created by the altar design. They are then taken from the altar, one by one, and placed in various locations around the home, where each one is activated and left in place until the candle has completely burned down.

If you have a large home and have additional flower offerings on a side table because there are too many to put on the altar without making it look cluttered, each time you take a flower offering off the altar, replace it with one from the side table. In that way, all the offerings will take a turn on the altar and form part of the symbolic representation of the focus of the ceremony.

Always leave the flower offerings that are in the most key positions on the altar until last, in order to maintain the symmetry and geometry of the design as long as possible. For example, for altar designs with a pronounced baseline of offerings forming a foundation that everything else rests on (New Beginnings, The Facilitator, and Establishing Foundations), this will mean taking flower offerings from the top and side areas of the altar first and leaving the offerings on the baseline until last.

How to position flower offerings around your home

Create a clear, uncluttered space for each flower offering by removing any other objects from the area. As much as possible, place each flower offering so that it is immediately visible when you enter a room or area, preferably on a raised surface such as a table. This creates a more uplifting effect and is generally safer too.

If you have a basement that has a concrete floor and is not used as a living area, it's fine to put the flower offering directly on the floor.

If you have a large home, you can use a tray to carry the flower offerings from the altar to the rooms. It doesn't have to be a special tray that you use only for space clearing purposes.

Important: Do not light the candle of any flower offering until you have placed it in the room where it will be located for the rest of the ceremony and you are ready to activate it.

The best order to place and activate flower offerings in your home

The altar
The kitchen stove

Then start from the basement, if there is one, and go up floor by floor, placing and activating the flower offerings in the following order on each floor before continuing to the next floor:

Living areas
The main bedroom
Children's bedrooms (in birth order, starting with the eldest)
Guest bedrooms
Other rooms, such as home offices, studies, playrooms, junk rooms, and so on, according to their level of importance or usage

Space Clearing, Volume 1

Finally, work your way back down the building, floor by floor, placing and activating a matrix flower offering in a central position on the landing, hallway, or foyer of each floor.

If your home has a basement that is used as a living area, include a matrix flower offering there too. If it is only used as a storage area, there is no need to do so because there will be no superastral layers to engage.

If you have a single-storey home, the order of placing and activating flower offerings is exactly the same. The only difference is that there will only be one matrix flower offering and it will be on the same floor as all the other offerings.

In a studio apartment, it is sometimes not necessary to use a matrix flower offering if the space is very small.

The altar

The first flower offering to activate is always placed in the centre-front position of the altar, vertically in line with your bell. This applies no matter which floor of your home the altar is on and which altar design you use.

The kitchen stove

The next offering to activate is always on the kitchen stove or in the food preparation area, if there is no stove (if you follow a raw food diet, for example). Do this no matter which floor of the home the kitchen is on.

The reason why the second flower offering is always placed in this location is that the kitchen is the heart of nourishment in a home. You may be fortunate to have always had enough food to eat, so you may take this for granted. A period of lean finances in your life or visiting a part of the world where people live from hand to mouth will soon make you understand how essential food is to our physical existence and why the kitchen stove offering is therefore so important.

After the ceremony has finished, it's fine to move this flower offering to one side if you wish to cook, then move it back again after you have finished. You don't have to blow the candle out or wait until it burns down.

Living areas

The best place to put a flower offering in a living area is somewhere central, such as a coffee table in the middle of the room or in the centre of a mantlepiece above a fireplace. In a room that has several clearly defined uses, such as one that has a living area, dining area, and an office area in one corner, place a flower offering in each area, in order of importance or usage.

Bedrooms

In a bedroom with a single bed, it is best to put the flower offering on a bedside table, unless the bed is awkwardly positioned, making it difficult to see the offering when you enter the room. In that case, place it on a raised surface elsewhere in the room, where it will be more visible.

In a bedroom that is occupied by more than one person and has a large bed or multiple single beds, place the flower offering so that it doesn't favour one person over any other. For example, if the room has a double bed with bedside cabinets on either side of the bed, don't put the flower offering on one of the cabinets. Place it in a central location in the room that both people will be able to relate to equally. If necessary, bring in a small table to use for that purpose. Never place a flower offering on a bed, as that could be a serious fire hazard.

Home offices and studies

In a room that has a desk as a prominent feature, the centre of the desk is usually the best place to put a flower offering. Move any items in the centre of the desk out of the way to give the offering a clear space.

Junk rooms

Be very careful when placing a flower offering in a room that is filled with junk. If there is no safe place to put it, don't put an offering in there at all.

Matrix flower offerings

These are the last flower offerings to be placed and activated, starting at the top of the property and going down, floor by floor. They need to be positioned in a central, prominent position on each floor, usually on a landing, in a hallway, or in a foyer. Place only one matrix flower offering per floor.

They are called matrix flower offerings because they have a different function to other flower offerings. They are used to link all the flower offerings into an energetic matrix.

Hold horizontal awareness of all the flower offerings on each floor as you activate each matrix flower offering. If there is more than one floor to your home, as you go down the building hold simultaneous awareness of all the flower offerings on each floor as you activate the matrix flower offering on that floor as well as vertical awareness of the matrix offerings you have already activated on the upper floors.

If your home has an entrance hall, that is usually the best place to put the final matrix flower offering, on a small table near the front door, for example. If there is no foyer, place it in a position from which you feel you can energetically access as much of the entire home as possible.

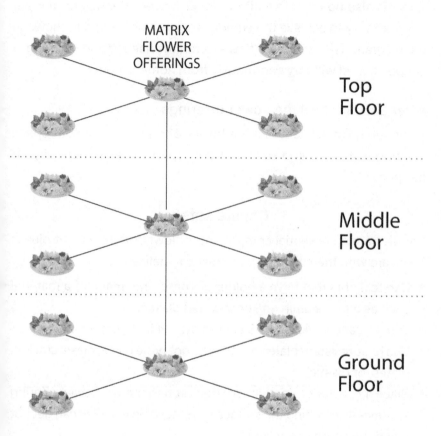

MATRIX
FLOWER
OFFERINGS

Top
Floor

Middle
Floor

Ground
Floor

Example of matrix flower offerings in a three-storey home

We have included this diagram to help you to understand how matrix flower offerings work. The matrix flower offerings are the ones at the centre of each level. Although the diagram shows them as being in a geometrically straight vertical line, there is no need to attempt to achieve this physically in your home because the matrix space is fluid dimensional and superastral in nature, not physical (if you're interested to know more about this, you can find more information in the chapter about how flower offerings work in *Space Clearing, Volume 2*).

There is also no need to limit the other flower offerings to four per floor or to try to achieve the equidistant positioning that is shown in the diagram. The number of flower offerings needed and where they are positioned will vary enormously from home to home.

After activating all the flower offerings

After you have activated all the flower offerings, place your space clearing water pot and saucer at the top of the altar, behind your harmony ball.

Candle safety

Candles are an essential component of flower offerings, but please take care with them by following these guidelines:

- Use tealights that have a holder of some kind, made of a material such as glass, aluminium, or recycled plastic.
- Trim all candle wicks to 0.5 cm (about 1/4 inch) before lighting.
- Use heat-resistant plates or saucers (not bone china, glass, cracked plates, or plastic).
- Place a coaster or heat-absorbing mat under each flower offering to prevent scorching the surface it is placed on (candles can get hot when they burn down low).
- Place flower offerings on raised surfaces such as tables, not on the floor, unless the home has no furniture so there is no other choice.
- If you live in an area that is prone to earthquakes, devise some method that will prevent the candles from tipping over and causing a fire if an earthquake happens.
- Always place flower offerings in such a way that a pet, child, or adult will not be able to cause an accident.
- Always place flower offerings well away from any draughts.
- Always place flower offerings well away from curtains, soft furnishings, and other flammable items.

- Never place a flower offering on a bed, sofa, chair, or other type of soft furnishing.
- Never place flower offerings near direct heat sources, such as open fires, or on warm surfaces, such as the tops of radiators.
- After you light a candle, don't move it before the end of the ceremony unless it's absolutely necessary.

Step 17
Do a circuit of clapping

☑ *Basic Space Clearing*
☑ *Essential Space Clearing*
☑ *Full Space Clearing*

Starting at the main entrance, walk around the inner perimeter of the space, stopping to clap in all the corners as you go and any other areas where stagnant energies can accumulate.

This is the point in the ceremony where the clearing work begins. It can be hard work in some homes, especially if the property is very old, has never been space cleared before, or is full of clutter. But it is well worth the effort involved.

The purpose of the clapping circuit

When done correctly, clapping is a powerful way to break up clumps of stagnant energies and surface layers of astral imprints in rooms. It also prepares the space to make the belling circuit that follows it more effective.

Why it doesn't work to substitute clap sticks or drums

Clap sticks consist of two pieces of wood that are banged together. If you have an enormous home, you may be tempted to use them instead of clapping with your hands. We explain in detail in *Space Clearing Volume 2* why we don't recommend this, or the use of drums or other percussive instruments. They are nowhere near as effective as clapping.

How to do the clapping circuit

If you have a large house or your hands are a bit dry, it can be helpful to moisturize your palms with some unscented, non-greasy hand cream before beginning the clapping circuit. This will help to make the clapping sound more resonant, which will make it more effective. It will also protect your hands so that your palms don't become sore.

How to start the clapping circuit

Go to the main entrance you began the hand-sensing circuit from. This time, stand squarely facing the door instead of sideways to it. Make sure your sleeves are still firmly rolled up above the elbow. Have your feet shoulder-width apart and your weight evenly distributed through your feet. Adjust your posture so that your spine and head are vertical.

Engage the etheric layer of the centre of the door by moving your hand near it a few times, as if you are gently stroking a cat.

When you feel you have made contact with the etheric layer, engage throat friction, raise your hands to somewhere between throat level and eye level (depending on what feels most comfortable to you) and do one loud, resonant clap to begin the clapping circuit.

After clapping, sweep your hand down over the area to smooth out the energy, turn sideways to the door, hook your hand into the clear energy at heart level, and carry it with you to the first corner of your home. This will be located to the left of the main entrance if you are right-handed and to the right if you are left-handed.

Walk around the inner perimeter of the space, stopping to clap where necessary

As you walk, keep your hand outstretched and your palm facing the wall, about 5 cm (3 inches) from it. Keep your hand soft and flexible, not rigid or tense. This looks exactly the same as the technique for hand sensing, except that you are no longer sensing.

When you arrive at the first corner, stop, face into it, engage throat friction, take a breath, and raise your hands as high up into the corner as you can comfortably reach. Then clap three times, loudly and sharply, as you move your hands down to waist level, directing the effect of the claps into the entire corner, from the ceiling to the floor.

The direction of clapping must always be from high to low. Don't start low down in a corner and clap upward to above your head as this will result in you being showered with all the stagnant energies that the clapping technique is designed to disperse.

After clapping a corner, smooth the energy down with the flat of your hand, from as high up in the corner as you can reach down to your waist level. Then, still keeping your palm flat, hook into the energy at heart level and continue around the space to the next corner, keeping your arm outstretched and your palm toward the wall, bringing the clear energy with you as you go.

Repeat this in each corner of your home, taking exactly the same path you took for the hand-sensing circuit. You can also clap out other areas where stagnant energies tend to accumulate, such as the gaps between furniture. If you want to be very thorough, open all your closets and clap them out too.

If there is a lot of clutter or stagnant energies in some areas, the clapping will sound dull. You may need to clap it out two or three times.

Soft furnishings such as beds, sofas, and armchairs absorb astral imprints more than other types of furniture, so if you have any of these in your home, you will need to give them special attention during this circuit.

Here are some examples:

- **Single bed**: Clap three times – once at the head of the bed, once in the middle, and once at the foot
- **Double bed**: Clap three times from head to foot on one side, then three times from head to foot on the other side
- **Chair**: Clap three times, starting at the top of the chair's backrest and ending at the front edge of the seat
- **Sofa**: Clap three times from the top of the backrest to the front edge of the seat in one part of the sofa, then repeat once or twice more in different sections of the sofa (depending on its size)

We need to mention here that people sometimes have an emotional reaction during the clapping circuit. That's because we are energetically connected to our home and the objects in it, so the process of clearing energies in our home can also help to clear corresponding areas of stuckness in ourselves.

If this happens to you, don't stop. Just keep going with the clapping circuit and let the tears flow. A few breaths will help to move the energy through. The emotions will quickly pass. If a member of your household who is present during the ceremony has an emotional upwelling, tell them to do the same.

How to clap

Be sure to get deep into each corner, as close to the wall as you can. Breathe with throat friction and firmly direct each clap from your belly, with will. This is not a lightweight technique. It needs oomph.

Your claps need to be loud and sharp. Soft claps will have no effect at all. Aim for the same level of intensity as a whip being cracked. One of the reasons why Richard's clapping technique is so good is that long before he learned how to do space clearing, he had already developed excellent clapping skills while living on a farm for a while. He used it as a humane way of herding cows and developed it to the level that it was just as effective as using an electric cattle prod.

Most people find that the reverberation of their claps sounds dull and muffled at first, especially if there is clutter in the room. If you are doing it right, the sound will gradually become crisper and clearer as you progress. There is often a significant change when you are about three-quarters of the way around the inner perimeter of a home.

There are many different rhythms you can clap in, and many different intensities and volumes. In large rooms, you will usually need to do much louder clapping than in smaller rooms, and you may find that less volume is more appropriate for the rooms of small children and babies. A slow, sedate pace may be needed in some areas and much faster clapping in other places. This constitutes a whole branch of study for professional space clearers. When doing the ceremony in your own home, just do what feels best to you.

The crocodile clap

This is a special technique that can be used in narrow spaces, such as between a wardrobe and a wall, where there is not enough room to do a conventional clap. Put your palms together with one hand flat on top of the other and extend your arms into the narrow space. Then pull your arms vertically apart, like a crocodile opening its jaws, and bring them back together again at speed so that your hands clap loudly together. Do this briskly several times until the sound reverberates clearly.

Long-distance clapping

This is a technique for clapping out grotty basements or areas that are so cluttered you can't walk around them. It's not as effective as getting in there and clapping out each corner individually, but it's sometimes the best you can do in the circumstances.

Stand at the entrance to the room and focus your attention on the first corner you want to clap out. Fix your sight at the top of the corner, where the walls meet the ceiling, and throw a sharp clap along the beam of your sight into the top part of the corner. Repeat twice more, moving your sight further down the corner each time.

Work methodically around the room in this way, throwing three claps into each corner of the space.

Note that this is not an invitation to do space clearing by long-distance clapping from your armchair. It's nowhere near as effective as physically walking around a space and clapping in all the corners.

End the circuit back at the main entrance

When you arrive back at the main entrance, turn to face the door. End with a loud clap, with your hands positioned somewhere between heart and eye level. Then use your dominant hand to splice the energies into the etheric layer of the door to complete the circuit, in exactly the same way as in Step 12 at the end of the hand-sensing circuit.

One clapping circuit is usually enough, unless you get back to the main entrance and haven't heard any improved resonance in the sound of your claps. If that happens, it will mean your clapping technique wasn't effective, you weren't doing it vigorously enough, or there was a heck of a lot of stuck energy to clear. Whatever the cause, you will need to go around the entire inner perimeter again, using more focus, more oomph, and making sure your claps are sufficiently sharp and clear.

As soon as you finish the clapping circuit, go straight to Step 18, which will only take a minute but is crucial.

Step 18
Wash your hands and forearms

☑ *Basic Space Clearing*

☑ *Essential Space Clearing*

☑ *Full Space Clearing*

Immediately after the clapping circuit, wash your hands and forearms under cold or cool running water.

Washing your hands and forearms straight after the clapping circuit will remove any clumps of stagnant energies that may have stuck to you and will leave you feeling fresh and ready to move on to the next step straight away. Please be sure to do this. It's a very important step in the ceremony to ensure that you don't pick up any unwanted energies.

Cold water works best. If you are doing the space clearing in cold weather and can't tolerate that, add a hint of warm water. Don't use hot water because it's not as effective.

With your sleeves rolled up well above your elbows, place the crook of one arm under the running water, then twist your arm so that it gets bathed in cold water all the way down to your fingertips. Use your free hand to pull the water down your arm, together with any stagnant energies you have picked up. Then repeat the entire process with your other arm.

Dry your hands and forearms on a clean towel.

If you are interested to know more about this etheric excretion technique, it is described in more detail in Chapter 4.12 of *Awakening the Third Eye* by Samuel Sagan.

Step 19
Do a circuit of belling

☑ *Basic Space Clearing*

☑ *Essential Space Clearing*

☑ *Full Space Clearing*

Starting at the main entrance, walk around the inner perimeter of the space, consciously directing the sound of your Balinese space clearing bell into the walls, corners, and other objects. Do not let the sound of the bell fade until the circuit is complete.

Most people find the belling circuit to be one of the most enjoyable parts of the ceremony. That's because Balinese space clearing bells are so beautifully resonant. They are also crafted in such a unique way that you can literally hear the energy of the space change as the belling circuit progresses.

The purpose of the belling circuit

This is the step where the deepest level of energy clearing happens. The belling technique is designed to shatter the astral imprints that have become embedded in the walls, floors, ceilings, fixtures, and fittings in a building, as well as the furniture and all the other items in it. The extent to which this succeeds will depend on the equipment used, the depth of imprinting, and the skill of the person doing the space clearing.

What type of bell to use

Always use a Balinese space clearing bell, for all the reasons we explain in Chapter 14. This is the one piece of equipment you absolutely must have to be able to do space clearing effectively.

It's also important to have the right size of bell for the space you are clearing:

- A small Balinese space clearing bell is effective in rooms up to 50 square metres (approx. 500 square feet).
- A large Balinese space clearing bell can be used in both small and large rooms up to 200 square metres (approx. 2,000 square feet).

How to do the belling circuit

Make sure your sleeves are firmly rolled up above the elbow. Pick up your bell from its bell stand on the altar and walk with it to the main entrance, taking care not to ring it on the way. A good way to prevent this from happening is to rest the dome of the bell on the flat palm of your free hand as you walk or simply hold the clapper inside the dome with your free hand.

How to start the belling circuit

Stand next to the main entrance, sideways to the door, and facing in the direction you will be walking. If you are right-handed, hold the bell in your right hand, with the right side of your body next to the door. If you are left-handed, hold the bell in your left hand, with the left side of your body next to the door.

Stand close to the door, but not so close that you could accidentally knock the bell against it when you ring it, which could damage the bell and possibly the door too.

Lift the arm you are holding the bell with out to your side up to shoulder height so that it is parallel to the ground. Then bend your arm at the elbow so that the lower part of your arm and your hand are extended forward, at a right angle to your upper arm and parallel to the ground.

Engage verticality and place your awareness above your head.

Look straight ahead, not at the bell or the door. Let your vision become soft and peripheral.

Engage throat friction (explained in Chapter 10) and breathe fluidly.

First ring

Nudge into the etheric layer of the door and ring the bell once in the same area where you started the hand-sensing circuit (the centre of the door, if it is made of wood, or it may be the door frame, if the door is made of glass).

Remember to keep your shoulder and elbow perfectly still, while rotating your wrist from side to side. This will cause the clapper inside the bell to move from side to side, which is the best way to produce a harmonious sound.

Second ring

Wait until just before the sound of the first ring of the bell fades, then ring it again.

Third ring

Wait until just before the sound of the second ring of the bell fades, then ring it a third time and start walking.

The belling circuit

Follow the inner perimeter of your home, ringing your bell every five seconds or so. Allow your awareness to ride on the sound of the bell. Consciously direct the sound into the corners of rooms, into the walls, and into any items of furniture that are positioned against the walls.

When you come to any soft furnishings in the middle of the room, such as beds, sofas, and armchairs, briefly move away from the wall and ring your bell over the padded areas, about 5 cm (2 inches) away from the surface:

- **Single bed**: Bell the bed from head to foot
- **Double bed**: Bell the bed from head to foot on one side, then repeat on the other side
- **Chair**: Bell the chair from the top of the backrest to the front edge of the seat
- **Sofa**: Start at one end of the sofa and bell it from the top of the backrest to the front edge of the seat, then repeat once or twice more in different sections of the sofa (depending on its size)

How to end the belling circuit

When you arrive back at the main entrance door, stand sideways to it and complete the circuit by ringing the bell once and tracing a horizontal figure of eight (the symbol of infinity) in the air at heart level. Finish with a brisk ring in the centre of the figure of eight where the two loops cross.

Then walk back to the altar, taking care that the bell does not ring, and place the bell back on its stand.

Very important: Never allow the sound of the bell to completely fade from the first ring until the last one, when you complete the figure of eight symbol. If that happens accidentally, the energy of the space will drop and you will have to start the entire belling circuit again from the main entrance.

Belling tips

- Develop a relationship with your bell in the same way that a musician develops a relationship with their instrument. The more you do this, the more you will discover what a Balinese bell truly can do and the level of insights it can facilitate.

- Keep your head vertical throughout the circuit and consciously engage throat friction.
- Breathe through your nose, not your mouth.
- Listen to the sound of the bell from above your head and direct it from there. Do not attempt to do belling from your mind, which is only capable of thoughts at the level of ordinary mental consciousness. Your ability to do this will determine to a large extent the depth of results you are able to obtain. Space clearing belling techniques ultimately involve a profound level of Point* mastery.
- If you find your arm gets tired during the belling circuit, unless you are very unfit this will be because you have dropped back into your mind instead of holding awareness above your head. When you ring a Balinese space clearing bell from verticality, it feels effortless.

Step 20
Harmony ball infusion and frequencing

☑ *Basic Space Clearing*

☑ *Essential Space Clearing*

☑ *Full Space Clearing*

Infuse your harmony ball with new, higher frequencies. Then walk around the inner perimeter of the space, shaking the frequencies out into your home.

The purpose of the harmony ball circuit

By this point in a space clearing ceremony, the clearing work has been done. The final part is to put new, higher frequencies into the area that has been cleared. It is vital to do this. If you miss this step out, it will leave an energetic void that will fill up with the same kinds of energies you had before.

The process is in two parts:

- Harmony ball infusion – infusing the harmony ball with new, higher frequencies
- Harmony ball frequencing – putting the new frequencies into your home

Harmony ball infusion

Take your personal harmony ball from its stand. If you are using neutral harmony balls in the ceremony (explained in Chapter 15), leave them on the altar for now.

Find a quiet place in your home where you can sit for about five minutes. Make yourself comfortable but don't slouch. You will get the best result if you keep your head and spine vertical. If you're comfortable sitting cross-legged on the floor in meditation posture (with your knees below the level of your pelvis, your spine straight, and your head vertical), that's the best position of all.

If you are doing the ceremony alone

Hold your harmony ball in one hand and cup your other hand over the top of it. Then rest your hands in your lap.

If another person is participating in the ceremony

If another person is participating in the ceremony, you can either use one personal harmony ball each, or you can share one or two harmony balls between you.

Important note: It must be one or both of the heads of the household who hold the main harmony ball(s), not a child. A child cannot take responsibility for infusing high spiritual frequencies for a whole family into a home.

How to use one harmony ball each

This is the best option if you lead independent lives. Sit in separate locations in the same room and hold your individual harmony balls as described above.

How to share a harmony ball between you

This method, known as a harmony ball sandwich, works best if you are emotionally close to each other and have a similar focus for the space clearing ceremony. Sit close together, side by side, and at the same height (on a sofa, for example).

- Ask the other person to hold out the hand that is nearest to you, palm facing up.
- Place your hand, palm facing up, on top of theirs, and place the harmony ball on it.

- Tell the other person to cup their free hand on top of the harmony ball.
- Then cup your free hand on top of theirs to form a harmony ball sandwich. Each of you will have one palm that is in direct contact with the harmony ball.
- Lower your hands to rest them comfortably between you.

When it comes to shaking the frequencies in the harmony ball around your home later in this step, only one person (you, the MC) can hold the harmony ball. That's fine, and it's also OK to put two personal harmony balls in the sandwich, if you prefer to do so, so that each person has a harmony ball to shake out.

If two or more other people are participating in the ceremony

Here's what to do if two or more members of your family or occupants of your home are participating in the space clearing with you.

If only one head of the household is participating

If you are the only head of the household present, hold the harmony ball in your hands, rest your hands in your lap, then invite everyone else present to put their hands around your hands. Each person will need to find a comfortable posture they can maintain without moving for about five minutes. It's fine to include children if they can do this, but not if they will fidget too much.

If joint heads of the household are participating

Create a harmony ball sandwich with the other joint head of the household, then invite everyone else present to put their hands around your hands.

You can use one, two, or even three personal harmony balls, if you want to, so that you, the joint head of the household, and one other person can all participate in shaking them out later. However, don't include neutral harmony balls in the sandwich. If you have any plans to use them to space clear any other place, they need to stay neutral so they can be used again.

If some members of the household are absent

If you share your home with other people whose areas of the home are included in the space clearing, but they are not able to be present for the ceremony, it is your responsibility as MC to include them. Consciously intend that everything you do in the harmony ball infusion and frequencing process will be done on their behalf too. (It is possible to do this because you know them very well, so higher parts of you will be connected to higher parts of them.)

Do not include anyone who has specifically said they want their areas of the home to be excluded from the space clearing.

How to MC the harmony ball infusion process

You will need to guide everyone through the harmony ball infusion process. Here are some tips about the most effective way to do this.

Stillness

Sit as still as you can to allow yourself to deeply involute. If other people are present, make sure they understand how important it is to stay still too. Any movement you make will take you out of the space. When doing this, it can sometimes feel as if hours have passed rather than minutes. It is possible to be so involuted that you lose track of time.

Throat friction

There is no need to teach anyone else present how to do throat friction. However, if you know how to engage silent throat friction, doing this yourself during the harmony ball infusion process will allow you to access deeper levels and open a much deeper space for others too.

Aspirations

The aim of the infusion process is to connect each person to higher parts of themselves and put the essence of their highest aspirations into the harmony ball(s). You do not need to know what their highest aspirations are. Your function, as MC, is to hold a space for this to happen.

It's essential to understand that aspirations are not the same as thoughts, emotions, wishes, intentions, visualizations, longings, yearnings, or any of the other types of desires that can be generated by your astral body. Aspirations come from a higher part of yourself that remembers your purpose in incarnating here on earth and knows what you are here to do, even if you have no conscious awareness of that yourself. When aspiring, there is no grasping or neediness, just a receptive turning upward and opening to the help of higher spiritual forces that have integrity.

The harmony ball infusion process

It's ideal if you can memorize the words of the harmony ball infusion process so that you can do it with your eyes closed. If you are doing the ceremony by yourself, you can do it silently. If other people are present, you will need to speak the words out loud.

There needs to be a pause between each of the steps to give yourself, and anyone who is doing the process with you, time to do it.

> Adjust your posture so that you are sitting comfortably. Make sure your head and spine are vertical and straight. Cup the harmony ball between your hands and rest your hands in your lap. Be as still as you can.

Close your eyes and take a few deep breaths. Use each out-breath to let go of any tension in your body.

Start by placing your awareness in your heart centre, in the centre of your chest. Take a few breaths in and out of your heart centre, breathing through your nose, not your mouth. Connect to the warmth of human spirit that naturally resides in your heart.

Continue to breathe through your nose a little deeper than usual, while moving your awareness to each area of your body in turn and breathing into it.

First, move your awareness into your lungs and chest...

Then down into your abdomen... pelvis... thighs... knees... lower legs... ankles... and feet.

Now, move your awareness back to your lungs and chest and from there up into your neck and head.

Then back to the lungs and chest.

From there, move your awareness into your shoulders... arms... hands... and into the harmony ball.

On each out-breath, fill the harmony ball with everything you're grateful for in your life – not in words, but in feelings or images.

Next, put into the harmony ball the essence of all your happiest memories. If less happy memories come up, just let them go. Focus on the happiest times, past and present.

Then put into the harmony ball feelings or images of yourself, radiantly happy, healthy, and successful in ways that are meaningful to you, surrounded by people you love and who love you.

Now, take a breath and move your awareness vertically upward. Find a place above your head where you can comfortably rest your consciousness. From there, turn up and aspire for help from high spiritual realms, silently, without words. Become an energetic flame of aspiration from the higher parts of yourself.

Aspire to be all that you can be, with no limitations, so that you can do what you have incarnated here on earth to do. You may not know exactly what that is, but higher parts of you do know. Take a few moments to do this.

Holding the space above your head, infuse the frequencies of your higher aspirations into the harmony ball.

Then, add into the harmony ball the frequencies of love, hope, joy, and happiness...

Add other life-enhancing qualities, such as kindness... compassion... courage... patience... confidence... enthusiasm... persistence... integrity... and any other qualities that are important to you.

When you are ready, take a deep breath, slowly open your eyes, and bring your awareness back to the room.

Harmony ball frequencing

The final stage is to shake the frequencies that have been put into the harmony ball(s) out into the space so that your entire home becomes imbued with the essence of the higher aspirations you have infused it with. Balinese harmony balls have a beautiful jingly-jangly sound that these frequencies can ride on.

If you are doing the ceremony alone

If you are right-handed, hold your personal harmony ball in your right hand. If you are left-handed, hold it in your left hand. To add more volume and oomph, you can also hold one or two neutral harmony balls in your other hand, if you wish to.

If another person is participating in the ceremony

As MC of the ceremony, you will lead the way and the other person will follow around behind you.

If you have shared a personal harmony ball, the other person will need to use a neutral harmony ball.

If you have a personal harmony ball each, you can both use one or two additional neutral harmony balls, held in your non-dominant hand, if you choose to. If the other person is physically incapacitated or does not wish to do the harmony ball circuit themselves for some reason, you can take their harmony ball and do it on their behalf.

If two or more other people are participating in the ceremony

As MC of the ceremony, you will lead the way, and the others will follow around behind you. If one of the other people is a joint head of the household, they will follow directly behind you, and the others will follow behind them. Distribute as many neutral harmony balls as you have between them.

Each member of the household who wants to participate can do so if you have enough neutral harmony balls to give them one each. This includes children, if they are old enough to be able to join in and wish to do so.

Please be discerning about giving harmony balls to very young children, though, because if they drop one, it will probably dent and cannot be repaired. It can still be used. It just won't look as beautiful as before.

If you do not have enough neutral harmony balls for each person to have at least one each, they can either silently follow you around the home or sit quietly near the altar while the circuit is in progress.

The harmony ball frequencing circuit

Start at the same main entrance and take exactly the same circuit as for clapping and belling. Shake the frequencies into the main entrance door, the walls, and any furniture and objects in the space. Spend extra time on soft furnishings, such as beds, sofas, and armchairs, which are very absorbent.

Keep your body, arms, and hands relaxed as you do this. It works best when done with fluid, joyous movements, not with astral intensity or meticulousness.

End the circuit back at the main entrance. If other people are participating in the ceremony, wait until everyone has arrived there, then count, "One, two, and three," so you can all stop shaking your harmony balls on "three".

That's it! Your home has now been filled with new, higher frequencies for you to enjoy and benefit from in the weeks and months ahead.

Put your personal harmony ball back on its stand on the altar. If you have used neutral harmony balls, collect these up and put them back on their plate on the altar or wherever they were being stored.

Step 21
Resense the energy

☑ *Basic Space Clearing*

☑ *Essential Space Clearing*

☑ *Full Space Clearing*

Resense the energy to assess the changes that have taken place.

Starting at the main entrance, do a final round of hand sensing to feel the difference the space clearing has made. If you have done it well, the space will also feel energetically lighter and brighter, and there will be a silky soft, vibrant layer of energy on the inner walls of your home.

Each space clearing ceremony is different. There are some changes that may be immediately noticeable and others that may become apparent in the days following the ceremony. To facilitate the changes, be sure to read the next chapter about what to do after a ceremony.

34

After a space clearing ceremony

Don't make the mistake of rushing back to your everyday life after a space clearing ceremony. You will get the most value from it if you can take some time to savour the new space and integrate the energetic changes.

Integration

Do your best to make arrangements to be at home for the rest of the day after a ceremony, either by yourself or with those you live with (don't invite any visitors that day or any guests to stay overnight).

The best way to spend your time is by reinforcing the effects of the ceremony in a meaningful way rather than watching television, surfing the internet, using your phone, or doing anything you habitually do. The form this takes will vary greatly from person to person and may include such things as meditating, taking stock of where your life is heading, giving some thought to how to prioritize the important things in your life, spending quality time with loved ones, and so on.

Some people feel energized after doing a space clearing. Others feel the need to rest or take a nap.

If you have a very busy life, you may choose to treat yourself to a long, relaxing soak in a hot bath, or go to bed and have an early night.

If the focus for doing space clearing was to kick-start clutter clearing, this can be a very good time to get started with that. Pick a small area of your home, such as a shelf or a drawer, and begin. People often comment that they find clutter clearing so much easier to do after a space clearing, as if the stuff walks out of the door by itself.

Space clearing can change the entire energetic fabric of your home, and it can take up to a week to integrate the changes it brings about. Much of this happens during the hours of sleep, which is why we recommend scheduling the ceremony for a time when you (the MC) will be sleeping at home every night for the next week.

Candles

Leave each candle in place until it has burned out so that the energy changes of the space clearing can fully integrate.

If you'd like to, you can extend this period and enjoy the flower offerings longer by replenishing the candles. To ensure continuity, light each new tealight from the flame of the one it is replacing. Flower offerings look strikingly beautiful when the light changes at dusk, so that's a wonderful time to enjoy them.

It's always best if you can stay at home for the rest of the day after a Full Space Clearing ceremony. If something unexpected happens and you have to go out, or you decide to take a nap, blow out the candles and relight them when you return, in the same order you first lit them. For fire safety reasons, and to maintain spiritual integrity in a space, never leave a burning candle unattended in your home.

The frequencies of each space clearing ceremony will be different, so only use brand-new tealight candles for each one. If you have to blow out the candles before they burn down, it's fine to use them a everyday candles in your home, if you wish to, but don't use them for a future space clearing.

How to dispose of any space clearing water

If you have any space clearing water left over at the end of the ceremony, it will only last for 24 hours at the most, so there's no point keeping it.

If your home has a front door at ground level, a lovely way to dispose of it is to open the door and throw the remaining space clearing water over your doorstep, to bless the entrance area to your home. It may not be practical to do this if you live in an apartment, so an alternative would be to pour it on your plants or simply pour it down the sink.

If you have used commercially grown flowers for the ceremony, we don't recommend drinking any leftover space clearing water or mixing it into your bathwater because of all the chemicals it may contain (see the next section).

How to dispose of flower offerings

The flowers used in a space clearing ceremony have no value after they have been used in the ceremony. After the candles have burned down, you can simply dispose of the flower heads in your garden waste later that day or the next morning.

Many types of commercially grown flowers, especially those that have travelled some distance to reach the part of the world where you live, contain levels of fungicides, herbicides, insecticides, preservatives, and growth regulators that are much higher than those permitted in food substances, so it's usually not a good idea to dispose of the flowers or stalks in your compost if you practise organic gardening.

35

How to space clear a very large home

If you live in a huge mansion, it may be too tiring to space clear the entire property in one go, especially if you are doing a Full Space Clearing rather than Essential Space Clearing or Basic Space Clearing. However, it won't work to do half the steps of the ceremony one day and the other half the next day. To be effective, MC-ship of the space needs to be held continuously from the beginning of the ceremony to the end.

What to do differently when space clearing a very large home

Space clear floor by floor

Split your property into separate areas, according to floor levels, which you can space clear over a period of one, two, or three days at the most.

Work from the bottom up, so that each floor you complete forms a foundation for the one above it. Space clear the basement first, if there is one, then the ground floor, and so on all the way up the house. Include the stairs leading down to the basement as part of the basement clearing, and the stairs leading to each of the higher levels as part of the next floor up.

The following steps are also done differently in a large house.

Preparations

When calculating the quantity of flowers to buy, allow for a fresh flower offering on the altar each day and the additional matrix flower offerings that will be needed on the final day.

Step 12: Do a circuit of hand sensing

Hand sense the entire property on the first day, starting and ending at the main entrance.

Step 13: Create flower offerings

Create fresh flower offerings each day for the floors you will be clearing.

Step 14: Create a space clearing altar

Position the altar in the entrance hall of the home, if there is one, or in a suitable location near to the main entrance. Leave the altar in place for however many days it takes you to space clear all the floors, adding a fresh flower offering each day to the altar and fresh flower offerings for the areas that will be cleared that day.

Step 15: Make some space clearing water

Make fresh space clearing water each day.

Step 16: Activate the flower offerings

First activate the flower offering on the altar. Then activate the other flower offerings in this order, if these areas are on the floor or floors you are clearing:

- The kitchen stove
- Living areas
- The main bedroom
- Children's bedrooms (in birth order, starting with the eldest)
- Guest bedrooms

- Other rooms, such as home offices, studies, playrooms, junk rooms, and so on, according to their level of importance or usage
- A matrix flower offering on each floor, starting with the uppermost floor of the area you are clearing that day

Remove all the flower offerings after the candles have burned down.

On the last day of the ceremony, when you activate the flower offerings on the top floor of the house, end by activating a matrix flower offering on that floor and fresh matrix flower offerings on each of the floors below it. This will help to connect the floors energetically and make your home feel more unified.

Step 17: Do a circuit of clapping

Start and end the clapping circuit at the main entrance to the house, no matter which floor(s) are being cleared.

This is easy if the main entrance is on the ground floor and you are space clearing the ground floor. It involves a bit more going up and down stairs when you space clear lower or upper floors. To maintain the energetic connection to the main entrance, keep your arm and hand in hand-sensing position while you are going up and down the stairs.

If you happen to have a lift/elevator installed in the property, it's fine to start the circuit at the front door, take the lift to an upper floor, do a round of hand sensing on that floor, then take the lift back down to the ground floor. Keep your arm and hand in hand-sensing position all the time you are doing this, including in the lift.

We recommend using unscented hand cream before you start the clapping circuit so the palms of your hands won't get too sore. You may also want to enlist the help of another capable person to share the task with you – you would do the first half of the circuit and then hand over to them to complete it (like the energetic equivalent of handing over a baton in a relay race).

Step 19: Do a circuit of belling

Start and end the belling circuit at the main entrance to the house, no matter which floor(s) are being cleared. Remember to keep ringing the bell as you go up and down the stairs (or lift/elevator, if there is one) so that the sound never dies.

Step 20: Do harmony ball infusion and frequencing

Wait until the last day of the ceremony to do this step. When shaking the frequencies out, do a circuit of the entire house, holding your personal harmony ball in your dominant hand and two neutral harmony balls in your other hand. If other occupants of the home participate in this part of the ceremony, they can follow around behind you using their personal harmony ball and a neutral harmony ball or balls.

Step 21: Resense the energy

Wait until the last day of the ceremony to do this circuit of the entire property. It will help to weave the energies of all the floors of your home together.

36

How to space clear someone else's home

Space clearing is a wonderful skill to have. The information in this book will teach you to safely and effectively space clear your own home. After you've obtained good results doing that, you can also space clear the homes of close friends and relatives, if they ask for your help and you feel able and willing to provide it.

There are various situations when someone may ask you to do this, such as if someone is unwell, disabled, pregnant, breastfeeding, grieving the death of a family member, has recently suffered a major loss of some kind, has had a traumatic experience, and so on.

Modifications to some of the steps of the ceremony will be needed. We have listed these later in this chapter.

Before agreeing to do the ceremony, you first need to be aware that space clearing someone else's home is more difficult than space clearing your own home. It requires a much higher level of knowledge, perception, and skill.

In addition to all the dos and don'ts explained earlier in the book, there are some other important aspects that need to be taken into account. To help you, we have compiled a complete checklist of all the factors you will need to consider before agreeing to do this.

Checklist before agreeing to space clear someone else's home

About the request to do space clearing

- Have you already space cleared your own home several times with good results?
- Do you know the home and everyone who lives in it very well?
- Has the person requested a space clearing without any persuasion from you?
- Is the person who requested the space clearing the sole head of the household?
- If other people live there, have they agreed to the space clearing?

About the home and its occupants

- Is anyone who lives there taking anti-anxiety or antidepressant medications?
- Does anyone who lives there have other mental health issues?
- Is the home so cluttered that it's impossible to walk around the inner perimeter of the space?
- Has there been a suicide, murder, violent crime, or other traumatic event there?

About your ability to do the space clearing

- Do you really want to do the space clearing and feel capable of doing it?
- Are you confident you can do the space clearing without putting your personal agendas or energies into the space?
- Are you in good health and fit to do space clearing?
- Are you taking any anti-anxiety, antidepressant, or strong pain medications, or sleeping pills?
- Are you still grieving the loss of someone who recently died and used to live in the home?
- Are you substantially overweight?

- Are you planning to sleep in the person's home the night before or the night after the space clearing?

If any of these aspects apply to you, be sure to read the relevant sections below.

Have you already space cleared your own home several times with good results?

It's vital that you do the Essential Space Clearing or Full Space Clearing ceremony in your own home a few times first and obtain good results before attempting to do the ceremony for anyone else. You need to be familiar with all the steps, the techniques, and the changes that space clearing can bring about.

Do you know the home and everyone who lives in it very well?

If you accept a request from a close friend or relative to space clear their home, only do so if you know everyone who lives there very well and are a frequent visitor to the place, so you are already familiar with the energies of the space. The information in this book is nowhere near enough to enable you to do space clearing in the homes of people you have never visited before, do not know very well, or do not know at all.

Has the person requested a space clearing without any persuasion from you?

No matter how much you would like to help a friend or relative, it's not OK to ask them if they want to have their home space cleared, tell them you think they need it, or space clear their home without their knowledge to surprise them or cheer them up.

You can certainly tell someone how space clearing your own home has helped you, and if they then ask you if you will space clear their home too, you can discuss this with them and perhaps do so. However, there must be no persuasion by you, and you must have no agenda to change the person or the energy of their space in any particular way. They must really want to have their home space cleared and actively participate in the process. They must not feel coerced into having it done or agree to let you do it because they don't know how to say no.

The reason we have listed all these cautions is because space clearing is very different to having a feng shui consultation where you are given advice about the design of your home. A feng shui consultant may suggest that you move your sofa to a new position or, in more radical cases, knock down walls or move your front door (this is more common in Asian countries). Whatever advice you receive, you can take it or leave it. And even if you go ahead and make the recommended changes, with some effort and expense they can usually be reversed if they don't produce the effect you were hoping for. Space clearing, on the other hand, cannot be reversed. When energies are cleared from a building, they cannot be reconstituted.

The fact is that many people really don't want to change. They may say they want to, but even if they are struggling in their life, they often prefer to stay exactly as they are rather than risk something new. No matter how much you would like to help someone or feel they need to change, you must not force it upon them.

> **Karen**: A good example of how this can go wrong comes from one of the first talks I ever gave about space clearing in the early 1990s, at the Mind Body Spirit Festival in London. Having attended many events of this type where the speakers tantalizingly tell the audience only scraps of information to entice them to take an entire workshop to learn more, I resolved to do it differently. I decided to compress the content of my two-day space clearing workshop into a

one-hour talk, with the intention of giving the 300 people present all the information they needed to go home and do space clearing immediately.

And I managed to do it. I talked very fast, skipped over sections I felt could be left out, minimized the practical demonstrations, and didn't take any questions.

Will I ever do that again? Definitely not.

For one thing, I now know from long experience that the most important thing Richard and I can pass to people when we teach in person is the practical demonstrations, so that people can see how the techniques are done and feel how the energy of the space changes as a result. It's not possible to convey this in anything like the same depth through books or even videos because the etheric component is missing. It's therefore one of the most vital aspects to include in an in-person talk or workshop.

I also now understand how important it is to set a context for what we teach. Space clearing is not a list of techniques that a robot could be programmed to do. There are certain things that need to be taken into account in each step of the ceremony, in much the same way that anyone can follow a cooking recipe, but a skilled chef will produce an entirely different result to a novice because they have a far more profound understanding of the alchemy of food.

What happened after this particular talk is that one man in the audience got so inspired by what he learned that he decided to space clear his grandmother's apartment. He had the keys to go in each day to feed her cat while she was in hospital having an operation, and he figured it would be a wonderful surprise for her to come home to an energetically, twinklingly clear place.

Well, it was a surprise. Just not the kind he had hoped it would be. She was so shocked when she arrived home and felt how different the space was that she had a relapse and went back to hospital, which felt more like home to her than her actual home did.

In my altruistic ambition to deliver the content of a two-day workshop in the space of an hour, one of the points I'd left out was how important it is for the owner to request space clearing because they want change and feel ready for it. His grandmother didn't want change at all. She had lived in her home for many years, and it was coated in layers of her own energies. Her grandson thought he was doing her a favour by giving her a completely fresh start. To her, it was a highly distressing transformation of her space and an invasion of her privacy.

Many older people feel this way. If you ask them, they will often say, "I like my life the way it is, thank you very much," and they will get into fierce battles if anyone suggests relocating them to make it easier. It's not just the tremendous upheaval that moving involves. It's also that they don't want to leave their own energy imprints behind and start afresh in a new place.

After hearing about this experience and reflecting on the many other important aspects I'd had to leave out, I realized that it really doesn't work to give short talks about space clearing, so I have never done one since. I also never write short articles about how to do space clearing. It really takes an entire book to teach someone how to do it well.

Is the person who requested the space clearing the sole head of the household?

If your friend or relative lives alone, they are free to make their own decision about having their home space cleared, without needing to consult anyone else.

If other people live there, have they agreed to the space clearing?

If there is more than one head of the household, the request for space clearing must come from all of them. It's not OK for one of the joint heads of the household to sneak you in to do space clearing without the knowledge and consent of the other head(s) of the household. That would be totally out of integrity.

If other people live there too, you will need to check if they have agreed to the space clearing, if they want their rooms to be included or not, and if they plan to be present for the ceremony or not. Space clearing a home that has multiple occupants is a LOT more complicated than one that has a sole occupant, so it would be wise to get experience of space clearing the home of a friend or relative who lives alone first.

Is anyone who lives there taking anti-anxiety or antidepressant medications?

Anti-anxiety and antidepressant medications have an anaesthetizing effect that will be reflected in the energy of a person's home.

When Karen started space clearing professionally in 1991, the use of these types of medications was far less widespread than it is today. The first time she ever came across it in a client's home, it had her completely puzzled. She did her usual round of hand sensing and couldn't feel anything. So she did another circuit. Still nothing. It was only after questioning the client that the reason for this emerged. The woman had been taking high doses of antidepressants for years. The emotional numbness caused by the drugs was mirrored in the energetic numbness of the walls, furniture, and objects in her home. The usual astral imprints were there, but they could not be read because they were covered by layers of numbness that helped her to remain oblivious to memories she wanted to forget.

Since that time, we've had a lot of experience of working with clients who are taking medications for anxiety or depression. We can spot this effect immediately when doing hand sensing. Depending on the type of medication, how long it has been taken, and how strong the dosage, there is always an anaesthetization of the energy of the space to some extent, which makes it difficult to know for sure what is happening as the space clearing progresses.

If you are taking anti-anxiety or antidepressant medications yourself, it's fine to space clear your own home because if it starts to feel too uncomfortable, you can simply stop. But it's a very different matter to space clear the home of someone else who is taking medications of this type.

The reason is that a home is not just a place where someone lives and stores their possessions. It's also where they anchor their energy and rest their consciousness. Space clearing changes these energies, so the person will not be able to rest their consciousness in the same way they used to. For most people, this is a good thing, but for someone who is taking medications for anxiety or depression, it can cause them to feel emotionally exposed and vulnerable, which they are usually not prepared to do.

To safely do space clearing in these circumstances requires a high level of expertise. For this reason, only the most experienced space clearing practitioners we have trained work with clients who are taking medications of this type. It's not a situation where a friend or relative can have a go, however well-meaning.

Does anyone who lives there have other mental health issues?

Space clearing the home of someone who has mental health issues can sometimes be helpful. It can also be very destabilizing for them. Please read Chapter 23 for more information about this.

Is the home so cluttered that it's impossible to walk around the inner perimeter of the space?

If your friend or relative has a lot of clutter, space clearing can clear out the stagnant energies that accumulate around clutter, which will make it easier for them to do clutter clearing. However, if there is so much clutter that you can't walk around the inner perimeter of the space or access some of the rooms, then it will be necessary for them to make substantial inroads into clutter clearing first.

Has there been a suicide, murder, violent crime, or other traumatic event there?

The information in this book will not equip you to do space clearing in such a place. Your friend or relative will need to engage the services of a professional space clearer who is also an experienced entity clearer.

Do you really want to do the space clearing and feel capable of doing it?

No matter how much a friend or relative may implore you to space clear their home, never agree to do so out of obligation or because you don't want to disappoint them.

Space clearing someone else's home is very different to space clearing your own home. You may encounter energies you are not equipped to deal with, such as entities, perverse energies, or the residues of violent, abusive, or traumatic events. If you don't know how to deal with these, you can mess up your own energy and create energetic chaos in the home of the person you are trying to help. Even if the space clearing goes well, there can also be the risk that the person may blame you for anything that goes wrong in their life after the ceremony, even though that may be purely coincidental and there may be no connection to it at all.

If you feel any fear or reluctance when asked, DO NOT override those feelings and go ahead because you wish to help. They are warning signals that you need to listen to.

Are you confident you can do the space clearing without putting your personal agendas or energies into the space

It takes a lot more skill than most people realize to do space clearing for other people at the level of integrity it requires. If you have any personal agenda when doing the ceremony, such as hoping that certain aspects of a person's life will improve, or even if you feel a lot of love or compassion for the person, you can unconsciously weave these frequencies into the ceremony and leave tinges of your own energies embedded in the space.

You must be able to do the space clearing from a completely neutral standpoint, for the highest good of the person and any other occupants of the home.

Are you in good health and fit to do space clearing?

Do not do space clearing in your own home or anyone else's home in any of the following situations, which we explained in detail earlier in the book in Chapter 21:

- If you are unwell
- If you are mentally or emotionally unstable
- If you are tired or energetically depleted
- If you are pregnant or breastfeeding
- If you are menstruating
- If you have any gynaecological health problems
- If you are energetically depleted after ejaculation
- If you have any open wounds, sores, or weeping eczema
- If you have taken any psychoactive drugs or intoxicants:
  - Marijuana/cannabis – in the preceding 1–4 weeks (depending on your level of usage)
  - Alcohol – in the preceding 72 hours
  - Opioids such as opium, codeine, morphine, oxycodone, methadone, heroin, and fentanyl – in the preceding 72 hours
  - Stimulants such as cocaine, methamphetamine, and amphetamines (including ADHD medications) – in the preceding 72 hours
  - Hallucinogens such as LSD, MDMA, psilocybin, ayahuasca, mescaline, THC, ketamine, and PCP – in the preceding 72 hours
  - Antipsychotics such as haloperidol and chlorpromazine – in the preceding 72 hours
  - Designer drugs such as synthetic marijuana, MXE, and mephedrone – in the preceding 72 hours
  - Sedatives, including sleeping pills and tranquilizers – in the preceding 48 hours

- Sugar – since waking that day
- Caffeine – immediately before or during a ceremony
- Nicotine – during the ceremony in the area being space cleared

Are you taking any anti-anxiety, antidepressant, or strong pain medications, or sleeping pills?

Anti-anxiety and antidepressant medications are designed to cause a numbing of emotions. Strong pain medications cause a numbness in the physical body, which will also affect your etheric body and your astral body because they are all interwoven. Sleeping pills cause a drowsiness that can persist for up to 48 hours after taking them.

Taking any of these substances will make it impossible for you to do hand sensing with any accuracy and will make it very difficult to feel any energy changes or hold the level of involution that is needed to get good results. The effects of these medications can also give you distorted view of what is happening energetically in a space, which can lead to unwanted or even chaotic space clearing results. We always advise against it.

Are you still grieving the loss of someone who recently died and used to live in the home?

Space clearing the home of someone who has recently died can put you at risk of picking up an astral fragment (also known as an entity), so a heightened level of energetic awareness and vigilance is needed. It will be impossible to hold the necessary objectivity if you knew the person who lived there, were close to them, and are still grieving. Even the most skilled professional space clearer would never do space clearing in such a situation.

Are you substantially overweight?

If you are substantially overweight, it's fine to do space clearing in your own home because you are already living with the energies there. However, we strongly advise against attempting to space clear anyone else's home. It can lead to a range of problems for both you and them.

The main reason for this is that body fat isn't just physical. There are always layers of stagnant energies embedded in it too, which will make you susceptible to picking up stagnant energies from the space (like attracts like). Being overweight will also create an etheric numbness that will make it difficult or impossible for you to feel this happening to you or feel if you pick up more toxic types of energies too.

We know from experience that overweight people generally ignore this advice. They tend to take the view that if they can't feel it, there's no problem. But there certainly is. We have therefore included this information here as much for the benefit of a potential recipient of a space clearing as for the person intending to do it. Hopefully, one or the other person will see the wisdom of not proceeding.

Are you planning to sleep in the person's home the night before or after the space clearing?

The etheric opening that happens when you sleep means that you become subject to the energies in the space around you. This is not something you can control by any kind of energetic shielding, intention or other method. It will happen, and there is very little you can do about it. It's one of the reasons why space clearing is such an incredibly useful skill to have when you're travelling, so that you can create clear space to sleep in.

If you stay in a hotel the night before doing a space clearing, you can take ownership of the space by space clearing the room and getting a good night's sleep. If you sleep in your relative's or friend's home to save money, you will not be able to take ownership of the space in the same way. Even if you space clear the room you sleep in, you will become permeated by the energies of the home you are there to clear, which will weaken your objectivity and ability to do so.

Staying in someone's home the night after a space clearing is also a no-no because it will interfere with the integration process that is supposed to happen for the occupants during the hours of the night after a clearing. You need to leave them to do that by themselves.

What to do differently if you space clear someone else's home

If you decide to go ahead and space clear someone else's home, there are some modifications that will need to be made to the ceremony.

Focus

You will need to ask the occupant(s) of the home to clarify their focus for the ceremony, not at the last minute but at least a few days in advance.

Step 6: Take a bath or shower and put on clean clothing

Do this in your own home, just before you travel to where you will be doing the space clearing. When you arrive at your destination and before you start the ceremony, wash your face, hands, and forearms to remove any energies you have picked up during the journey. If you're not sure if a freshly laundered, unscented towel will be available for you to use to dry yourself, take a hand towel of your own with you, or use some tissues or a paper towel.

Step 14: Create a space clearing altar

Creating a space clearing altar for someone else requires more advanced skills than creating one for yourself because it needs to be done top-down, not bottom-up. This means you can't use logic or reason. You need to be able to tune into higher parts of the person and match their focus of the ceremony to the archetypal altar design that will help them the most in their current situation. This becomes a lot more complicated if there is more than one occupant in the home. We strongly recommend that you get experience of space clearing for a friend or relative who lives alone before even considering more complex situations.

Step 16: Activate the flower offering(s)

We explained earlier in this book that learning how to activate flower offerings on behalf of a client is one of the most profound and challenging parts of the ceremony professional space clearing practitioners have to learn. It takes years to develop the subtle body structures that are needed for this skill.

Teaching those skills is far beyond the scope of this book, which is why we say it's essential you know the home and the person or people who live there very well. You will at least be able to tune into them at a more intimate level than with a person or people you don't know at all.

Be especially vigilant, when activating flower offerings, not to weave any of your own frequencies or agendas into the space. This means you must have done enough personal work to be able not to do that.

Step 20: Do harmony ball infusion and frequencing

If you space clear for a relative or friend, a new personal harmony ball will be needed so that they can fully infuse it with their own frequencies. Leave it with them after so they can do their own repeat ceremonies, when necessary. Don't use your own personal harmony ball for this because it will have your frequencies in it.

If more than one person lives in the home, it's fine for each person to have their own personal harmony ball if they wish to.

You'll need at least one neutral harmony ball to use yourself during the ceremony. The recommended number is three so that during the frequencing circuit you can hold one harmony ball in one hand and the other two in your other hand, to create dynamic qualities of sound.

37

How often to do space clearing

In the same way that your home feels better after a major spring clean, then gradually loses its sparkle in the weeks that follow, so the effects of space clearing will dwindle over time as energetic residues build up again.

How to know when it's time to do space clearing again

The length of time the effects of a space clearing last will depend on a number of factors, including your skill as a space clearer, the design of your home, what is happening in your life, what kind of person you are, and so on.

We generally recommend that you do an Essential Space Clearing or a Full Space Clearing ceremony at least once a year to keep the energy of your home in optimum condition. You can, of course, do the ceremony sooner than that if you have a major change in your life, feel stuck in some way, or have some other reason for wanting to refresh your space.

Is it possible to space clear too much?

It's possible to overdo physical cleaning, clutter clearing, and space clearing too. Space clearing daily or weekly, when there is no real need, is not recommended.

In most homes, it's only necessary to do a Full Space Clearing ceremony when you first move in and then once a year after that, with an Essential or Basic Space Clearing a couple of times in between, if needed. If you space clear too often, it can make it difficult to build a nurturing space, just as washing your hands too often can strip your skin of its natural oils.

When it can be helpful to do space clearing more frequently

If you have a lot of changes happening in your life all at the same time, it can be very helpful to do an Essential or Basic Space Clearing once a month or even once a week for a while to help you to move forward and integrate the new developments.

If you teach workshops or seminars and have an event that lasts several days, daily space clearing can be very helpful to maintain the space of the meeting room during that time. Similarly, if you work as a therapist or health professional, daily or weekly space clearings can help enormously to maintain the energies of the room where you see clients. The techniques for these types of space clearings are different to those described in this book, so we have included information about them in *Space Clearing, Volume 2*.

How to maintain the effects of a space clearing

There are a number of things you can do that will help to sustain the effects of a space clearing for longer.

Integrate the changes

The hours of the day and the night after a ceremony, as well as the week following a ceremony, are crucial times for integrating the changes it has brought about. The more closely you can follow our recommendations about this, the better (see Chapter 34).

Maintain your home in a good state of repair

Don't expect to be able to maintain a high-level space in your home unless you take care of the other aspects of home maintenance too. Keep it in a good state of repair and refresh any areas that are in need of renovation.

Keep your home clean, tidy, and organized

Cleaning your home each week and keeping it tidy and organized will help to prevent stagnant energies from accumulating.

Keep your home clutter-free

Have regular clear-outs to let go of things you no longer need so the space of your home stays up to date with who you are and where you are headed in your life.

Harmony ball infusion and frequencing

Harmony ball infusion and frequencing is most effective when done as part of a space clearing ceremony. If you notice the energy levels in your home start to drop, it can also be done in between space clearings to help to uplift the energy of the space.

Basic Space Clearing

The best way to maintain the effects of a space clearing is to refresh the space, as needed, by doing a Basic Space Clearing between Essential or Full Space Clearings.

PART SEVEN

Resources

38

How to learn more about space clearing

If you have enjoyed this book and wish to learn more, the next step is to read *Space Clearing, Volume 2: How space clearing works*.

It includes:

- The story of how we developed our space clearing knowledge and skills from when Karen was 4 years old to the present
- Deeper understandings of how the space clearing techniques work
- An introduction to spiritual connections
- How to develop more etheric and superastral awareness
- Advice about energetic protection
- A debunking of the most common energy clearing misconceptions
- In-depth descriptions of the many uses of space clearing, together with recommended altar designs

Clutter clearing

If you need help to clear your clutter, we recommend you first read our book *How to Clear Your Clutter* and, for more in-depth information, Karen's book *Clear Your Clutter with Feng Shui*.

Explore our online courses

We have pioneered the development of special techniques for conducting online courses, classes, and personal sessions through high-level virtual spaces.

It began in 2003 when Karen was living in Bali and needed to find a way to share developments with her network of certified space clearing practitioners around the world. Then in 2013, after we moved to the UK, we adapted those techniques to teach online courses. Since then, participants from over 70 countries have taken courses with us on a range of topics.

To our knowledge, there is no one else in the world teaching public online courses through consciously created virtual spaces in the way that we do. We are pioneering this technology, and happily so. We feel very strongly that it is important for some forerunners at this time to develop the use of internet technology to pass teachings at this level so that this knowledge will be available to future generations. What a sad world it will be when we all live in virtual reality (which is rapidly evolving now) if it is allowed to become devoid of spiritual dimension. We are doing our bit to help to make sure that does not happen.

Many of the participants who take our online courses are tangibly able to feel the virtual space we create for each event. Others experience it as a feeling of depth and safety, because of the remarkable heartness that forms in the camaraderie between participants. Whatever the case, it is such a unique experience that many return to access a deeper level of our teachings with each course, class, or personal session they take.

Information about upcoming courses and classes

www.clearspaceliving.com

Sign up to receive Karen's newsletters

We warmly invite you to sign up to receive Karen's free monthly newsletters, which contain links to articles about space clearing, clutter clearing, conscious living, and related topics:

www.clearspaceliving.com/newsletters

It's the best way to stay in touch with us, and you'll also be the first to hear when new books, events, and special offers are announced.

39

Professional space clearing

There are likely to be people who read this book who may feel inspired to become a professional space clearing practitioner. You can find information about what this involves at www.clearspaceliving.com, together with a list of the prerequisites that need to be fulfilled before applying for training.

How to train to become a professional space clearing practitioner

Professional training

"I thought I knew what space clearing was, but now I realize I had NO IDEA."

This is a typical comment made by a trainee halfway through Part One of our Professional Space Clearing Practitioner Training, after witnessing a space clearing in a client's home for the first time. Having read the book and received five days of training by this point, they are in a position to glimpse the depth of what really goes on during a ceremony.

The books, and even the professional training, are only the tip of the iceberg of this unique field of expertise. Each year brings many advances in space clearing skills, and there is no sign of this stopping or slowing down.

The fascinating thing is that, from the outside, space clearing looks pretty much the same to an uninformed onlooker as it always did. The ceremony itself has hardly changed over the years. However, the knowledge, skills, and levels of consciousness with which it is performed at practitioner level have moved on tremendously, resulting in correspondingly profound advances in the results that our professionals can obtain.

Why this book is not a professional training manual

The challenge for us in writing about space clearing has been how to give enough information to make it possible for someone to do the ceremony safely and effectively in their own home and the homes of close friends and relatives, yet not to give the misleading impression that this slice of knowledge is enough to enable anyone to instantly become a professional. A huge amount of additional information and skills are needed to safely and effectively space clear the homes of people you don't know very well or have never met before. Please use what you learn from us responsibly.

People are very connected to their homes. Doing a professional space clearing means you access the energies in a person's space at a very deep, intimate level. Without in-depth training, you are likely to make unfortunate blunders that can mess up people's lives. You also run the risk of harming your own health and wellbeing.

This book contains only about 20% of what we cover in our Professional Space Clearing Practitioner Training, and *Space Clearing, Volume* contains only about another 20%. That leaves a massive 60% gap between what you can learn from reading our books or taking online courses with us and the advanced knowledge and skills needed to space clear the homes of paying clients.

We know there are sure to be people who will completely disregard our advice about this. They will decide they know better and will set themselves up as a professional space clearer anyway. They will take methods that are only supposed to be for personal usage and probably throw in a few of their own inventions or things they've picked up from other teachers along the way.

Realizing this was likely to happen, Karen deliberated long and hard before publishing her first space clearing book in 1996. In the end, she decided it was better to put the information out there for people with integrity to use for themselves, and let karma take care of those who knowingly misuse it. In any case, we've discovered that most untrained space clearers don't last very long. They don't know how to manage their own energy in the spaces they go into, so they tend to encounter problems such as getting sick, putting on weight, or finding they are not able to attract enough clients to be able to make a living from it.

Prerequisites for professional training

The first space clearing practitioner training Karen ever taught was in 1997. The trainees were accepted purely on the basis of their enthusiasm to learn, which didn't work at all. It quickly became apparent that none of them were able to understand the teachings, let alone learn the skills required to practise them. Not one of them had a sufficiently awakened etheric or the subtle body structures to be able to begin the training, never mind complete it.

This was very disappointing for them and for Karen, so she had to make a decision at that point. Did she want to lower the standard so that anyone who had the time and money could become a professional space clearer of sorts? Or did she want to uphold the integrity of what she knew was required to do professional-level space clearing and train only a few people to a high level?

Well, she chose the latter, and she has never regretted it. When Richard joined her as a teacher–trainer in 2005, he was in full agreement with this too. We now therefore have a list of prerequisites that each person needs to fulfil before even applying for training, including training first as a clutter clearing practitioner. This has greatly increased the success rate. We have no wish to waste anyone's time, money, or energy, or our own time or energy either, so we now do everything possible to ensure there will be full compatibility before accepting anyone for training.

We can say with absolute confidence that our Professional Space Clearing Practitioner Training is the most advanced that is available anywhere in the world at this time. The level of knowledge, skill, and perception is in a completely different league to other trainings. At the time of writing, it consists of around 300 hours of tuition spread over 12 months, including two residential courses and in-depth online liaison with each trainee as they progress through their case studies to put the skills they learn into practice.

And it doesn't end there. As every space clearer we have ever trained will attest, the initial training is just the beginning. The difference in skills between someone who has just graduated and someone who has been practising professionally for years is huge. Training to be a space clearer is not about obtaining a certificate and hanging it on the wall and that's that. Active participation in annual continuing professional development (CPD) courses is essential to maintain and develop practitioner-level skills.

About hiring a professional space clearing practitioner

If you search the internet for space clearers, you'll find many who claim to have been trained by us but have, in fact, only read a book or attended a weekend workshop. There are also some who did indeed take our training years ago but were not able to complete it. Or they did complete it, but their skills lapsed because they did not want to or were not able to maintain the annual CPD that we require.

We've heard some very unhappy stories from people who have engaged the services of space clearers who are self-taught, trained by other teachers, or have trained with us and left our network. When it comes to inviting a space clearing professional into your home, you need to have the same care and discernment you would use if you were handing it over to someone to decide on the colour scheme or furnishings. The difference is that if you don't like the new décor, it can be changed at some expense. If you don't like the results of a space clearing, it's not reversible and not easy to change unless you know someone you can call on who has much better skills.

For your peace of mind, if you are thinking of hiring a space clearing practitioner, see the link to our International Directory of Practitioners at the end of this chapter.

Practitioner skills

In the early years of training practitioners, many of Karen's trainees gave up because they weren't prepared to do the personal work required to develop the ability to accurately read energies through hand sensing. We're happy to report that all the professional space clearing practitioners we train now are able to access deep levels of information in this way. The more accurately they can read imprints, the more effectively they can clear them and transform the energy of a space. Most people find this to be one of the most interesting, insightful, and valuable parts of the ceremony.

If you ever invite a professional to space clear your home, you therefore need to be wary if they do space clearing without doing hand sensing because that will mean they are doing it blindly.

Also beware of anyone who does hand sensing, or reading the energies of your home using a different method, in such a way that you cannot verify any of the information they give you. This is a very precise skill that has nothing to do with intuition, psychic channelling, guesswork, or logical reasoning. We have included more information about the hand-sensing technique in *Space Clearing, Volume 2*.

Feng shui consultants who offer space clearing

Space clearing is categorized as a specialized branch of feng shui. However, that does not mean that anyone who has a feng shui qualification necessarily has any ability to do space clearing. Professional space clearing skills are much more advanced than those required to achieve feng shui certification, which is why our space clearing practitioners are often called in to help when a feng shui professional has tried everything they know, yet their client's situation hasn't improved.

Many cultures in the world have a form of feng shui. The Chinese system is the most elaborate, structured, and well known. It offers advice about every aspect of siting, designing, constructing, furnishing, and utilizing buildings. Other cultures have their own versions, such as the Vastu Shastra system used in India and the Asta Kosala Kosali system used in Bali. There are now also many other systems of feng shui that are based on watered-down traditional techniques or have varying degrees of New Age teachings mixed in.

From studying these feng shui systems, certain core principles emerge that can be found in them all, the most important of which is that they help to enhance the flow of etheric energies in the environment. Other aspects are clearly based primarily on superstitions, beliefs that are local to the culture in which they are practised, convoluted intellectual versions of the original teachings, or recent inventions.

Unfortunately, there is no modern school of feng shui we know of that teaches students how to awaken their etheric body in order to be able to directly feel the energies that feng shui principles are based on, as we do when we train space clearing practitioners. Instead, the students learn theories and then apply them to the situations they encounter as best they can, which accounts for some of the very strange feng shui advice we've seen applied in clients' homes on many occasions.

We're very sure that the adepts who first developed feng shui in ancient China did not do so by performing mathematical calculations, applying formulas, or using intuitive guessing, as those who learn it today are taught to do. They would have been able to see, feel, and work directly with the etheric energies that lie at the heart of feng shui. The formulas they left behind were their attempt to leave their knowledge to students who were not capable of perceiving or working directly with the energies of spaces themselves.

The core principles of feng shui are excellent and have stood the test of time. We are not saying there are no reputable feng shui consultants in the world today, just that they are very rare. Most consultants do no personal work at all to awaken their etheric, which means they have no first-hand awareness of *chi*.

A good first question to ask anyone you may consider hiring to do feng shui or space clearing in your home, therefore, is what personal work they have done to develop their subtle body structures. That will at least separate out those who have first-hand experience of energies from those who have only studied theoretical principles.

Gifting a professional space clearing ceremony to someone

Booking one of the space clearing professionals we have trained to do a ceremony in the home of someone you know and care for can be a wonderful gift. However, please be aware that all the arrangements will need to be made with the recipient(s) of the space clearing rather than with you.

Because the desire for the space clearing did not initially come from the recipient(s), the first topic that will always need to be discussed is whether they truly want the depth of changes that the ceremony can bring about and are ready for that. Sometimes the person will be very enthusiastic and receptive. Sometimes they won't be. Make sure they feel free to decline the offer if they wish to, without any awkwardness or bad feeling.

How to find a certified space clearing practitioner

You can find an up-to-date list of our certified practitioners in our International Directory of Practitioners at www.clearspaceliving.com. practitioners.

If a person's name does not appear there, they will be offering a different type of space clearing or a very different standard to what is practised by the currently certified practitioners we have trained to such a high level, each of whom is required to complete annual CPD to maintain and develop their skills.

40

Recommended reading

Books by Karen Kingston

Clear Your Clutter with Feng Shui (Piatkus, first published 1998) – the 25th Anniversary Edition of this book was published in the UK in 2024 in paperback and ebook. It has been translated into 26 languages, and the 2013 edition is also available in audiobook format, narrated by Karen.

Books by Karen Kingston and Richard Kingston

How to Clear Your Clutter (Clear Space Living, 2023) – this concise book is designed as a quick and easy introduction to the clutter clearing systems described in detail in *Clear Your Clutter with Feng Shui*.

Space Clearing, Volume 2: How space clearing works (Clear Space Living, 2024)

Articles by Karen Kingston

You can find a wealth of articles about space clearing, clutter clearing, conscious living, and related topics at www.clearspaceliving.com/blog.

Books by Samuel Sagan

Awakening the Third Eye (Point Horizon Institute, 2013)

Entities: Parasites of the Body of Energy (Clairvision School Foundation, 1994) – published in the United States as *Entity Possession: Freeing the Energy Body of Negative Influences* (Destiny Books, 1997)

Regression: Past-life Therapy for Here and Now Freedom (Clairvision School Foundation, 1996)

Atlantean Secrets, Volume 1: Sleeper Awaken! (Clairvision School Foundation, 1999)

Atlantean Secrets, Volume 2: Forever Love White Eagle (Clairvision School Foundation, 1999)

Atlantean Secrets, Volume 3: The Gods Are Wise (Clairvision School Foundation, 1999)

Atlantean Secrets, Volume 4: The Return of the Flying Dragon (Clairvision School Foundation, 1999)

Bleeding Sun: Discover the Future of Virtual Reality (Clairvision School Foundation, 1999)

Planetary Forces, Alchemy and Healing (Point Horizon Institute, 2016)

Samuel Sagan's books are available direct from clairvision.org, which ships from the United States. We also stock all these titles in our online shop at www.clearspaceliving.com, which ships from the UK.

PART EIGHT

Glossaries

41

ALTMC Glossary

A Language to Map Consciousness (known as ALTMC for short, pronounced alt-em-see) is available to read at clairvision.org. For ease of reference and with the kind permission of Samuel Sagan and the Clairvision School, we have listed here abridged definitions of terms that we have included in this book, with information in brackets, where necessary, to add small clarifications.

What is ALTMC?

The introduction to ALTMC explains:

> This book presents some of the discoveries made by the Clairvision Foundation, as well as a set of principles that can be used by anyone interested in engaging in an exploration of consciousness based on direct experience. Note that the power of what is presented here lies in the fact that it isn't the product of one individual trying to share his/her vision of the world, as is often the case with books of esotericism, but the result of a collective "mapping". No view was adopted until it could be confirmed and objectified through the experience of the whole Foundation, as well as hundreds of students following the courses of the Clairvision School.

ALTMC definitions

Aquarium effect

A form of connection in which you are immersed in the presence. Rather than sitting in your column above, the connection floods the room, sometimes giving you the impression of floating in an "aquarium of presence".

Archetypes

Archetypes are the perfect prototypes out of which the seeds of things and beings originate.

Aspiration

Turning upwards in an attitude of active receptivity. Aspiration creates a receptacle for high spiritual beings to give help.

Astral body

The astral body is the subtle body that is the vehicle of thoughts and emotions.

Astrality

In the fourfold model of subtle bodies developed by Samuel Sagan and the Clairvision School, the astral body is the vehicle of thoughts and emotions, sometimes referred to as ordinary mental consciousness. Astrality is the fabric of this consciousness.

Central channel

The central channel of energy that extends from the top of the head to the root of the body (the perineum). It is the principal channel of the etheric body.

Central thread

The line of energy at the centre of the column above that begins at the vertex (the top of the head) and from there ascends vertically.

Chakra

In Sanskrit texts, chakras are wheel-like structures that govern subtle bodies and a whole range of functions of consciousness.

Column above

The column of energy that extends infinitely above the head, as in an upwards extension of the crown chakra. Ordinary astral consciousness is synonymous with the mind and personality. Superastrality is the more subtle frequencies of higher consciousness, accessed through the centres above the head. Just as the mind is the organ of ordinary astral consciousness, so the column above is the vehicle for superastral levels of consciousness, and their corresponding functions of perception. Verticality, as a key quality of the column above, is a direct way to access these levels.

Column below

The column of energy that extends below the body. The column begins just below the perineum and extends infinitely down.

Combinessence

A oneness of essence. A coalescence of beings. A state of unity shared by two or more high spiritual beings.

Connection

A link of consciousness to a non-physical being or beings, or the world. A connection is experienced as a presence. Connections can also take place with your Higher Self, or higher parts of yourself.

De-exvolution

A de-exvolution is an involution. Calling it de-exvolution emphasizes the fact that in its original state, human consciousness was far more involuted than it is now. So in de-exvoluting, there is a return towards more primordial and less fallen states.

Dragon

On the individual level, the dragon is the power of the lower chakras, which manifests in the potential of life force and desires, passions, belly drive, raw energies, including the sexual force, intensity, underground vitality, and resources, and ultimately willpower. Behind and beyond the individual dragon lies the universal Dragon, the unlimited power that is the matrix of the entire creation.

Individual dragon = the power of your lower chakras, the power in your column below.

The Dragon = the universal Dragon power, of which your dragon is an emanation.

Elementals

Tiny beings that conglomerate to form matter. Classically, it is elementals that form the four elements of earth, air, fire, and water.

Entity

A term used to refer to parasites of the body of energy. Most entities are fragments, issued from the astral body of the dead. To speak of parasitic entities, many healers use the term "attachment".

Etheric

See: Etheric body and Ethericity. (When used as a noun, etheric is short for etheric body. When used as an adjective, it means relating to the etheric body or qualities of ethericity.)

Etheric body

The vehicle of life force. The etheric body can be equated with the *prana-maya-kosha*, "envelope made of *prana*" of the Hindu tradition, and with the *qi* (also known as *chi*) of the Chinese tradition.

Ethericity

The quality of the etheric or life force. Anything that is alive has an etheric body and therefore a quality of ethericity. Ethericity can also refer to the subtle substance of life force, distinct from an etheric body. For example, a plant has an etheric body that gives it life. A garden has ambient ethericity that can be felt apart from the life force of any individual plant.

Etheric sensing

A form of perception based on sensing energetic characteristics of plants, animals, or people through your own etheric body. Etheric sensing is a resonance from etheric to etheric. The knowing coming through etheric sensing is therefore primarily related to life force.

Exvolution

A turning outwards of consciousness, towards grosser levels of existence. The opposite movement of involution. Excessive exvolution is one of the central characteristics of the present human condition. Dwelling in a human body, consciousness is constantly drawn outwards through the senses, towards the material world. Consciousness loses touch with its inwards essence, its non-manifested roots. This engrossment in the senses is an exvolution, an extroversion by which consciousness forgets its own nature of infinity and becomes assimilated to physical limitations. Human beings forget they are immortal Spirits, they believe themselves bipeds bound by the constraints of a three-dimensional universe. Consequently, to know itself consciousness must follow a path of involution.

Fragment

Fragments are issued from the shattering of the astral body of the dead. Made of astral substance and sometimes coated with etheric energy, they can act as entities.

Infra-etheric

Levels of the etheric body that lie closest to the physical and are beyond the present range of perception.

Involution

A turning inside of consciousness. Consciousness letting go of the senses and internalizing itself, turning towards its source and cognizing itself. The opposite of involution is exvolution. Just as a glove can be turned inside out, so consciousness is turned outside in through involution. However, it would be more accurate to say that consciousness is turned inside out through exvolution, and that involution brings it back to its original state. Hence the key direction: consciousness knows itself through involution.

Lower complex

Because the etheric body remains tightly bound to the physical body until death, the two are often grouped together under the term "lower complex" when discussing subtle bodies. See also: Upper complex.

Mind

The layer of thoughts and emotions. The astral body is the vehicle of the mind.

Ordinary mental consciousness (OMC)

The waking consciousness of present-day human beings. The discursive mind.

Packed thought

A condensed thought, the content of which is not explicit or expressed but concentrated into a seed. Ordinary mental consciousness operates with unpacked thoughts, supermind with packed ones. For example, when you turn towards a glass, you immediately identify its shape and know that it is a glass without having to repeat to yourself "this is a glass". The instant silent knowing that identifies the object is an example of packed thought. If, after this, your mind indulges in commenting "this is a glass" then this commenting is an unpacked thought. Abstract intelligence operates through packed thoughts.

Pancake

A Clairvision term for a perverse energy that lands on your face or some other body part after floating in the etheric environment.

Personal stage

The present stage of human evolution in which human beings have developed a sense of individuality and a certain degree of self-determination, but have lost their unity with the Divine and are disconnected from spiritual realms. See also: Prepersonal stage and Transpersonal stage.

Perverse energy

An etheric substance that has crept into the human system and nested in it, to the detriment of vitality and health.

Point

Perceived above the head, the Point is the standpoint from where consciousness can operate non-dimensional functions of superastrality as well as resonate with higher angelic frequencies. The Point is like a prism through which the non-dimensional astral body is projected into the dimensional etheric and physical bodies.

Power of the Point

Super-focused states of consciousness. The power of the Point operates with packed thoughts and can access archetypal forces and superastrality. It can therefore resonate with the supermental consciousness of gods and angels.

Prepersonal stage

A stage of existence in which human beings have a poor sense of their own individuality, or no sense of individuality at all. In the early prepersonal stage, human beings were one with the Divine but without any sense of individuality. Then comes the personal stage, in which individuality is acquired at the expense of a near-complete disconnection from spiritual worlds. Finally, in the transpersonal stage, human consciousness is to regain its unity with the Divine, while retaining individuality. See also: Personal stage and Transpersonal stage.

Presence

The flavour of consciousness that characterizes a being, whether a high angel or a small parasitic being such as an entity.

Ritual

A practice through which a connection is established with non-physical beings. This definition contrasts with the loose modern use of the term "ritual", which covers circumstances such as losing your first tooth or burning your personal journal. These may have symbolic significance but, strictly speaking, they do not qualify as rituals.

Root charge

The root charge is the powerhouse behind all emotional charges and desires. It is held in the toroid, a doughnut-shaped master structure of energy located just below the perineum and the anus. The voltage held in the root charge is a limited manifestation of the power of the Dragon.

Samskara

Samskaras are imprints left in the psyche by emotionally charged experiences.

Structure

Structure refers to the ability to go from A to B, meaning to carry out elaborate tasks, manage complex situations, solve problems, and organize. Structure brings a know-how of achieving. In the supermind work, structure is equated with superastrality.

Structures

Structures refers to various subtle organs or structures such as chakras, gateways, etc.

Subtle bodies

The non-physical layers which, together with the physical body, constitute a human being. Subtle bodies form the non-physical hardware of consciousness.

Subtle bodybuilding

In the present condition of human beings, subtle bodies aren't completely shaped – not unlike unused atrophied muscles that do not respond to the conscious will. The term "subtle bodybuilding" adequately reflects the sustained effort by which subtle bodies and their constituting structures are perceived, shaped, crystallized, made operational, integrated to your consciousness, and submitted to the rulership of your Higher Self.

Superastrality

Superastrality refers to levels that stand above ordinary mental consciousness. It is accessed through verticality. Structure and superastrality are one and the same thing.

Third eye

Organ of inner vision and command centre of the body of energy. The third eye gives direct perception of non-physical realities, leading to first-hand experiences instead of having to rely only on theories. Rather than a patch of energy on the forehead, the third eye is a tunnel that extends from the back to the front of the skull. It includes several centres of energy, including the frontal eye (between the eyebrows) and the atom (at the very middle of the third eye tunnel).

Throat friction

A simple but extremely powerful technique that consists of making a friction sound while both inhaling and exhaling. Its effect is to crystallize structures of energy and to induce high states of vision and connection. The throat friction technique is described in detail in Chapter 2 of Samuel Sagan's book *Awakening the Third Eye*.

Transpersonal stage

The prepersonal, personal and transpersonal stages are three phases in the evolution of human consciousness. In the prepersonal stage, human beings have little or no sense of individuality, but there is union with the Divine. In the personal stage, a sense of individuality has appeared, but at the cost of a loss of connection with the Divine and with spiritual worlds. In the transpersonal stage, the sense of individuality is retained and unity with the Divine has been regained. See also: Prepersonal stage and Personal stage.

Unpacked thought

A thought expressed in some form of inner discourse, as opposed to a silent knowing. The discursive mind (ordinary mental consciousness) operates through unpacked thoughts.

Uplifting

Uplifting consists of pulling energies up along the central thread of the column above. It is one of the cardinal techniques taught by the Clairvision School.

Upper complex

The astral body and the Higher Self working together. See also: Lower complex.

Verticality

Verticality is simply the quality of being vertical. It is easily perceived in the vertical column of energy (known as the column above) that extends upwards above the head. Superastrality is accessed through verticality. See also: Column above.

Vision

A superior function of consciousness. A direct perception of reality, which bypasses the senses and cognizes the essence of things.

Visionful

An object of perception is said to be visionful when it engages subtle vision through the richness of its qualities (inner light, vibration...) or because of the archetypal forces behind it. It is a very useful concept for developing non-physical perception.

42

Space Clearing Glossary

Ambient etheric

See: Ethericity* in the ALTMC Glossary.

Astral imprint

An astral frequency that is embedded in a physical substance. The technique used in space clearing to read astral imprints is called hand sensing. The primary technique used in space clearing to clear astral imprints is called belling.

Basic Space Clearing

An abridged version of space clearing, described in detail in *Space Clearing, Volume 1*. It is conducted using a Basic Space Clearing kit and is the version most people start with.

Belling

A range of techniques using the unique sound of a Balinese space clearing bell to clear astral imprints and revitalize energies in buildings during a space clearing ceremony.

Clapping

A range of techniques involving striking the palms of one's hands together to break up clumps of stagnant energies and surface layers of astral imprints in buildings and objects.

Colourizer

A strip of handwoven gold-threaded material, available in a range of colours. Used in the creation of an altar for a Full Space Clearing ceremony.

Essential Space Clearing

This version of space clearing is described in detail in *Space Clearing, Volume 1* and is conducted using an Essential Space Clearing kit. It is more effective than Basic Space Clearing and not as comprehensive as a Full Space Clearing, although it is quicker and easier to do.

Etheric debris

Elemental* energies resulting from the energetic excretions of living organisms. Etheric debris feels cruddy and unclean. It is often intermingled with stagnant energies and may have a physical component such as dust, grime, mould, or grease.

Flower offering

When activated during a space clearing ceremony, the purpose of a flower offering is to create an anchor for spiritual forces and help to facilitate taking energetic ownership of a space. A classic flower offering consists of a small saucer or plate with a tealight candle at the centre and small flower heads placed around the candle, pointing outward. A rose petal flower offering consists of a small saucer or plate with rose petals placed around a tealight candle and a few flower heads on top of the rose petals, pointing outward.

Full Space Clearing

The most effective version of space clearing described in this book, conducted using a Full Space Clearing kit.

Hand sensing

The art of sensing etheric* and astral* energies with the palm of one's hand and interpreting them through specific subtle body structures that can be developed above the head.

Harmony ball

A small, brass-plated ball that makes chiming sounds when shaken. It is used in the final part of a space clearing ceremony to facilitate putting new, higher frequencies into a space.

Island

An independent floor-to-ceiling structure found in some homes, such as a freestanding fireplace in the centre of a living room or sometimes an entire room within a room.

Matrix flower offering

Matrix flower offerings are used in a Full Space Clearing ceremony to create a superastral* matrix that links all the flower offerings on each floor horizontally and also links all the matrix flower offerings to each other vertically. The method of activating matrix flower offerings is substantially different to that for other flower offerings.

MC

MC is short for Master of Ceremonies. The MC of a space clearing ceremony is the person who takes overall responsibility for it, practically and energetically.

MC-ship
Holding the position of MC.

Personal belling
A centring and uplifting technique using the sound of a Balinese space clearing bell.

Space clearing flower offering mudra
The ritual movement used to activate a flower offering in a space clearing ceremony while holding a flower head between the forefinger and middle finger of one hand.

Space clearing water
Water that has been ritually presenced for use in a space clearing ceremony.

Stagnant energies
Etheric energies that accumulate in areas where energies do not flow well, similar to the way water can stagnate in a pond. Stagnant energies often accumulate around clutter.

The Seven Levels of Consciousness
A model created by Karen Kingston and Richard Kingston of the level of consciousness that are accessible while incarnated in a human body

White Gold
The spiritual connection that facilitates the space clearing method described in this book.

Index

Page numbers in *italics* relate to photographs and illustrations.

Made in the USA
Monee, IL
01 June 2024

59229761R00233